The World of the

DRUIDS

The World of the
DRUIDS

MIRANDA J. GREEN

With 291 illustrations, 51 in color

THAMES AND HUDSON

For Stephen

Author's note
I wish to express my appreciation to the following individuals and institutions for their help to me in writing this book: Professor W.H. Manning, for reading and commenting on the text; Professor Michael Fulford, Alex Gibson, Philip Macdonald, David and Pamela Johnston, Tony Rook and Mathew McCabe for making particular illustrations available to me. Kenneth Brassil, Brian Davies, Tecwyn Ellis, Raymond Howell, Tristan Gray Hulse, John Kenyon and Wynne Lloyd provided me with advice and information on the Druid Renaissance and the Welsh tradition; Raymond Howell and Chris Sobol helped me with some Welsh translations; Philip Carr-Gomm, Mathew McCabe, and Marian Bowman provided helpful comments on modern Druidism. I am also grateful to John Franklin, Liz Murray, Michel Raoult, Philip Shallcrass, the Pagan Federation, the Royal National Eisteddfod Office, Celtica, English Heritage and the Museum of Welsh Life at St Ffagans. I am indebted to staff at University of Wales College, Newport and at Thames and Hudson for all their encouragement and support. Finally, my warmest thanks go to Nora Chadwick and Stuart Piggott (alas both now deceased), whose seminal works on the Druids laid the foundations and acted as vivid sources of inspiration for this volume.

On the jacket, from left to right: Druids celebrating the Summer Solstice at Stonehenge, Wiltshire. Greg English/Link ©; G. Henry and E. A. Hornel, The Druids: Bringing in the Mistletoe, 1890. Glasgow Museums: Art Gallery and Museum, Kelvingrove; Killary Harbour, Connacht, Ireland. Photo Edwin Smith; Pewter mask, c. 1st century AD. Roman Baths Museum, Bath. Photo courtesy of Bath Archaeological Trust; Gold collar, Gleninsheen, County Clare, c. 700 BC. National Museum of Ireland, Dublin; 18th-century engraving of Druids by Grasset de Saint-Sauveur, Les Druides: Costumes de Théâtre. Bibliothèque des Arts Décoratifs, Paris. Photo Jean-Loup Charmet, Paris; Cavenham crown, 2nd–3rd century AD. Ipswich Borough Council Museums and Galleries.

Half-title: Drawing by Paul Jenkins
Title-page: 'The Druid',1896, watercolour by Sir Hubert von Herkomer (1849–1914), the Forbes Magazine Collection, New York. All rights reserved.

© 1997 Thames and Hudson Ltd, London

First published in the United States in 1997 by Thames and Hudson Inc., 500 Fifth Avenue, New York, New York 10110

Library of Congress Catalog Card Number 96-61291

ISBN 0-500-05083-X

Printed and bound in the United States

CONTENTS

I

FINDING THE DRUIDS

How Do We Know About the Druids?   8

The Druids in Celtic Society   10

The Geography of the Celtic World   11

An Outline History of the Druids   14

The Oak and the Mistletoe   18

Timeline for Druidism   20

II

THE CELTS AND THE SUPERNATURAL

The Nature of Celtic Religion   24

The Celtic Pantheon   26

A God in Every Place   29

Druids in Context   31

Druidic Organization   32

Ceremonies and Festivals   34

The Farming Year   37

III

THE DRUIDS IN CLASSICAL LITERATURE

The Chroniclers   40

Druids and the Social Order   44

Healers and Magicians   46

The Druids and Education   48

Philosophers and Scientists   50

Immortality and Rebirth   51

Druids and Romans   52

IV
DIGGING UP DRUIDS

Priesthoods in European Prehistory   56
Images of the Druids   58
Ceremonial Regalia: Badges of Office   60
Gifts to the Divine Powers   64
Cauldrons and Holy Water   66
Death, Burial and the Afterlife   68

V
SACRIFICE AND PROPHECY

The Concept of Sacrifice   72
Sacrifice in Action   74
Ritual Murder   76
Flesh for the Gods   78
Bodies in the Bog   80
The Danish Bog Victims   82
Animals as Sacrificial Victims   85
Divination: Telling the Future   88
Prophets and Oracles   90

VI
THE FEMALE DRUIDS

Women in Celtic Society   94
Druidesses and Wise Women   97
Witches and Magic   98
Priestess and Prophetess in Irish Myth   101
Virgin Priestesses   103

VII
SACRED PLACES AND THEIR PRIESTS

Sacred Groves and Pools   108
Shrines and Temples   110
The Sacred Spring at Bath   112
Priests in Celtic Sanctuaries   115

The Sacred Healers   118
Enclosing Holy Space   120

VIII
DRUIDS IN IRISH MYTH

The Learned Class   124
The Early Myths   125
Cathbadh of Ulster   128
Sacral Kingship and Druidic Prophecy   130
Druidism and Christianity   134

IX
DRUIDS RESURRECTED

The Druidic Revival of the Renaissance   140
Stukeley and His Peers   142
The Stonehenge Connection   144
Realists and Romantics   146
Druids as Illustrated   150
Birth of a Welsh Myth   152
Druids, the Eisteddfod and Welsh Identity   156

X
DRUIDS TODAY

Neo-Paganism and the Old Religion   160
Witches and Druids   162
Ceremony and Celebration   166
Modern Druid Organizations   169
Stonehenge Prohibited   172
The Modern Druid Doctrine   177
Guardians of the Planet   179

Directory of Modern Druid Organizations   180
Gazetteer   182
Further Reading   184
Acknowledgments   186
Index   188

I

FINDING THE DRUIDS

'Philosophers ... and men learned in religious affairs are unusually honoured among them and are called by them Druids. They further make use of seers, thinking them worthy of high praise. These latter by their augural observances and by the sacrifice of sacrificial animals can foretell the future and they hold all the people subject to them.... And it is a custom of theirs that no one should perform a sacrifice without a "philosopher" ...'

Diodorus Siculus, *Library of History* V, 31, 2–3

T HE TERM 'DRUID' means different things to different people. For some, it conjures up images of venerable white-robed and bearded gentlemen gathering at Stonehenge or at the Welsh National Eisteddfod. Others, with more awareness of the past, think of Druids as cruel religious Celtic fanatics, striking down hapless victims of human sacrifice by stabbing or burning. For others, again, Druids are somehow mixed up with secret forest groves, mistletoe, magic and spells. So what is the reality? Who were these mysterious people? When and where did they manifest themselves? And how do we know anything about them?

The available contemporary evidence presents a complex picture: Druids were involved in politics, sacrificial ritual, prophecy and the control of the supernatural world. They were teachers, keepers of oral tradition, royal advisers and, in some instances, they were themselves rulers. Like the prophets of the Old Testament, they were feared and venerated because they had the ear of the divine world.

A modern Druid ceremony at Primrose Hill, London, at the autumn equinox. The musical instrument in the centre is a 'Hirlas Horn', or Horn of Plenty.

CLASSICAL COMMENTATORS, writing about the Celts during the first century BC and the first few centuries AD, initially mention the Druids as prominent members of Celtic society. They are discussed by several writers, some of whom – such as Caesar (*Gallic War*), Strabo (*Geography*) and Pliny (*Natural History*) – speak at great length about the various functions of the Druids, while others make only brief allusions to them.

The second body of primary literary evidence concerning the Druids is contained in the myths of Wales and Ireland. These were written in the vernacular (that is, in Welsh or Irish, rather than in Latin) during the medieval period. The Ulster Cycle of prose tales, compiled in written form some time between the seventh and twelfth centuries AD, but probably deriving from much earlier oral tradition, contains what are arguably the earliest vernacular mythic texts.

Page from the twelfth-century Irish Leabhar na h-Uidhre *(the* Book of the Dun Cow*), which contains most of the* Táin Bo Cuailnge *(the* Cattle Raid of Cooley*). The tale consists of the mythical account of the conflict between Ulster and Connacht. The most famous Druid described in the* Táin *is Cathbadh, who belonged to the royal court of King Conchobar of Ulster.*

One of the most prominent characters in these tales is the Druid Cathbadh, who was attached to the court of King Conchobar of Ulster. Another group of texts, known as the Mythological Cycle, compiled in the twelfth century, describes a divine race of Ireland, the Tuatha Dé Danann, who were steeped in Druidic lore and magic. In a different set of stories, the Fenian Cycle, also written down in the twelfth century, the central character is Finn, leader of the Fianna, a war-band sworn to guard the king. As a child, Finn was reared by two holy foster-mothers, one described as a 'wise woman', the other a Druidess. Finally, the early chronicles of Saint Brigit allude to the rearing of that great sixth-century Irish saint in a Druid's household; and chronicles of Saint Patrick refer to his encounters with Druids.

References to the Druids in the early Welsh literature are more scarce. However, there is an interesting parallel to the Irish *Life of Saint Brigit* in the twelfth-century *Life of Saint Beuno*, the sixth-century canonized abbot, which contains an account of his death: on arrival at the gates of Heaven, he encountered Saint Peter, the other Apostles *and* the Druids.

Only literary evidence, whether from the Classical world or from the vernacular mythic tradition, can give us direct evidence of the Druids. These documents alone mention them by name: we have no inscriptions or any images which can certainly be identified as Druidic. Thus, any attempt to use archaeological material as evidence for the Druids must be made with an awareness that we are dealing with supposition and inference rather than fact. Perhaps the most important archaeological document which can be quite firmly linked with the Druids is the Coligny calendar, an incomplete bronze sheet, dating to the first century AD, inscribed in Gaulish with a list of auspicious and inauspicious days. This was clearly a religious text which priests may have consulted when making their predictions (p. 37).

Other archaeological material relates not specifically to the Druids but to priests or cult officials in general. There is evidence of their presence in sacred structures, sacrificial deposits and regalia such as headdresses, badges of office and sceptres. Certain images in stone and bronze may represent clergy rather than the gods themselves, but in the absence of accompanying dedications, we cannot be sure.

(Above) Bronze figurine of a dancer, perhaps associated with a cult ceremony, from a hoard of religious bronzes (which included boars, a horse, a stag and a male figure who has been tentatively identified as a Druid) found at Neuvy-en-Sullias, Loiret, France, near a temple site. First century BC.

(Left) Eighteenth-century engraving of two Druids, dressed in the manner of Romans, in togas and laurel wreaths.

THE MEANING OF 'DRUID'

'The magicians perform no rites without using the foliage of those trees [oaks] ... it may be supposed that it is from this custom that they get their name of Druids, from the Greek word meaning 'oak.'
Pliny, Natural History XVI, 95

It is often thought that the word 'Druid' comes from the Indo-European word 'dru' for oak. Indeed, in his Natural History, written in the first century AD, the Roman writer Pliny the Elder makes this connection. But many scholars now believe that the word 'Druid' means 'wisdom'. Even if this is so, however, the link between 'Druid' and 'oak' may have been made by the ancient Celts and the Romans because of the recognized association between the Druids and their sacred tree (right).

THE DRUIDS IN CELTIC SOCIETY

During his stay in Gaul, Julius Caesar wrote a commentary on the Gaulish campaigns. His account provides us with many interesting references to the Druids, including their high standing within Celtic society.

JULIUS CAESAR WAS appointed by the Roman senate as governor of southern Gaul in 59 BC. He immediately began a series of campaigns to conquer the Gallic heartlands, and finally completed his task in 50 BC. Although his commentary on the Gallic Wars was primarily an account of the military campaigns themselves, he was interested in Gaulish culture as well and, in Book VI, he recorded detailed observations on the customs and religious practices he encountered. Caesar's account of the Druids is the fullest and most informative we have:

'Throughout Gaul there are two classes of men of some dignity and importance.... One of the two classes is that of the Druids, the other that of the knights. The Druids are concerned with the worship of the gods, look after public and private sacrifice, and expound religious matters. A large number of young men flock to them for training and hold them in high honour. For they have the right to decide nearly all public and private disputes and they also pass judgment and decide rewards and penalties in criminal and murder cases and in disputes concerning legacies and boundaries. When a private person or a tribe disobeys their ruling

they ban them from attending at sacrifices. This is their harshest penalty. Men placed under this ban are treated as impious wretches; all avoid them, fleeing their company and conversation, lest their contact bring misfortune upon them; they are denied legal rights and can hold no official dignity.... It is thought that this [the Druidic] system of training was invented in Britain and taken over from there to Gaul, and at the present time diligent students of the matter mostly travel there to study it.

'The Druids are wont to be absent from war, nor do they pay taxes like the others.... It is said that they commit to memory immense amounts of poetry. And so some of them continue their studies for twenty years. They consider it improper to entrust their studies to writing.... I think they established this practice for two reasons, because they were unwilling, first, that their system of training should be bruited abroad among the common people, and second, that the student should rely on the written word and neglect the exercise of his memory.... They are chiefly anxious to have men believe the following: that souls do not suffer death, but after death pass from one body to another; and they regard this as the strongest incentive to valour, since the fear of death is disregarded. They have also much knowledge of the stars and their motion, of the size of the world and of the earth, of natural philosophy, and of the powers and spheres of action of the immortal gods, which they discuss and hand down to their young students.'

Caesar, *Gallic War* VI, 13–14

Caesar and his contemporaries portray the Druids as enjoying extremely high status within Gallic society, of a rank akin to the *equites* (knights), who were the highest nobility below the tribal chief magistrate or king. Indeed, the tribe of the Aedui, which occupied part of what is now Burgundy, was in Caesar's time split into two factions led by two brothers: Dumnorix, an anti-Roman agitator, and the pro-Roman Divitiacus, who was a Druid.

A human sacrifice watched by Gaulish soldiers. Caesar tells us that the Druids performed human sacrifices and occupied a high rank in Gaulish society, equal to that of the warrior-aristocracy.

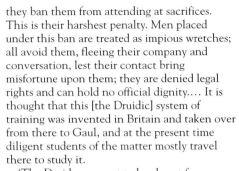

ANY ATTEMPT AT defining the world of the ancient Celts depends upon three categories of evidence, all of which need to be be used cautiously because they are incomplete and sometimes ambiguous. The texts of Classical commentators, archaeology and the early evidence of language all appear to combine to provide us with a picture of a Celtic culture or tradition which, by the third century BC, stretched from Ireland to Hungary and from Scotland to northern Italy.

Let us look at each of these three sources of evidence a little more closely. Observers from the Greek and Roman world speak of the Celts living in a large region of territory north of the Alps. We need to be a little careful of nomenclature here. Many writers speak not of Celts *sensu stricto* but of *Galli* or *Galatae*. But the Greek author Herodotus, who has been dubbed the 'Father of History', commented upon *Keltoi* residing in the area of the Danube in the fifth century BC, and Polybius, writing in the second

century BC, also uses this term. However, Caesar describes the Celts as being just one ethnic group living in a specific part of Gaul: he does not equate all Gauls with Celts, nor does he (or any other writer, for that matter) refer to the Britons as Celts, although he acknowledges those of the southeast to be similar to the Gauls in customs and lifestyle. We need to pose the (ultimately unanswerable) question as to whether the European Celts possessed any degree of ethnic consciousness or whether the term 'Celts' was merely a convenient but somewhat vague label used by Mediterranean chroniclers to identify essentially heterogeneous groups of people living north of the 'civilized' world of Greece and Rome. The precision with which the term 'Celts' was used by Classical writers may, of course, have varied quite widely.

Early evidence for the presence in Europe of people speaking languages which are recognizably Celtic is scarce because, before the Roman period, northern Europe was virtually non-

Map showing the territory occupied by Celts (or people influenced by Celtic culture), from the fifth century BC to the Roman conquest.

Bilingual inscription written in Gaulish and Latin; from Todi in Umbria, north Italy.

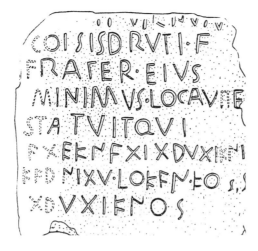

The village and lake of Hallstatt, Austria, the site of a great cemetery which has given its name to the material culture of the earliest Iron Age in temperate Europe.

literate. The few pieces of linguistic material that have been found consist of the names of places and people contained within Classical literature and inscriptions: some of the latter consist simply of single words, usually names, on coins. But some quite long inscriptions in Gaulish, dating to the later first millennium BC, have been discovered in recent years, in southern France, Spain and Italy.

In archaeological terms, the emergence of Celtic culture coincides with the adoption of iron technology in temperate (non-Mediterranean) Europe. The first phase of the Continental Iron Age is generally dated to between about 750 and 500 BC and has been named 'Hallstatt' after the great cemetery at Hallstatt in Austria, the burial place of the local salt-mining communities of the *Salzkammergut* ('salt-route') around modern Hallein. Certain distinctive elements of Hallstatt material culture, particularly metalwork, occur widely in Europe and are even present, though rarely, in Britain. The main archaeological phase of the Celtic Iron Age is called 'La Tène', after the great deposit of metalwork found, with other material, in the water at the margins of Lake Neuchâtel in Switzerland. The La Tène phase is dated from the fifth century BC to the Roman occupation of Britain and continental Europe in the first centuries BC and AD. The archaeological record of the La Tène Iron Age presents a picture of a typically heroic, highly stratified society in which warfare, feasting and flamboyance were closely associated with aristocratic power. Perhaps the most distinctive and unifying feature of the Celtic La Tène tradition is its art,

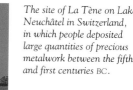

Bronze plaque decorated with a bird-headed triskele (a three-pronged pattern radiating from a common point), first century BC, from the sacred lake of Llyn Cerrig Bach, Anglesey, which may have been a Druidic holy site.

which displays a unique attitude to visual expression while, at the same time, taking inspiration from the Mediterranean and Near Eastern worlds. This essentially abstract, non-realistic art, full of tension, energy and meandering patterns which sometimes resolve themselves into human faces or other pseudo-representational designs, can be found all over temperate Europe, from Ireland to Romania.

The Classical writers, linguistic evidence and archaeological material all contribute to the identification of the Celtic world. But what do we mean by this concept? We need to consider to what extent the expansion of the Celts from their central European heartlands meant actual migrations. Classical authors certainly allude quite specifically to episodic folk movement, but that probably does not entirely account for the presence of Celtic material and linguistic culture in such a vast area of Europe. Some 'Celtic expansion' must have been the result of the spread of ideas and traditions rather than of ethnic Celts.

What happened to the Celts during and after the Roman occupation of their territories? Roman influence undoubtedly led to substantial changes in Celtic culture but not to a total submergence of indigenous tradition. Instead, a dynamic and exciting hybrid Romano-Celtic culture emerged.

When, in the early fifth century AD, the Roman empire's central administrative system collapsed in the West, Celtic culture seems also to have disappeared, except in the far west and

north of Britain and in Ireland. Elsewhere, the old Celtic world was overrun by new, alien cultures such as those of the Saxons and the Franks. But in the 'Celtic West' (Ireland, Scotland, Wales, Cornwall, the Isle of Man and Brittany) Celtic languages and culture survived and flourished. Wales and Ireland produced a fascinating early vernacular mythic tradition; and Celtic Christianity was the stimulus for a resurgence in Celtic art, which manifested itself above all in carved stone crosses and illuminated manuscripts.

Map showing the Celtic West (excluding Brittany), where Celtic language and culture flourished from the fifth century AD onwards.

Nineteenth-century bronze statue of the Gaulish leader Vercingetorix, who fought against Julius Caesar for Celtic freedom at Alesia in 52 BC.

THE EARLIEST WRITERS about the Druids, whose texts have survived (chapter 3), were from the Greek and Roman world, and their testimony dates no earlier than the first century BC. Our most informative sources – Strabo, Diodorus Siculus and (above all) Julius Caesar – were all writing in the mid- or late first century BC. However, we can push the literary evidence for Druidism back somewhat further, inasmuch as all these historians undoubtedly drew on a single earlier source, Posidonius, a Greek philosopher from Syria, who flourished during the early first century BC. But the earliest literature to mention Druids may have been the work of Timaeus, a Greek historian who lived in the mid-fourth to mid-third century BC, and who was used as an authority by many later chroniclers, including Diodorus.

An even earlier date for Druidism could be argued: literary references to the Celts can be traced back as early as the sixth century BC, when Greeks such as Hecataeus of Miletus spoke of them, followed by the great fifth-century historian Herodotus. Although these early writers did not mention the Druids specifically, they were clearly well established by at least the second century BC in order for their brotherhood to have attained such prominence by the time Caesar and his peers encountered them.

During the first century AD, authors such as Lucan, Pliny and Tacitus refer to Druids: all three associate them with secret ceremonies enacted in secluded forest groves. Most of the historians of the first centuries BC and AD speak with some distaste of divinatory human sacrifice, as perpetrated by the Druids.

'Free' Druidism before the Romans

Many Graeco-Roman writers give the Druids a thoroughly bad press, commenting with unctuous self-righteousness on the savage practices of human sacrifice carried out by a 'barbarian' priesthood. They describe the arcane cult ceremonies taking place in secluded groves, away from profane and alien eyes. Other writers present an opposite image of the Druids as 'Noble Savages', profound thinkers, intellectuals and philosophers, scholars of the universe, teachers and custodians of oral culture.

The messages conveyed by the ancient chroniclers are multi-stranded, sometimes contradictory, often anecdotal. Some of their reporting quite clearly derives from a curious but uninformed 'touristic' attitude, on the part of Mediterranean observers, to a culture which was evidently something of a mystery to them.

It is quite possible that by the time the Graeco-Roman world took an interest in the Druids, in the first century BC, Druidism was already on the decline. Gaul was effectively conquered by the mid-first century BC, and it is arguable that the consequent fragmentation of Celtic society, and the diminished power of the noble families, severely curtailed the functions of the continental Druids. What is very striking is the difference between the comments made by writers of the first century BC and those of the first century AD. Caesar, Strabo and Diodorus project a positive, active image of the Druids engaged in official capacities as judges, teachers and presiders over ritual matters, including sacrifice. But if we examine the testimony of Tacitus, Lucan, Pliny and Pomponius Mela, all of whom wrote in the first century AD, we find new notes creeping in: the association of Druids with secret, hidden places such as forests, and more pejorative, emotive descriptions of savage rites. Pliny presents the Druids as magicians; Mela speaks of Druids teaching in remote and secret places, such as caves and groves.

So we may be faced with the frustrating situation that almost as soon as observers from the Classical world began commenting on the Druids, the role and status of this learned class began to change and diminish. Thus, we may have no witnesses to the Druids in action at the height of their powers, influence and prestige. This in itself may lend the remarks of the ancient writers a kind of 'folkloric' tone, in which certain Druidic practices are communicated as curiosities belonging not only to an alien world but also to the past.

Persecution under the Roman emperors

We learn from the texts of Suetonius, Tacitus and Pliny that the early Roman emperors of the first century AD frowned upon Druidism and tried to suppress it. Suetonius was an author (and scandal monger) who lived in the late first and early second century AD and who composed a series of imperial *Lives*. He alludes to Augustus' ban on Druidism for Roman citizens. There is a clear indication here of the emperor's disapproval, but this did not extend to any attempt at full-scale eradication. Pliny, however, informs us that Augustus' successor Tiberius issued an edict designed to get rid of the Druids 'and that class of seers and doctors' entirely, thus indicating either increasing disquiet at their (evidently still active) nationalistic influence in Gaul or simply imperial bigotry.

Pliny and Suetonius give conflicting messages about Druidism under the emperor Claudius: Suetonius says that he 'completely abolished the barbarous and inhuman religion of the Druids in Gaul'; Pliny speaks of the execution of a Gaulish chieftain because he wore a Druidic talisman (the so-called 'serpent's egg') while conducting legal business. On the other hand, we can infer from Tacitus that the Druids continued to have an active role as agitators in Britain during the time of the Boudican rebellion of AD 60/61, in Nero's reign, when the Roman governor Paulinus attacked the Druids' holy stronghold on Anglesey; indeed, the influence of the British Druids as a focus of Celtic nationalism is frequently cited as one of the major factors in the decision of the Roman government to conquer Britain. In the 'Year of the Four Emperors', AD 69, when Rome itself was experiencing enormous upheavals in the imperial succession after the death of Nero, the Druids were – opportunely – engaged in inciting the Gaulish tribes to a mass uprising.

Evidence for the persecution of the Druids is clear up to, and including, the reign of Nero. But comments about them dry up before the end of the first century AD, only to reappear in the third century, and there exists no testimony to their systematic annihilation.

Druidic survival: Gaul

If the Romans did seriously attempt to wipe out Druidism in Gaul, it appears that they were not entirely successful. The documents known as the *Augustan Histories* speak of Druid prophetesses (p. 97) who acted as fortune-tellers for emperors such as Severus Alexander and Diocletian in the third century AD. The fourth-century Bordeaux poet Ausonius wrote in his *Commemoratio Professorum Burdigalensium* ('Remembrance of the Teachers of Bordeaux') of Druids in Brittany and Aquitaine, who were outstanding rhetoricians. Ausonius describes a contemporary of his called Delphidius as being descended from the Druid stock of Bayeux in northern Gaul. Delphidius' grandfather was apparently called Phoebicius, a priest of Bordeaux attached to the temple of Belenus, an important Celtic healer-god associated with Apollo in Gaul. Phoebicius was a prominent teacher of rhetoric at the University of Bordeaux. Ausonius records that not only he,

Cameo of the Roman emperor Claudius, who was completely against the Druidic religion. Suetonius claims that Claudius abolished Druidism throughout Gaul; a claim that is slightly suspect since Druids continue to be mentioned in Roman accounts for some time after Claudius's reign.

but also his son Patera and his grandson Delphidius, were famous for their eloquence as rhetoricians. This is important for it bears witness to the continued reputation of the Druids as instructors, orators and – by implication – keepers of oral tradition.

Druidic survival: Ireland

With the collapse of the western Roman empire at the beginning of the fifth century AD, literary references to the Druids in Gaul and Britain come to an end, but the new written tradition of Ireland, from its first introduction to the island (so it is alleged) by Christian monks in the fifth–seventh centuries to the High Middle Ages, is full of allusions to Irish Druids (chapter 8). Mythic texts, such as the Ulster Cycle and the Mythological Cycle (p. 8) contain numerous references to the Druids, particularly as prophets. In addition, the seventh-century *Lives* of Saint Brigit and Saint Patrick describe a period at the interface between paganism and Christianity, when Druids are variously presented as accepting of, or hostile to, the new faith.

In some Irish texts, the learned class is divided into three: Druids, Bards and Filidh (seer-poets), a tripartite division strongly reminiscent of that described in Classical testimony, such as that of Strabo. There is evidence that sometime before AD 1500, the Insular functions of the Druids and Bards were subsumed within those of the Filidh, who retained roles as seers, teachers, political advisers and poets until the seven-

teenth century, when free Ireland became subject to the English government.

Druidism reborn

Druidism *sensu stricto* came to an end with the demise of the Irish Druids in the early modern period. But in England and on the Continent, there was a revival of interest in Druids with the rediscovery of Classical texts in the sixteenth century. In Britain, seventeenth- and eighteenth-century antiquarians, such as John Aubrey and William Stukeley, reconstructed the Druid order (chapter 9) and linked it with megalithic stone circles like Stonehenge. Also during the eighteenth century, the Welsh Bard Iolo Morgannwg constructed connections between Druids, the ceremony of the Gorsedd (a Welsh word meaning an assembly-place traditionally associated with enthronement) and the National Eisteddfod.

Between the eighteenth century and the present day, Druidic tradition has been maintained through the various modern orders, such as the Order of Bards, Ovates and Druids. These latter-day Druids have little in common with those of Classical antiquity, although they conduct ceremonies and wear clothes which allegedly show links with the past. In 1908, Winston Churchill was initiated into the Albion Lodge of the Ancient Order of Druids. Today, the Council of British Druids wishes to create a National Eisteddfod at Stonehenge, a desire doomed to failure as all major ceremonies there are banned for reasons of conservation.

(Opposite) A nineteenth-century engraving of St Patrick. In the seventh-century Life of Saint Patrick, *the saint's struggles with the pagan Druids in Ireland are related. As Christianity spread through Ireland, the Druids were increasingly seen as evil and even ridiculous figures.*

The eighteenth-century antiquarian William Stukeley's drawing for the title page of his unpublished book, The History of the Temples of the Ancient Celts, *written in 1723. Due to Stukeley's growing obsession with all things Druidic, he later changed the book title to* The History of the Religion and Temples of the Druids, *and changed the title page accordingly (p. 144).*

THE HISTORY OF THE TEMPLES OF THE ANTIENT CELTS.

THE OAK AND THE MISTLETOE

PLINY THE ELDER, writing in the first century AD, describes a religious ceremony in Gaul in which white-clad Druids climbed a sacred oak, cut down the mistletoe growing there, sacrificed two white bulls and used the mistletoe to cure infertility (see Box). Pliny was primarily interested in natural history and some scholars have dismissed his testimony in relation to the Druids as largely fanciful, particularly as he is the only Classical author to mention this ceremony. But

it is worth examining Pliny's comments because they contain a good deal of potentially significant information, which will be touched upon elsewhere in this book. To begin with, Pliny specifically associates the Druids with oak trees. We will see in the following chapters that trees, and particularly oaks, were held sacred both by Druids and Celts generally.

Central to Pliny's statement is the sanctity of mistletoe, both as a healing agent and as an aid

DRUIDS, BULLS AND MOON-WORSHIP

'The Druids – that is what they call their magicians – hold nothing more sacred than mistletoe and a tree on which it is growing, provided it is Valonia Oak…. Mistletoe is rare and when found, it is gathered with great ceremony, and particularly on the sixth day of the moon…. Hailing the moon in a native word that means "healing all things", they prepare a ritual sacrifice and banquet beneath a tree and bring up two white bulls, whose horns are bound for the first time on this occasion. A priest

arrayed in white vestments climbs the tree and with a golden sickle cuts down the mistletoe, which is caught in a white cloak. Then finally they kill the victims, praying to God to render his gift propitious to those on whom he has bestowed it. They believe that mistletoe given in drink will impart fertility to any animal that is barren, and that it is an antidote to all poisons.'
Pliny, Natural History XVI, 95

This portrait of white-garbed Druids, wielding sickles of gold to cut down clumps of sacred mistletoe from great oaks, is one of the best-known and enduring images of Druidism that has come down to us. Indeed, it is an image that has undoubtedly influenced the way that the Druids have been presented in modern times, from the sixteenth century to the present day. William Stukeley's Druids at Stonehenge, the Welsh Druids of the Gorsedd and Neo-Pagan Druidry all contain elements of Pliny's description.

to fertility. Both these concerns are emphasized in Celtic religious expression. Interestingly, in the modern pharmacopoeia, mistletoe is reputed to be beneficial to sufferers of insomnia, high blood-pressure and certain malignant tumours. Moreover, that mistletoe may have possessed important symbolism for the Celts is suggested by its presence as a motif in early Celtic art. Human heads bearing curious leaf-shaped crowns are common decorative themes on both jewellery and stone monuments (p. 59). The lobed shape of the leaves on these objects closely resembles the leaves of European mistletoe and, if such an identification is correct, it may be that the faces depicted in this pre-Roman art are those of gods or priests; perhaps even the Druids themselves.

In Pliny's comments, three other points of significance concern feasting, the moon and bull sacrifice. All three are familiar to the repertoire of Celtic religion. Ritual banquets are represented in some rich tombs of both the early and late Iron Age of Celtic Europe: the Hallstatt chieftain's tomb at Hochdorf (p. 69) was furnished with a set of nine drinking horns and a nine-piece dinner service, for the Otherworld banquet, as well as a huge cauldron of mead. Certain shrines exhibit abundant evidence of ceremonial banquets: excavators of the sanctuary at Mirebeau, in northern France, found a veritable carpet of bones from butchered animals and broken pots, which appear to be the remains of feasting. Pliny makes allusion to the moon as an instrument of healing: here again we have corroborative evidence, in that Celtic goddesses associated with healing and regeneration are sometimes depicted wearing lunar amulets; and the great temple of the healer-goddess Sulis Minerva at Bath bears a carving of the Roman moon-goddess Luna. Among the finds at Bath was a lunar pendant (p. 112), possibly once part of a priest's sceptre. Finally, bull sacrifice – mentioned by Pliny in association with Druidic ritual – is attested in other evidence. Cattle were commonly used as sacrificial animals: the shrine of Gournay in Picardy was the scene of repeated ox sacrifice, and cattle were ritually slaughtered in numerous Celtic sanctuaries. Bull sacrifice is twice depicted on the Danish Gundestrup cauldron, which was probably made in the first century BC. In Irish mythology, the *Tarbhfhess*, or 'bull sleep', was a ritual closely associated with Druidism: a selected individual was fed on bull flesh before being chanted to sleep by four Druids; while he slept, he dreamed of the next rightful king of Ireland and when he awoke, he gave this information to his Druid attendants.

Bronze figurine of a bull, sixth century BC, from a cave at Býčiskála, Moravia. The cave was the scene of complex ritual activity which included the slaughter of forty people (mostly women) and two horses. Pliny mentions the association between Druids and bull sacrifice.

Quadrangular pillar carved with foliate designs and human heads decorated with mistletoe-leaf crowns, from Pfalzfeld St Goar, Germany; fifth–fourth century BC. Pliny links the Druids with mistletoe, and it may be that the leaf-crowned heads on this pillar represent holy men, akin to the Druids.

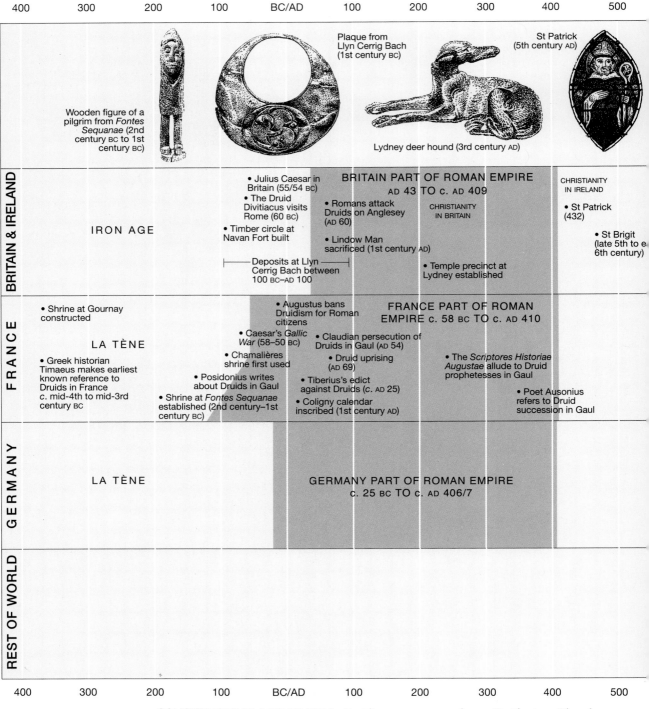

Wooden figure of a pilgrim from *Fontes Sequanae* (2nd century BC to 1st century BC)

Plaque from Llyn Cerrig Bach (1st century BC)

Lydney deer hound (3rd century AD)

St Patrick (5th century AD)

BRITAIN & IRELAND

IRON AGE

- Julius Caesar in Britain (55/54 BC)
- The Druid Divitiacus visits Rome (60 BC)
- Timber circle at Navan Fort built

— Deposits at Llyn Cerrig Bach between 100 BC–AD 100

BRITAIN PART OF ROMAN EMPIRE AD 43 TO c. AD 409

- Romans attack Druids on Anglesey (AD 60)
- Lindow Man sacrificed (1st century AD)
- Temple precinct at Lydney established

CHRISTIANITY IN BRITAIN

CHRISTIANITY IN IRELAND

- St Patrick (432)
- St Brigit (late 5th to e[...] 6th century)

FRANCE

LA TÈNE

- Shrine at Gournay constructed
- Greek historian Timaeus makes earliest known reference to Druids in France *c.* mid-4th to mid-3rd century BC
- Posidonius writes about Druids in Gaul
- Shrine at *Fontes Sequanae* established (2nd century–1st century BC)
- Caesar's *Gallic War* (58–50 BC)
- Chamalières shrine first used
- Augustus bans Druidism for Roman citizens
- Claudian persecution of Druids in Gaul (AD 54)
- Druid uprising (AD 69)
- Tiberius's edict against Druids (c. AD 25)
- Coligny calendar inscribed (1st century AD)

FRANCE PART OF ROMAN EMPIRE c. 58 BC TO c. AD 410

- The *Scriptores Historiae Augustae* allude to Druid prophetesses in Gaul
- Poet Ausonius refers to Druid succession in Gaul

GERMANY

LA TÈNE

GERMANY PART OF ROMAN EMPIRE c. 25 BC TO c. AD 406/7

REST OF WORLD

| 400 | 300 | 200 | 100 | BC/AD | 100 | 200 | 300 | 400 | 500 |

CONSTRUCTING A TIMELINE for Druidism presents a special challenge, particularly from its beginnings to AD 400. This is because our main sources are the testimonies of Greek and Roman historians, some of whom commented retrospectively about the Druids, while others – like Caesar and Strabo – relied on an earlier lost source, such as Posidonius. Therefore, any chronology for early Druidism must be made with caution.

The timeline above implies that the *floruit* of ancient Druidism was from the first century BC to the first century AD. But this picture is misleading; what the timeline, in fact, displays is

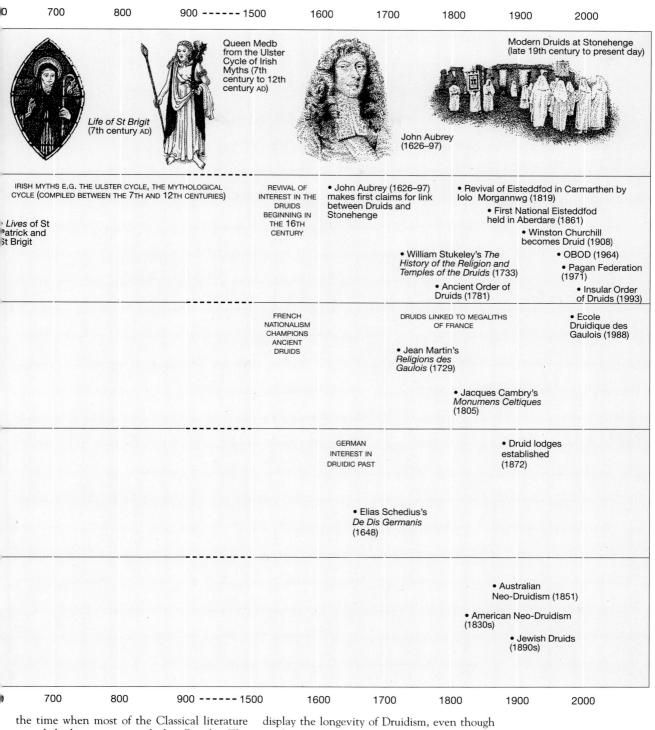

Life of St Brigit (7th century AD)

Queen Medb from the Ulster Cycle of Irish Myths (7th century to 12th century AD)

John Aubrey (1626–97)

Modern Druids at Stonehenge (late 19th century to present day)

IRISH MYTHS E.G. THE ULSTER CYCLE, THE MYTHOLOGICAL CYCLE (COMPILED BETWEEN THE 7TH AND 12TH CENTURIES)

• Lives of St Patrick and St Brigit

REVIVAL OF INTEREST IN THE DRUIDS BEGINNING IN THE 16TH CENTURY

• John Aubrey (1626–97) makes first claims for link between Druids and Stonehenge

• William Stukeley's The History of the Religion and Temples of the Druids (1733)

• Ancient Order of Druids (1781)

• Revival of Eisteddfod in Carmarthen by Iolo Morgannwg (1819)

• First National Eisteddfod held in Aberdare (1861)

• Winston Churchill becomes Druid (1908)

• OBOD (1964)

• Pagan Federation (1971)

• Insular Order of Druids (1993)

FRENCH NATIONALISM CHAMPIONS ANCIENT DRUIDS

DRUIDS LINKED TO MEGALITHS OF FRANCE

• Jean Martin's Religions des Gaulois (1729)

• Jacques Cambry's Monumens Celtiques (1805)

• Ecole Druidique des Gaulois (1988)

GERMAN INTEREST IN DRUIDIC PAST

• Elias Schedius's De Dis Germanis (1648)

• Druid lodges established (1872)

• Australian Neo-Druidism (1851)

• American Neo-Druidism (1830s)

• Jewish Druids (1890s)

| 0 | 700 | 800 | 900 ----- 1500 | 1600 | 1700 | 1800 | 1900 | 2000 |

the time when most of the Classical literature recorded the presence of the Druids. The absence of literary references to the Druids in the earlier Iron Age does not mean that they did not exist long before Caesar's time.

Despite the inherent difficulties of constructing an accurate and complete timeline, it does display the longevity of Druidism, even though its character underwent radical changes between its first mention in Gaul and Britain, at the end of the first millennium BC, and the Neo-Pagan Druidry currently practised in Britain, Europe and the rest of the world. Druidism, then, has existed in some guise for over two millennia.

THE CELTS
AND THE
SUPERNATURAL

*'The whole Gallic people is exceedingly given to religious
superstition.... Of the gods they most of all worship Mercury.
He has the largest number of images, and they regard him as
the inventor of all the arts, as their guide on the roads and in
travel, and as chiefly influential in making money and in
trade. Next to him they worship Apollo, Mars, Jupiter and
Minerva. About these gods they hold nearly the same views as
other people do: that Apollo drives away disease, that Minerva
first instituted the arts and crafts, that Jupiter rules the
heavens and Mars the issue of war.'*

Caesar, *Gallic War* VI, 16–17

CAESAR IS ONE of the few Roman writers to discuss the
gods venerated by the Celtic Gauls. But his testimony is
curious in that he presents the Gaulish pantheon as
though it were identical to that of Rome. This is, of
course, impossible since Caesar was writing during the mid-first
century BC, when Gaul was in the throes of conquest by Rome
and there simply had not been enough time for Roman religion
to have been adopted and absorbed by the new province. Caesar
seems to have indulged in something known as *interpretatio
romana*, a phrase coined by Tacitus, whereby Roman observers
equated native deities with their own, presumably because they
recognized features of similarity between certain Classical and
indigenous gods. Caesar may have used Roman names for
Gaulish gods either because he was ignorant of their true names
or, and more likely, because he wished to make his observations
comprehensible to his audience back in Rome.

This chapter explores the nature of Celtic religion, using both
ancient literature and material culture. If we can gain some
understanding of the way in which Gauls and Britons perceived
the supernatural world, we can begin to place the Druids in their
proper context, to see how they functioned within the
framework of pagan Celtic belief-systems and rituals.

*Stone relief of the antlered god, Cernunnos, from Rheims, France; first–second
century AD. Cernunnos was one of the native Gaulish gods worshipped before the
Roman period. Depictions of an antlered god occur in Iron Age imagery: on coins
and in Italian rock art.*

THE NATURE OF CELTIC RELIGION

Iron Age wooden figures: (left) female figure from Ballachulish, Argyll, Scotland, and (right) male figure from Teigngrace, Devon, England. These are interesting in that the Roman epic poet Lucan specifically mentions wooden images of the gods in Gaulish sacred groves.

WHILE GREEK AND ROMAN culture revolved around urban life, Celtic society was predominantly rural. The close link enjoyed with the natural world is reflected in what we know of the religious systems of Celtic Europe during the late first millennium BC and early first millennium AD. As in many polytheistic (multi-god) systems, the spirits worshipped were those of both the wild and cultivated landscapes and their inhabitants. Cults focused upon features of the landscape, mountains and forests and on animals. Divine powers associated with the fertility of humans, livestock and crops were objects of veneration. Tribal territories were themselves held sacred, and the ground which received the dead was imbued with sanctity and revered by their living relatives.

The spirits of watery places were invoked, as givers of life and as links between the earthly and other worlds. The celestial powers, especially the sun and thunder, were acknowledged as divine, and propitiated. Inscribed dedications and iconography, in the Roman period, show that these spirits were perceived as personifications of natural features: Taranis' name indicates

not that he was the god of thunder: he *was* thunder; Sequana was the River Seine at its spring source; Sulis was the hot spring at Bath, not simply its guardian or possessor. Certain spirits were very close to the animals with which they were associated: the names of Artio, the bear-goddess, and Epona, the horse-goddess are based on the Gaulish words for bear and horse.

The evidence for Celtic religion

Our evidence for the nature of Celtic religion comes partly from ancient literature (from the Classical commentators on the Celts, and from the vernacular mythic sources of Ireland and Wales) and partly from archaeological evidence, especially in the Roman period when inscribed dedications and religious images contribute considerably to our knowledge. What we lack (because of the virtual non-literacy of Iron Age Celts) is written testimony from the Celts themselves.

We need to exercise some care in our use of all three of these sources for Celtic religion. The Classical historians were inevitably subject to bias, distortion, ignorance, misunderstanding, literary convention and 'barbarian' stereotyping, all of which combine to present a picture of Celts and Celtic religion which is somewhat skewed and, to a certain extent, unreal.

Because of their chronological separation from the pre-Christian period, the early Welsh and Irish vernacular (written in the Welsh or Irish language) sources must be scrutinized with even more rigour than the Classical sources in assessing their validity as evidence for pagan Celtic religion. While it is possible to single out specific texts which – because of their pagan content – can be strongly argued to encapsulate genuine echoes or resonances of the pre-Christian past, the earliest mythic stories of Ireland and Wales, such as those contained in the *Mabinogi* (Wales) and the *Táin* (part of the Irish Ulster Cycle), were not compiled in written form until the medieval period. Opinion is divided as to whether these texts contain substantive material derived from oral tradition or whether they were a creation of the medieval monastic authors.

The archaeological evidence does not contain the bias inherent in the literary sources. Nonetheless, our interpretation of this evidence is inevitably coloured by our late-twentieth-century mindset.

Stone severed head, from Caerwent, South Wales. The head was found in a shrine, in the grounds of a late Roman house in the town. Ritual head hunting was practised by some Celts during the Iron Age, and may well have involved Druid participation.

Bronze stag, showing the antlers in velvet, first century BC, from a hoard of religious bronzes at Neuvy-en-Sullias, Loiret, France.

inscriptions or were included in contemporary texts. The ancient name for the River Marne was Matrona (Mother); the Seine was Sequana; the Severn, Sabrina; the Wharfe, Verbeia; and the Saône, Souconna, and there are countless others. Natural springs were foci for healing cults: Aquae Sulis (the waters of Sulis) were venerated at Bath; the goddess Arnemetia was invoked at Aquae Arnemetiae (Buxton in Derbyshire).

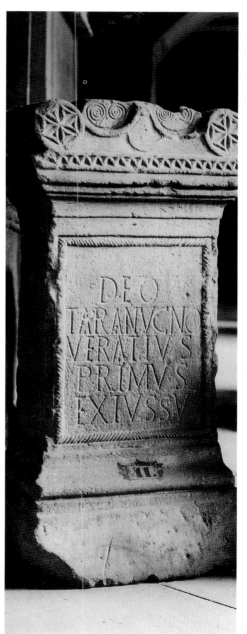

Stone altar of Roman date, with inscribed dedication to the Celtic thunder-god, Taranucnus (a derivative of Taranis), Böckingen, Germany. Taranis was one of the three Gaulish gods mentioned by Lucan as requiring appeasement by means of human sacrifice.

Bronze figurine of the Celtic sun-god, first–second century AD, from Le Châtelet, Haute-Marne, France. He resembles depictions of the Roman sky-god Jupiter, and holds a thunderbolt and lightning flashes, but the wheel is a Celtic solar symbol.

Elemental forces of the supernatural

Two of the most important groups of divine powers were those associated with the sky and water. Archaeological evidence suggests that the sun and thunder were perceived as especially potent. From as early as the Bronze Age, people in much of temperate Europe used the motif of the spoked wheel to represent the sun and, by the later Iron Age and Romano-Celtic periods, solar deities were represented with wheel-symbols. The Romans imported their own celestial god, Jupiter, to Celtic lands, and his imagery was merged with that of the native sun-god to produce a hybrid sky-deity who resembled the Roman god but had the additional native solar attribute of the wheel.

The Celts also had a native thunder-god Taranis, the Thunderer. Inscriptions to him have been found in Britain, Gaul, Germany and the former Yugoslavia, and the Roman poet Lucan mentions him as a savage god who demanded human sacrifice (p. 78).

There is abundant evidence for the veneration of water by the Celts (and, indeed, by their Bronze Age forebears). In the pre-Roman Iron Age, lakes, rivers, springs and bogs received special offerings of metalwork, wooden objects, animals and – occasionally – human beings (chapters 4 and 5). By the Roman period, the names of some water-deities were recorded on

THE CELTIC PANTHEON

IDENTIFYING THE GODS

For evidence of identifiable gods in the pre-Roman Iron Age we are reliant upon a relatively small number of images. Examples include the cross-legged stone figures from Roquepertuse (far right) and Entremont which came from shrines decorated with human skulls; these images wear armour and carry carved human heads in their hands: the inference is that the statues represent war-gods receiving appropriate cult offerings. The bronze statuette (right) from St Maur, Oise, France, is armed to the teeth: we assume that he is a warrior-god but, in the absence of a dedication or sacred context, he may represent a tribal chief rather than a deity.

The Roman presence generated considerable changes in the material culture of Celtic religion. Now, for the first time, people wrote the names of their gods on altars and images. Moreover, the amount of iconography was vastly increased, in line with Graeco-

Roman traditions of representation, and images were now frequently endowed with particular attributes or symbols which identified their function.

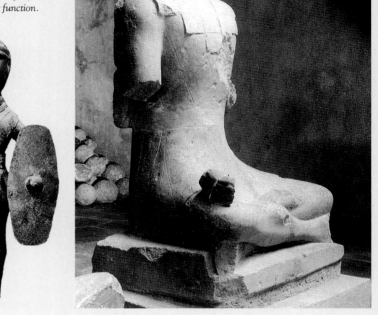

IS IT POSSIBLE to speak of a Celtic pantheon, when we have so little evidence for named pre-Roman divinities? We have two clues, both from ancient literature: one is Caesar's statement, with which we opened this chapter. If we examine his list of Gaulish divinities, we can see that there is an uncanny similarity between them and the information provided by archaeology for Romano-Celtic Gaul and Britain. Caesar says that Mercury was venerated above all: if we look at the evidence for Mercury or his native counterpart during the Roman period in western Europe, he was indeed the most popular god. Likewise Apollo, Mars, Jupiter and Minerva were all conflated with Celtic deities. Healing cults associated with Apollo in his native guise as Belenus, Moritasgus, Grannus, along with other titles, were very prevalent in Romano-Celtic Gaul; the sky-god Jupiter was equated with indigenous solar- and thunder-gods, as we have seen; Mars and Minerva, too, were both

objects of veneration. These two divinities were primarily associated with war and, interestingly, there is abundant evidence for war-deities of both sexes in the pre-Roman Celtic world.

A plethora of gods

Evidence from the Roman period presents a bewildering array of gods and goddesses who are represented by images or inscribed dedications. Sorting these multifarious and numerous divine beings into some kind of hierarchy is necessary, though not always easy, if we are to make any sense of the religious systems in place in Celtic Europe. By examining the frequency and distribution of images and god-names, it is possible to make distinctions between deities who were venerated all over the Celtic world, those who were popular in more restricted regions – perhaps corresponding to tribal boundaries – and those who were linked to a specific locality, sometimes worshipped only at a single sanctuary.

Stone relief, of Roman date, showing three Mother-Goddesses, from Vertault, Burgundy, France. The goddess on the left nurses a baby, the central one holds a towel or napkin and the third has a basin and sponge.

The establishment of patterns of frequency and distribution may point to the relative popularity of certain gods, but not necessarily to any order of importance. For example, in east-central France, the local Burgundian healing-goddess Sequana was probably more influential, in the minds of her devotees, than the Mother-Goddesses, who were worshipped all over Britain, Gaul and the Rhineland.

Certain cults transcended tribal boundaries and were followed everywhere. Examples of universal divinities include the Mother-Goddesses, the sky-god and the horse-goddess Epona, who was invoked by devotees living as far apart as Britain, Rome and Bulgaria. A distinctive feature of the Mother-Goddesses was their frequent appearance as a triad: they were perceived as a triple entity in many parts of

LUCAN'S THREE CELTIC GODS

*I*n his Pharsalia, *the Roman poet Lucan provides us with the names of three Gaulish gods with Celtic names or titles. One was Esus, a word meaning 'Lord' or 'Master'; the second was Taranis, the 'Thunderer'; the third was Teutates, a name denoting his function as a tribal god. Lucan's singling out of three gods implies that they were of particular importance, this may be borne out by a number of inscriptions to each of these three gods. Seven altars to Taranis come from scattered parts of the Celtic world; Teutates is known from some British dedications, such as the silver feather plaque (right) with inscribed dedication to Mars Toutatis (above, right) found in Hertfordshire; and Esus is mentioned on an inscription accompanying a distinctive image of a woodcutter in Paris (far right). There is an almost identical, though uninscribed, sculpture from Trier.*

MARTI
IOVIAII
TICLAVDIVS PRIMVS
ATII LIBER
V · S · L · M

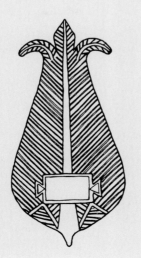

Britain, in Gaul and on the Rhine, although it is possible to identify strong regional differences between them.

The Celtic sky-god, too, had variations in the way he was perceived and his cult expressed. But the link between the Celtic Jupiter and the solar wheel is maintained over wide areas: altars decorated with wheels were set up to Jupiter by Roman soldiers on Hadrian's Wall and also by supplicants in Cologne and Nîmes.

Regional divinities can sometimes be identified, perhaps especially associated with tribal or sub-tribal territories. Specific to the Remi of northwest Gaul is a distinctive group of stone carvings depicting a triple-faced god, with shared facial features and luxuriant beards. In the Iron Age this same tribe issued coins with three faces, a motif found nowhere else in Gaul. The inference is that a specifically Remic divinity is represented. Another tribal god was Lenus, venerated by the Treveri. He was worshipped at a number of Treveran sanctuaries, the most splendid of which was at the tribal capital of Trier itself. But he was occasionally exported to other areas: Lenus had altars set up to him in faraway Britain, at Chedworth in Gloucestershire, and Caerwent in south Wales.

Some Celtic divinities, however, were extremely localized, sometimes occurring in just one shrine, perhaps because the spirit concerned was the personification of a particular place. In Gaul, over 400 different Celtic god names are recorded, of which 300 occur just once. Sequana was confined to her spring-shrine near Dijon; Sulis belonged to Bath; the divine couple Ucuetis and Bergusia were worshipped solely at Alesia in Burgundy. The British god Nodens is associated above all with the great sanctuary at Lydney on the Severn, but he appears at one other site, Cockersand Moss in Cumbria. Two other native deities – Cocidius and Belatucadrus – were both linked with war and were each worshipped in clearly defined territories in the region of Hadrian's Wall.

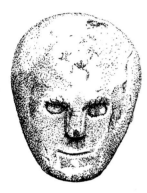

Front and side view of a stone triple head from Corleck, County Cavan; first century BC–second century AD. Three was considered a magical and sacred number by the Celts. The head probably represents a god worshipped by the Irish Celts during the late Iron Age.

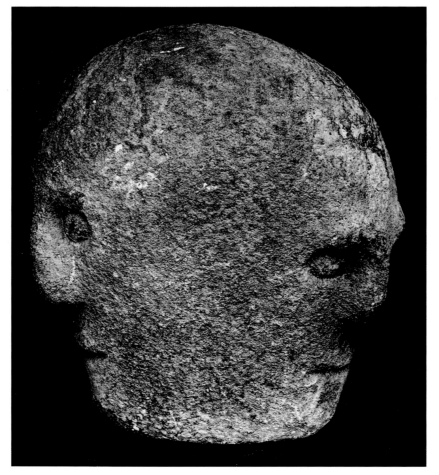

THE PAGAN CELTS perceived the presence of supernatural power as integral to their world. The sky, the sun, the dark places underground all had their spirits. Every mountain, river, spring, marsh, tree and rocky outcrop was endowed with divinity. Nemausus was the Gaulish name not only for the settlement at Nîmes in France but also for the presiding spring-god. He had a set of three female counterparts, the Nemausicae. In the same region, the town of Glanum possessed a god called Glanis: an altar from a sacred spring is inscribed 'to Glanis and the Glanicae'. Other gods whose names betray their origin as topographical spirits include Vosegus who presided over the mountains of the Vosges, Luxovius of the spa settlement of Luxeuil, and Vasio to whom belonged the town of Vaison in the Lower Rhône Valley.

Divine hunters and the wild

Hunter-gods were venerated in Celtic Europe, and they often seem to have had an ambivalent role as protector both of the hunter and his victim. From France, the armed deer-hunter depicted on an image from the temple of Le Donon (Vosges) lays his hand in benediction on the antlers of his stag companion; the hunter-god from Le Touget (Gers) carries a hare tenderly in his arms. Arduinna, the eponymous boar-goddess of the Ardennes, rides her ferocious quarry, knife in hand; whilst the boar-god of Euffigneix (Haute-Marne) is portrayed with the motif of a boar, bristles erect, striding along his torso, which implies conflation between the human and animal perception of divinity.

As is the case in many traditional societies, the hunt was probably hedged about with prohi-

Stone statue of a hunter-god, with a hare in his arms; first–second century AD, from Le Touget, Gers, France. Hunting was both a sport and a ritual activity among the Celts: the symbolic significance of hares was perhaps due to their March antics and because they forage at night. In addition, the British queen Boudica sacrificed a hare to her goddess of victory, Andraste, in the mid-first century AD.

SPIRITS IN THE LANDSCAPE

Sometimes topographical spirits were clearly associated with the fertility of the land. The triple Mothers were addressed on dedications by territorial sobriquets, particularly in the Rhineland: the Matronae Aufaniae around Bonn and the Vacallinehae at the sanctuary of Pesch are just two examples. These Germanic Mothers were especially responsible for the earth's bounty: they are depicted on altars with baskets of fruit on their laps and accompanied by acolytes bearing garlands of flowers.

Apart from features in the landscape itself, the sacred was perceived to be powerfully present in the wild and domestic animals that inhabited both farmland and wilderness. The names of some deities show their intimate association with the beasts for which they were responsible. We have already met Epona and Artio, divine protectresses of horses and bears. Mercury Moccus looked after pigs, Apollo Cunomaglus was a hound-lord, and there were many others.

Stone statuette of the horse-goddess Epona, first–third century AD, Alesia, Burgundy, France.

Stone carving of a boar-god, second–first century BC, from Euffigneix, Haute-Marne, France. The figure wears a heavy torc around his neck; a great eye is depicted along his left side, and a bristling boar strides along his torso.

communication could take place in everyday life: a family preparing its meal would, perhaps, lay aside a portion of food and drink for the spirit guardians of hearth and home. Prayers and the promise of gifts might attend preparations for the hunt, the harvest, war, marriage or birth. The gods might receive offerings at funerals, to facilitate the passage of the deceased from one world to the next. Dead ancestors might be remembered with reverence on their birth- or death-days. There is some evidence that ancestors were venerated within Celtic society: an obscure Alexandrian poet of the third century BC, known as Nicander of Colophon, alludes to the Celts' practice of communicating with their dead in order to predict the future: to this end, they would spend the night beside the graves of family members, hoping for enlightenment during sleep. The ritually dismembered human bodies found in the Iron Age sanctuary of Gournay in Picardy, France, suggested to the excavator, Jean-Louis Brunaux, that some kind of funerary ritual, perhaps connected with an ancestor-cult, had been practised there. The single human bones found in grain silos at Danebury may represent the symbolic presence of ancestors returning home after ritual exposure of the bodies elsewhere.

Sandstone statue of a horned or leaf-crowned god, with janiform head; from Holzerlingen, Germany; sixth–fifth century BC. The double-faced image could look both into the earthly and supernatural worlds.

bitions and rituals. The Greek author Arrian, writing in the second century AD, said that the Celts never went hunting without the gods' blessing, and that they made payment of domestic animals to the supernatural powers in reparation for their theft of wild creatures from the landscape. Hunting itself may have been perceived as a symbolic, as well as practical, activity, in which the spilling of blood led not only to the death of the beast but to the earth's nourishment and replenishment.

Communicating with the spirits

The available evidence suggests that the ancient Celts lived in a world which they shared with multifarious spirits, and, this being so, it is reasonable to suppose that attempts were made to reach and interact with that spirit world. Such

IT IS AGAINST the backdrop of pagan Celtic religion outlined in the preceding pages of this chapter that we have to set the Druids and, indeed, other religious officials. An important characteristic of pagan priests in antiquity was that they were not concerned with ethics or morality, but with the wielding of power by means of religion. There is an enormous difference between the nature of Christian priests – whose duty it is to guide and counsel their parishioners as to the correct path to follow, in order to gain salvation – and most pagan priests of the ancient world.

Perhaps, in part at least, because the Druids of Gaul and Britain have only been observed and recorded through Classical eyes, it is possible to discern considerable similarities between Druids and Roman priests. Both were involved in the control of supernatural forces by means of divination; both were closely associated with secular power; both were heavily involved with sacrifice; and both were concerned with controlling the populace.

A professional pagan clergy

A striking characteristic of Celtic society was the close link between religion and politics, a phenomenon which we find also in the Roman world. Election to Gaulish magistracies was accompanied by religious ceremonies, which took place on consecrated ground, attended by priests and other tribal leaders. We can cite close parallels in Britain today when a new monarch is crowned in Westminster Abbey in the company of the most senior prelates in the land.

Classical writers record several instances of Gaulish royal involvement in religious affairs: Dio Cassius speaks of King Ambigatus of the Bituriges, who carried out divination and sacrifice. Likewise, the Galatian king, Deiotarus, is reported by Cicero as being both warlord and the most powerful religious leader in the land. Even the name of this king links him with sanctity, since it is etymologically related to the word for god. Only he was endowed with the ability to interpret certain omens. Caesar's friend Divitiacus, of the royal Aeduan house (the Aedui were an eastern Gaulish tribe), was both ruler and Druid.

We need to pose the question as to how far religious officials in Gaul and Britain formed a professional group, distinct from any secular office. We also need to explore definitions of 'priest' and to see whether such a term is appropriate for the Druids. Is it possible, for instance, to make a distinction between priests and prophets or between Druids and magicians? To try and answer such questions, we have to go back to the descriptions of the Druids in the ancient literature, particularly the detailed account given by Caesar. Anthropologists find it difficult to arrive at a universal determination of 'priesthood': in both ancient and modern traditional societies, the term defies restrictive definition. Some scholars, notably Nora Chadwick, in her seminal work *The Druids*, published in 1966, deny that the Druids were priests at all, and stress their political role. But, given the seemingly inevitable links between politics and religion in antiquity, and given the very clear religious role of the Druids (according to Caesar, Strabo, Diodorus, Lucan and many others), I find no problem in referring to the Druids as priests: after all, Caesar categorically states 'The Druids expound religious matters …' (VI, 13).

The testimony of the Graeco-Roman writers demonstrates that the Druids were concerned with a wide range of politico-religious functions, and that they were involved with prophecy and the practice of magic, as well as the more straightforward priestly responsibilities of cult-organization, prayer and sacrifice.

Caesar informs us that the Druids were definitely a professional class, in that they were trained specialists (taking as long as twenty years to learn their craft), set apart from the common people in their exemption from both fighting and taxation: 'The Druids are wont to be absent from war, nor do they pay taxes like the others' (VI, 14).

PRIESTS AND POLITICS

The politico-religious responsibility of the Aeduan chief Divitiacus is directly comparable to Julius Caesar's own situation in Rome: in 63 BC, Caesar gained the office of Pontifex Maximus (chief religious official), which was as much a political as a religious position and one to which he was elected, just as with any of the major state magistracies. The power accrued to him through this 'religious' office was political, and it is interesting that woven into the establishment of the Principate (the rule of Rome by an emperor) by Augustus, in the late first century BC, was the office of Pontifex Maximus, as one of the usual imperial titles. The close connection that seems to have existed between priest and politician among the Celts and the Romans has its modern equivalent, notably in some of the Islamic states, particularly Iran. Even in today's secular Britain, the Queen is both head of state and head of the Anglican Church.

Bronzes from religious hoards in Britain. (Top) Model bronze wheel and boar figurine, from a hoard at Hounslow near London; first century BC. (Below) Raven figurines and a model wheel found with other bronzes, deposited in a pot with mid-third century AD coins, from Felmingham Hall, Norfolk. Hoards like this may well have been temple furniture buried for safe keeping by Druids or other clergy at a time of danger.

DRUIDIC ORGANIZATION

Priestly colleges existed in many Indo-European societies, including Italic and Indo-Iranian systems. Caesar's description of the annual gathering among the Carnutes hints at their presence in Gaul. People achieved Druidic status by merit and training rather than by belonging to a dynasty, although Caesar implies that only noblemen could aspire to such high office. The situation may have changed by the fourth century AD when the poet Ausonius described a Druidic dynasty based upon family succession.

There must have been religious officials other than Druids, and Classical writers mention sacerdotes, gutuatri, vates and others (p. 115). The divisions in the priesthood may have been partly to do with central or local organization, and partly to do with rank. It is likely that each shrine had some kind of custodian, and the individuals who undertook the butchering of sacrificial animals were probably of lower status than the Druids themselves.

Caesar's statement concerning Druidic exemption from war and taxation is important: such dispensation must have been confined to few people. Their exemption from warfare may have been due to the need for Druids to be unpolluted by death (the Roman Flamen Dialis – or High Priest of Jupiter – could not be defiled by the sight of dead bodies). If this were the case for the Druids, however, such a prohibition cannot have extended to human sacrifice!

> *'The Druids have one at their head who holds the chief authority among them. When he dies, either the highest in honour among the others succeeds, or if some are on an equal footing they contend for leadership by a vote of the Druids, but sometimes even in arms.'*
> Caesar, *Gallic War* VI, 13

CAESAR'S COMMENTS MAKE it clear that, in mid-first-century Gaul, elevation to the highest Druidic office was through merit rather than heredity. It is interesting to note that the Druidic exemption from fighting did not mean a total prohibition on combat.

The testimony of writers such as Caesar helps us to build up a picture of how the Druids may have been organized and the extent to which the Druidic system spanned the Celtic world. Caesar tells us that: 'At a fixed time of the year they [the Druids] meet in assembly in a holy place in the land of the Carnutes, which is regarded as the centre of the whole of Gaul' (VI, 13) (p. 45).

The implication is that the Druids existed all over Gaul and that there was some kind of network which linked them all. Analogous to this Gaulish holy place among the Carnutes (which was probably somewhere around the modern town of Chartres) was Drunemeton (the 'Oak Sanctuary') in Asia Minor, described by Strabo, in which the Galatian Council met. It may be, therefore, that the Druids were also present here in Asia Minor. We know, too, that Druids operated in Britain: 'It is thought that this system of training was invented in Britain and taken over from there to Gaul, and at the present time diligent students of the matter mostly travel there to study it' (Caesar VI, 13). Caesar is equally definite, however, that the Druidic system did not pertain in Germany (i.e. beyond the Rhine): '… they have no Druids in charge of religious matters' (VI, 21).

The Druids as mediators

One of the main functions of pagan priests was to act as mediators both between the spirit and human worlds and between different human groups. Similarly in the modern world, Christian clergy on the one hand act as a link between God and people – by prayer, the administration of the sacrament and other sacral activities – and, on the other, frequently take the role of political mediators, for example in Northern Ireland, Bosnia, South Africa and other trouble-spots in the world.

The Druids also possessed the dual responsibility of mediating between gods and humans, and between disputing groups of peoples. The act of divination, which played such a pivotal role in Druidic activity, was a mediation-exercise in which communication with the supernatural powers was effected.

Mediation between the gods and people may have given the Druids authority to negotiate in secular matters as well. Caesar tells us that they acted as judges, arbitrators and negotiators in disputes of all kinds. Indeed, that was one of the functions of the Druids' annual assembly. The Druids' influence in mediation may also have been linked to their role as keepers of oral tradition, which was both the tribe's history and its identity.

Prayer and propitiation

Before the Roman period, we have very little evidence for the use of prayer among the Celts, though invoking the spirit world must have been common practice. Sacrifice – of which much is made by Classical writers – is a form of prayer, and was presumably practised in order to 'win over' the gods, to persuade them to help rather than harm their devotees, and to thank them for blessings received.

Prayers were presumably said in sanctuaries and at other cult foci. It may be that images of the gods provided a focus for prayer, as did altars in the Roman period and carved stone crosses in early Christian Ireland. Indeed, inscriptions on Gaulish and British altars sometimes testify to the devotion of supplicants, for they frequently bear the information that the stones were the gifts of pilgrims 'in willing fulfilment of a vow'. In this, the pagan Celts of the Roman empire were following Roman practice, but often addressing their own native divinities. The lead curses found in shrines like Bath, exhorting the goddess Sulis to punish malefactors, are also a form of prayer (p. 114).

We have to assume that, just as occurs today, there were organized and private prayers. The Druids and their peers would have conducted solemn prayer rituals for the whole tribe or community on important occasions. Lesser priests might lead small communities in prayer, and the head of the household perhaps led private family prayers.

SHAMANISM IN CELTIC BRITAIN?

*I*n many traditional societies, including those of some North American Indians and in Siberia, religious officials known as shamans take on the guise of animals, in order to make contact with the spirit world (right). We have no unequivocal evidence for shamanism among the pagan Celts, but indirect evidence, such as a newly discovered antler headdress from Hook's Cross in Hertfordshire (p. 58), the figure with a similar antler headdress shown on the Gundestrup cauldron (below, right), and the 'pantomime horses' depicted on the late Iron Age bucket (below) from Aylesford in Kent, may indicate the existence of shamanistic practices. Antler headdresses could have been worn by a priest or Druid who used the guise of a stag to reach the spirits of the wild; the Aylesford horses, with their human legs, could represent men dressed in horse-skins taking part in a ritual dance. In any case, it may well have been that priests entered into ecstatic trances (perhaps aided by intoxicating or hallucinatory substances) wherein they were addressed by the gods. We know that narcotics were available to Iron Age peoples: cannabis has been found in the Hallstatt tomb at Hochdorf in Germany. Some scholars have recently interpreted the curious, surreal, images which appear in pre-Roman Celtic art as possibly being executed by artists while in a drug-induced trance.

CEREMONIES AND FESTIVALS

Bronze head of a bull-horned god from Lezoux, France; first–second century AD. Many Celtic gods are depicted in semi-human, semi-animal form, as if to emphasize the close links which were perceived between humans and the natural world.

ANCIENT LITERATURE MAKES numerous references to assemblies and ceremonies, generally associated with religious or quasi-religious activities. The annual Druid 'synod' among the Carnutes in Gaul (p. 45) was probably an occasion for festivities as well as solemnities. Athenaeus, drawing on the work of Posidonius and so referring to the early first century BC, tells of a central Gaulish chieftain called Louernius, ruler of the Arverni, who held a festival, where 'in an attempt to win popular favour, [he] rode in a chariot over the plains distributing gold and silver to the tens of thousands of Celts who followed him', and hosted a sumptuous feast that lasted several days (Athenaeus, *Deinosphists* IV, 37). Irish vernacular mythic texts also refer to politico-religious assemblies and festivals, notably the great Assembly of Tara (the sacred place of royal investiture) where fairs, markets, horse-races and other social events took place.

It is the early Irish literature that has given us the names of the four great seasonal festivals, some of which were closely associated with the Druids. The celebrations marked important points in the farming calendar, and their functions were to propitiate the divine powers for healthy crops and livestock, to mark the passage of the seasons and to allow the people to relax after their intensive agricultural labour. The names of these four great Irish festivals were: Imbolc, Beltane, Lughnasadh and Samhain.

Imbolc and spring

The festival of Imbolc took place in spring on 1 February, and celebrated the lambing season and the lactation of ewes. The name means 'purification' (perhaps associated with the pure white of milk) and Imbolc was particularly associated with the pagan Irish goddess Brigit, who later became a Christian saint but she retained both her old festival and her responsibility for the dairy. Imbolc seems primarily to have been a purificatory festival, perhaps to ward off harm from the pregnant ewes, their lambs and their milk.

Beltane and summer

Beltane is the great Celtic May festival, still celebrated under that name in Scotland and Ireland, and known as Calan Mai in Wales. It was celebrated on 1 May, and marked the official beginning of summer, when livestock was moved onto high pastureland. Beltane was, and is, a fire festival. In his Glossary, the ninth-century Irish writer Cormac firmly links Beltane with the Druids; he speaks of the two great fires they made, between which cattle were driven as a symbolic protection against disease. The name Beltane probably derives either from 'bil' (luck) or 'bel' (light).

The chief assembly at Tara, the official centre of Ireland, took place at Beltane. Many Irish myths associate fire, Beltane and the Druids. The *Book of Invasions* contains a story concerning the Druid Mide, founder of Meath, who was the first Druid to light a Beltane fire. The twelfth-century Irish text known as the *Dinnshenchas* tells how his great fire spread all over Ireland, and he thus incurred the enmity of the other, native Druids. Mide cut out all their tongues and ritually burnt them, presumably because a Druid unable to speak would thereby lose all his power. Speech, including prophecy and satire, was an important Druid tool.

The May festival of Beltane, showing the Druidic fire ritual which celebrated the beginning of summer. Cattle are shown being driven between two bonfires, in an act of fertility – and as a purification ritual.

Lughnasadh and autumn

The harvest-festival of Lughnasadh was celebrated on 1 August and for the fortnight preceding and following. It is named after the great Irish divinity Lugh, a god of light, war and craftsmanship, who founded the festival in honour of his foster-mother, Tailtiu. Lughnasadh was celebrated at various great Irish centres: Emhain Macha in Ulster; Carman in Leinster and at Tara for the whole of Ireland. The *Dinnschenchas* describes Lughnasadh as a festival of assembly where political and legal matters were settled, but it was also a forum for other pan-tribal activities, such as games and feasting. Ritual events to promote successful harvests would also have been enacted and were probably presided over by Druids or other religious officials.

Samhain and winter

The fourth major Insular festival was Samhain, which was celebrated on 31 October/1 November. The word 'samhain' may derive from the Irish 'samrad' or Gaulish 'samon', terms which refer to the warm season of the Celtic year; thus Samhain may signify the end of warm weather and the beginning of winter. A great assembly at Tara was held at this time, and the origin of the festival may have been linked with the rounding up and selection of domestic animals for winter culling, food-provision or breeding. Samhain was a dangerous time, like its successor Hallowe'en, it was a period in which the conventional boundaries of space and time were temporarily suspended and where the spirits of the Otherworld mingled freely with the living. Traditionally Samhain is associated with the Celtic New Year, but doubt has recently been cast on this particular connection.

Samhain was a time of immense spiritual energy, when momentous events were liable to take place. The Ulster hero Cú Chulainn had Otherworld encounters at this festival, as did the superhuman war-leader Finn in the Fenian Cycle. At Samhain, the tribal god, the Daghda, mated with the raven war-goddess, the Morrigán; and the ceremonies associated with sacral kingship were linked with the winter festival.

The Druids were associated with Samhain: their mediatory powers were required to control the supernatural energy flowing from the open Otherworld. The ancient Irish goddess Tlachtga, the daughter of a Druid, gave her name to a hill where a great assembly was held at Samhain.

Stone janiform head, joined at the centre by the beak of a bird of prey, from the shrine of Roquepertuse in southern France; fourth–third century BC. The head, mounted at the entrance to the sanctuary, may be an image of the presiding god, whose double gaze could survey both the sacred and the profane worlds.

AS WE HAVE SEEN, all four of the great Celtic religious festivals – Imbolc, Beltane, Lughnasadh and Samhain – were linked to events in the farming calendar involving agricultural or pastoral activities. This situation has its parallels in the Roman calendar of festivals, which combined ritual observances with celebration of the different phases of the year.

Peter Reynolds' work on the Butser Iron Age Farm Project in Hampshire, England, has sought to reconstruct the Celtic farming year. Based on his experiments, he has shown that activities undertaken at certain times of the year were crucial to the success and even survival of rural communities.

Winter was the period when a great deal of woodland management took place. Alongside the provision of fuel went the production of timber for building and tools.

The beginning of spring was the time for ploughing and sowing. Grass began to grow and livestock could be turned out to pasture; calves, lambs and kids were born.

Sheep-shearing (or plucking) took place at the beginning of summer, in early June. This would have been followed by the washing, spinning and weaving of the wool. In early July, haymaking started: hay was essential for winter fodder. Harvesting of crops occurred in August; this was a labour-intensive process. Once the harvest was in, livestock would be let out into the fields to graze, trample and manure the denuded ground. An early autumn task would be the arrangements for the storage of grain over the winter: in southern England, underground silos or storage-pits were used. Autumn was the time that animals were sorted out; the surplus males and the weak stock would be slaughtered, and the meat smoked or salted down. Manuring, followed by autumn ploughing would begin, probably to be completed just before Samhain.

Calendars and sacred festivals

Seasonal religious celebrations were naturally closely linked to the annual calendar. The Roman official calendar was actually drawn up by the College of Pontiffs: it contained the dates of all the cult festivals, along with the days on which markets were held. Some days were regarded as unlucky for religious activities, others auspicious. One example of a surviving Italian town calendar is the tablet from Antium, which marks out each day, together with instructions as to the right and wrong times to perform sacrifices and other rituals.

The Antium calendar has a close parallel in a fragmentary Gaulish bronze tablet, dating to the first century BC, from Coligny in central France, which appears to be a timetable of religious festivals and cult events (p. 89). The Coligny calendar is our best evidence for the supposition that the great Irish seasonal festivals of Imbolc, Beltane, Lughnasadh and Samhain were also celebrated elsewhere in the Celtic world: the word 'Samonios' occurs on the tablet, and this is cognate with Samhain. In addition, the first-fruit festival entered on the calendar for 1 August, under the term 'Rivros' ('Great Festal Month', according to Anne Ross), may be cognate with Lughnasadh, which was held at this time.

The Druids were almost certainly involved in the drawing up of the Coligny calendar, just as the Roman priests were responsible for the calendars at Antium and elsewhere. Each major Gaulish and British town or tribe may have had its own sacred timetable which was perhaps normally inscribed on wood and so has not survived. Alternatively, of course, at least in the less romanized regions or before Roman influence, these Celtic religious calendars would have been kept in the heads of the priests, a knowledge which would have enhanced their status and power within their communities. We should remember Caesar's statement about the Gaulish Druids: 'They consider it improper to entrust their studies to writing …' (VI, 14).

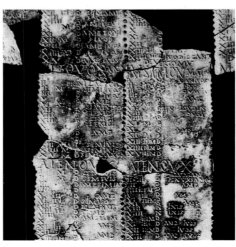

FARMING AND THE GODS

*A*ll parts of the farming year were critically important. If the weather was hostile or if crops or animals were blighted by disease, disaster could strike the farmer, his family and the community. So the gods had to be propitiated with the correct prayers, ceremonies and sacrifices. The right or wrong days for ploughing, sowing and reaping had to be calculated, and the divinatory powers of the Druids would have been central to such predictions.

That the gods were themselves associated with agricultural activities is suggested by the comments of two ancient authors. One is Tacitus who, in his Germania, recounts a ceremony in which a sacred wagon belonging to the earth-goddess Nerthus was wheeled round her territory to a place of celebration, where feasting went on for several days. The second writer is Gregory of Tours, a sixth-century bishop who wrote of a rite and festival which took place in Autun, France, in the third century AD: the goddess Berecynthia was carried in a wagon round the countryside 'for the preservation of their fields and vineyards'.

The Coligny calendar, from near Bourg-en-Bresse, France, first century BC, consisting of a fragmentary bronze plaque inscribed in Gaulish with a calendar of sixty-four months. It was probably used by the Druids to calculate the most auspicious days for ceremonies, festivals and important political events. The calendar was deliberately broken before its deposition in the earth.

III

THE DRUIDS IN CLASSICAL LITERATURE

*'Philosophers, as we may call them, and men learned in religious affairs are unusually honoured among them [the Gauls] and are called by them Druids....
And it is a custom of theirs that no one should perform a sacrifice without a "philosopher"; for thank-offerings should be rendered to the gods, they say, by the hands of men who are experienced in the nature of the divine, and who speak, as it were, the language of the gods....'*

Diodorus Siculus, *Library of History* V, 31, 1–5

FROM AS EARLY AS 200 BC the Druids were a subject of fascination to writers from the Graeco-Roman world. These chroniclers, locked into their own culture, observed both the Celts and the Druids – almost from the point of view of tourists – as curiosities, very different from themselves. But at the same time, they noted aspects of Druidism which were also features of their own religion, particularly prophecy and divination. It was the practice of human sacrifice, however, that marked out the Druids as outlandish barbarians.

The Druids are only mentioned for certain in Gaul and Britain. There are references, for example, by Diogenes Laertius in the third century AD, to Druids among the Galatai, but the term may refer to Gaul rather than Galatia in Asia Minor.

Collectively, the Classical literature presents us with a complex picture of the Druids. They are variously described as religious officials, teachers, thinkers, healers and magicians. The attitudes of the Greek and Roman writers to the Druids are far from uniform and display major contradictions. For some, the Druids were savage, uncouth barbarians who had to be eradicated, but for others, the Druids were worthy of respect as intellectuals and high-minded philosophers. Pomponius Mela called them 'Masters of Wisdom'.

The writings of the Classical chroniclers had a strong influence on the representations of Druids in paintings of the eighteenth and nineteenth centuries, such as 'The Druids' Ceremony' by Noel Halle (detail, left), c. 1737–44.

THE CHRONICLERS

THE DRUIDS DAMNED
'The Druids, too, took advantage of the armistice to resume the barbarous rites of their wicked religion …'
Lucan, *Pharsalia* I, 422–65

'… the groves devoted to Mona's [Anglesey] barbarous superstitions he demolished. For it was their [the Druids'] religion to drench their altars in the blood of prisoners …'
Tacitus, *Annals* XIV, 30–31

'For the principate of Tiberius Caesar did away with their Druids and that class of seers and doctors …'
Pliny, *Natural History* XXX, 4

'… the Druids, in addition to natural philosophy, study also moral philosophy. The Druids are considered the most righteous of men …'
Strabo, *Geography* IV, 4, 4

THE CLASSICAL WRITERS fall, by and large, into pro-Druid and anti-Druid camps, though some authors include elements of both. The earliest surviving literature is sometimes known as the Posidonian Tradition. Posidonius was a Syrian-born Greek philosopher, living around 135–50 BC, who travelled in Gaul and whose work only survives in the literature of later writers. Of these, Caesar (100–44 BC), Strabo (*c.* 60 BC–AD 20–25) and Diodorus (fl. first century BC) – all writing during the first century BC – are the most important. Sometimes they specifically acknowledge Posidonius; in other writings his

influence can be identified. The descriptions of the Druids in all these texts are remarkably similar in many respects, but Caesar's testimony is the most detailed and perhaps benefits from his lengthy sojourn in Gaul in the 50s BC.

All three of these writers present a mixed image of the Druids, though the emphasis is on their barbarism. Caesar quite clearly had respect for their power, whilst both Diodorus and Strabo allude to their philosophical activities and their association with the barbarous practice of human sacrifice, almost in the same breath: 'Philosophers, as we may call them.… It is in consonance with their savagery that they practise a unique impiety in their sacrifices …' (Diodorus Siculus V, 31, 3, 32, 6).

Hostility to the Druids: Pliny, Lucan and Tacitus

The Roman authors Pliny, Lucan and Tacitus were writing over 100 years later than Caesar, at a time when Gaul was becoming fully integrated into the Roman empire and Britain was in the process of pacification. All three are unsympathetic to the Druids. Lucan and Tacitus speak of dreadful rites involving human sacrifice in secluded groves. Pliny sneers at Druidic magic. The testimony of all of them is influenced by the

(Above) The Roman emperor Tiberius tried to eradicate Druidism in the Celtic world by issuing an edict banning the practice of the Druidic religion.

(Right) Some Greek scholars – such as Hippolytus and Clement of Alexandria – created an idealized notion of the Druids as 'Noble Savages', emphasizing their roles as learned thinkers and mystics, and downplaying any reference to their involvement in human sacrifice.

image of primitive barbarism, an offence to the civilized world and worthy of eradication.

Respect for the Druids: Alexandrians and others

Among Greek scholars educated in the schools of Alexandria in the early Christian period, there arose the idealized notion of the Druid as an example of the 'Noble Savage', the simple yet powerful mystic, untainted by the trammels of civilization. These writers do not mention human sacrifice, but emphasize the Druids' role as learned thinkers. The scholars who expounded such images of the Druids – men such as the Christian Hippolytus (AD 170–c. 236), Clement of Alexandria (AD 150–c. 212) and Cyril of Alexandria (Archbishop AD 412–444) – had no empirical knowledge nor eye-witness accounts of Druidism, but were library researchers whose material was all second-hand. All these Greek authors acknowledged earlier sources, such as Timaeus (356–260 BC) and Polyhistor (born c. 105 BC), for their work.

Other writers, too, used Alexandrian sources: Diodorus Siculus and the great fourth-century AD writer Ammianus Marcellinus cite the work of Timagenes, an Alexandrian who came as a captive to Rome in 55 BC.

(Left) A number of Roman writers – such as Pliny, Lucan and Tacitus – were hostile and unsympathetic to the Druids, giving them a thoroughly bad press. These chroniclers emphasized the Druids' role in barbaric activities such as bloodthirsty human sacrifice in secret forest groves.

The Alexandrians had a profound interest in what they saw as the pure and simple wisdom of the barbarians. Their view, like that propounded in the Book of Genesis, was that Man had fallen from Grace and that developed society was deficient compared to the Golden Age of the past. They shared this opinion with many other thinkers of Classical antiquity, notably the eighth-century BC Greek poet Hesiod and the first-century AD Roman, Lucretius.

How reliable were the Classical authors?

On the face of it, we should expect the earlier sources to be the most trustworthy, because they were written at, or just after, a time when Druids were still an active force. Posidonius visited Gaul, and Caesar spent nearly ten years there. Pliny, Lucan and Tacitus were all contemporary with the early imperial attempts to eradicate Druidism. But these earlier chroniclers of the Druids all had an agenda other than mere historical recording. Each was bound not only by the conventions of Mediterranean culture but also by literary convention, which allowed for exaggeration, romanticism, invented speeches and the unacknowledged use of other sources. The archetypal or stereotypical barbarian image is always present, to a greater or lesser extent. Stock characterization influences the descriptions of Celts and Druids. Certain phrases, which are apparently meaningful, have to be treated with scepticism. Thus Strabo's remark that the Druids were 'the most righteous' of men is a stock Greek literary attribute for foreigners, and may possess no more profound meaning than that.

The writers of the Posidonian and Alexandrian traditions may have been affected by the current philosophies of the Graeco-Roman world. So the Druids were perhaps artificially credited with Stoic and Pythagorean thinking, and we have seen that the idealized Alexandrian portrait of the 'Noble Savage' had a wider arena than its application to Druidism. What is interesting is that Christian writers were sympathetic to pagan Druids.

Caesar is our most useful source for the Druids. Although his *Gallic War* had a politico-

BRITAIN AND THE DRUIDS

'It is thought that this [the Druidic] system of training was invented in Britain and taken over from there to Gaul, and at the present time diligent students of the matter mostly travel there to study it.'
Caesar, Gallic War VI, 13

Caesar is not unique among Roman writers in his comments on the presence of Druids in Britain. His statement is important, not only because of its implications for the status of British Druids, but also because it makes a close link between Gaulish and British society.

More than a hundred years later, Pliny the Elder wrote similarly of the sharing of Druidic practice between Gaul and Britain: 'But why should I speak of these things when the craft [of Druidism] has even crossed the Ocean and reached the empty voids of Nature? Even today Britain practises magic in awe, with such grand ritual that it might seem that she gave it to the Persians' (Pliny, Natural History XXX, 4).

Pliny is saying the reverse of Caesar. But the point here is the mention of Britain as being so remote from civilization as to be virtually off the edge of the world. Thus the image of the Druids as 'beyond the pale' is enhanced.

The Roman historian Tacitus, too, speaks of Druids in Britain, specifically on Anglesey, to which island stronghold they may have been driven after the Roman occupation which began in AD 43 (see below). Tacitus is a relatively objective chronicler and there is no reason to doubt his testimony that the Roman governor attacked the Druids' sanctuary in AD 60/61.

(Above) Reconstruction of a sacrificial scene outside the temple of Sulis Minerva at Bath, with the officiating priest and a supplicant.

mentioned in the ethnographical section, in Book VI, as if this account is a digression from the historical chronicle of the Gallic Wars contained in the other books. Indeed, the picture of Gaulish society presented in Book VI may have been a deliberately 'native' ethnographical piece of reporting. This would explain why he used the Gaulish term 'Druid' in Book VI rather than *sacerdos*, his term for 'priest' in the other sections. However, *sacerdos* and Druid are not synonymous: Caesar's description of Druids presents them as quasi-priests/quasi-magistrates and scholars have rightly pointed out that Caesar's Druids have much in common with the politico-religious role of high-ranking magistrates in late republican Rome.

The Classical accounts of the Druids probably contain elements of truth and fantasy. That the Druids were both politically influential, at the height of their power, and central to religious affairs need not be questioned. But we must be aware of embroidery, exaggeration and false accreditation.

propaganda purpose, his description of the Druids is dispassionate, detailed and contemporary. He was present in Gaul before the Druids lost political power. However, Caesar's testimony has problems: the Druids are only

(Left) The Roman poet Lucan described a Druidic grove near Marseille, which was destroyed by Caesar's soldiers in the mid-first century BC. He commented upon the ghastly wooden images of the gods which lurked among the trees (rather in the manner of Haitian Voodoo dolls), terrifying visitors to the sacred wood.

(Right) King Arthur's mentor, the Druid Merlin, tricked into climbing into a chasm. Illustration c. 1905 by Henry Justice Ford (1860–1941).

DRUIDS AND THE SOCIAL ORDER

Divitiacus: Druid and ruler

The great Roman orator and author, Cicero, was a near contemporary of Caesar who met Divitiacus in 60 BC, when the Aeduan noble-man visited Rome in an abortive attempt to elic-it Roman help against the incursions into Gaul by the German king, Ariovistus. Cicero's com-ment is important because, although Caesar speaks of Divitiacus at great length, only Cicero calls him a Druid. Cicero's remark was made in the context of a discussion of Roman republican rule by the senate, through the authority of religion.

According to Caesar, Divitiacus was a pro-Roman Aeduan chieftain and a personal friend. He shared power with his younger brother Dumnorix, who led the anti-Roman faction and was a passionate nationalist. Divitiacus was immensely influential in Gaulish politics and, moreover, was a frequent mediator between Gaulish leaders and Caesar. He attended the convention of Gaulish states, and it was this body that sent him to Rome to plead on behalf of all the tribes. Divitiacus negotiated with Rome for pardons both for his own brother and for the rebel tribe of the Bellovaci. His image is that of an urbane, reasonable politician, an ele-gant rhetorician and diplomatist and a skilled and persuasive arbitrator.

Dumnorix the freedom fighter

Divitiacus' brother Dumnorix is an interesting character and he, too, may have been a Druid. When Caesar was planning his second visit to Britain in 54 BC, he decided that any potentially treacherous chieftains should go with him, rather than be left to foment rebellion behind his back. One of these was Dumnorix who said that he did not like sea-travel and, significantly, 'that religious considerations prevented him'.

Judges and arbitrators

'The Druids are considered the most righteous of men and on this account they are entrusted with the decision not only of the private disputes, but of the public disputes as well; so that, in former times, they even arbitrated in

THE CLASSICAL TEXTS make it clear that – just as in the belief-systems of many societies in antiquity and the present – Celtic religion and politics were closely linked, and that the Druids were the main focus for such connections. Caesar says that the only two classes of any con-sequence in Gaulish society were the Druids (whom he puts first) and the *equites* (knights). He goes on to discuss their manifold responsibil-ities which included political and military nego-tiations, the conduct of sacrifices, religious instruction and training. Dio Chrysostom (AD 40–c. 112) speaks with respect for the political and intellectual powers of the Druids, compar-ing them to Persian *magi*, Indian Brahmins and other influential learned classes.

cases of war and made the opponents stop when they were about to line up for battle, and the murder cases, in particular, had been turned over to them for decision …'

Strabo, *Geography* IV, 4, 4

Strabo, Diodorus and Caesar all refer to the Druids' responsibilities in judging criminal and civil cases, but Strabo speaks as though military arbitration belonged to the past at the time he was writing. Yet his near contemporary, Diodorus, is definite in his mention of current Druidic involvement in war:

'Nor is it only in the exigencies of peace, but in their wars as well that they obey, before others, these men and their chanting poets, and such obedience is observed not only by their friends but also by their enemies; many times, for instance, when two armies approach each other in battle with swords drawn and spears thrust forward, these men step forth between them and cause them to cease, as though having cast a spell over certain kinds of wild beasts. In this way, even among the wildest barbarians, does passion give place before wisdom, and Ares [Greek god of War] stands in awe of the Muses.'

Diodorus Siculus, *Library of History* V, 31, 1–5

Caesar comments on the Druids' role as judges for all manner of crimes or civil disputes, from murders to legacies. They presided over cases involving both individuals and communities, and intervened in matters involving property-boundaries. One of the principal roles of the great annual Carnutian assembly of Druids was to settle disputes. A particular form of control over men, exercised by the Druids, involved banning them from sacrificial ceremonies, a kind of excommunication which effectively outlawed the malefactor from society. Strabo is out of step here, and it may be that his change of tense, halfway through his narrative, may have been a deliberate introduction of archaism, to give the piece a 'once upon a time', fairy-tale dimension.

(Above) A Galatian warrior kills his wife and himself to evade capture.

(Below) The Druids held an annual assembly in the tribal territory of the Carnutes, the symbolic centre of Gaul.

45

A lead curse tablet dedicated to Nemesis, the goddess of justice and vengeance, found in the amphitheatre at the legionary fortress of Caerleon, south Wales. The tablet may have been dedicated by a Roman soldier placing a bet at the games or by a gladiator, hoping thus to win his contest and survive. Such curse tablets may have been written by religious functionaries.

'The Druids of Gaul have recorded that it [the selago plant] should be kept on the person to ward off all fatalities, and that the smoke of it is good for all diseases of the eyes.'
Pliny, *Natural History* XXIV, 62

CLEARLY MAGIC WAS involved here: earlier in the passage, Pliny discusses the strange manner in which the plant had to be collected: 'It is gathered without iron with the right hand, thrust under the tunic through the left arm-hole, as though the gatherer were thieving ...' It is interesting that Pliny should link magic and medicine and that he mentions afflictions of the eyes: it is clear from the votive objects found at many curative shrines (p. 115) that cures for eye problems were often sought from the gods.

The more famous passage in Pliny, which refers to the Druidic ritual of mistletoe gathering, begins thus: 'The Druids – that is what they call their magicians – hold nothing more sacred than mistletoe and a tree on which it is growing, provided it is Valonia Oak' (Pliny, *Natural History* XVI, 95). Like the selago plant, mistletoe had to be collected in a particular manner, and it may be significant that the sickle used to cut it was, again, not iron but 'golden' (probably gilded bronze because pure gold would have

The writings of the Graeco-Roman commentators tended to reduce the importance of the Druids' roles in Celtic society. They perceived any powers that the Druids possessed as just quackery, stereotyping the Druids as mere Medicine Men (right) uttering ineffective mumbo-jumbo spells.

THE DRUID'S EGG

*P*liny makes reference to a curious Druidic talisman, called an anguinum, an egg-like object allegedly made from the spittle and secretions of angry snakes. This 'Druid's Egg' was used as an amulet to help the bearer gain victory in the law courts. Pliny describes it as 'round, and about as large as a smallish apple'. In his 1968 book, The Druids, Stuart Piggott suggested that these anguina were in fact fused empty whelk cases which, although common sights on the sea shores of northwest Gaul and Britain, would have been exotic to the Mediterranean world.

(Above) Egg amulet made of serpentine, probably of Roman date, from Bu Sands, Orkney, Scotland.

been too soft). The mistletoe was used, like the selago, in healing: it was given to the sick person in a drink, and believed to be an antidote to all poisons and efficacious in the treatment of infertility.

Later writers, too, allude to the Druids' practice of the magical arts. The Alexandrian Hippolytus, writing in the late second–third century AD, refers to the Druids as magicians; and Diogenes Laertius (third century AD) speaks of the 'riddles and dark sayings' of the Druids.

We need to exercise a degree of caution about the image, projected by Graeco-Roman commentators, of the Druids as Merlin-like magicians. Sorcery and magic were perceived by the Romans as sub-religious activities which were sometimes regarded as quackery and, at a more sinister level, as harmful 'black magic'. So it would be natural for the religious leaders of a 'primitive' culture to be stereotyped as 'Medicine Men', uttering mumbo-jumbo spells and imprecations. If the Druids did practise magic, then that has to be viewed within the context of similar behaviour which took place in the Classical world. The custom of writing curses and offering them to the gods, a widespread practice in Mediterranean antiquity, was – after all – a form of magic.

This painting – 'The Druids: Bringing in the Mistletoe' – by George Henry and Edward Atkinson Hornel, 1890, shows how the mistletoe was collected with a 'golden' sickle.

THE DRUIDS AND EDUCATION

Stone relief of a schoolroom scene; Roman date, from Neumagen, Germany. Many Classical writers speak of the Druids as educators; they were in charge of teaching oral tradition, religious doctrine and the history of the tribe.

'A large number of young men flock to them [the Druids] for training and hold them in high honour.... The Druids are wont to be absent from war, nor do they pay taxes like the others.... Attracted by these prizes many join the order of their own accord or are sent by parents or relatives. It is said that they commit to memory immense amounts of poetry. And so some of them continue their studies for twenty years. They consider it improper to entrust their studies to writing, although they use the Greek alphabet in nearly everything else, in their public and private accounts.'
Caesar, *Gallic War* VI, 13–14

OF ALL THE CHRONICLERS writing in the first century BC, only Caesar alludes specifically to the educational role of the Druids. His testimony implies that only aspiring Druids came for training. But Pomponius Mela, in the first century AD, says that the students attending Druidic schools were the sons of noblemen and he does not make it clear whether these were all expected to become Druids: 'They teach many things to the noblest of the race'. He goes on to describe the secrecy in which the teaching took place: '... in sequestered and remote places during twenty years, whether in a cave or in secluded groves ...' (*De Chorographia* III 2, 19).

The need to hide away may have developed in the first century AD, when the pervasive Roman presence was inimical to open Druidic practice.

As to what the Druids actually taught their students, we only gain snippets from the Classical writers. Caesar says that they learned about the gods, about the past and about the natural world. Ammianus suggests that the Druids were historians of the Gaulish people. Druidic teaching had little or nothing to offer in terms of morals, of retribution for misdeeds or rewards for good conduct, in the form of a hell or heaven. But Diogenes Laertius makes the interesting comment that the Druids used the triad (or triple phrase) in their teaching: 'to honour the gods, to do no evil and to practise bravery' (*Lives of the Philosophers* I, Prologue 6). Only in the second instruction is there a suggestion of an ethical code.

We know little of where the Druidic teaching took place, except for Mela's comment about caves and groves. But Tacitus speaks of the old Celtic school at Bibracte in Burgundy, which was superseded, in 12 BC, by a Roman school founded by Augustus at Autun. Could the former establishment have been a Druidic academy?

The keepers of oral tradition

'They consider it improper to entrust their studies to writing.... I think they established this practice for two reasons, because they were unwilling, first, that their system of training should be bruited abroad among the common people, and second, that the student should rely on the written word and neglect the exercise of his memory. It is normal experience that the help of the written word causes a loss of diligence in memorizing by heart.'

Caesar, *Gallic War* VI, 14

Caesar goes on to say that the second reason for this stress on oral learning was connected with the secrecy attached to Druidic teaching. The Christian writer Origen also comments on the absence of known Druidic writing. But we should not be surprised at such a method of teaching: learning by heart was a customary educational practice in the ancient world, and was common in Greece and Rome.

An interesting feature of Caesar's statement concerning oral teaching is his reference to verses, as if the Druids had some role akin to that of the Bards mentioned by other authors. Caesar, indeed, is the only writer not to mention both poets (Bards) and Druids. Strabo says: '… there are three classes of men held in special honour: the Bards, the Vates and the Druids. The Bards are singers and poets' (*Geography* IV, 4, 5), and Diodorus records: 'They have also lyric poets whom they call Bards. They sing to the accompaniment of instruments resembling lyres, sometimes a eulogy and sometimes a satire' (*Library of History* V, 31, 2). Later on in the same passage, Diodorus alludes to the close link between Druids and Bards. Lucan also speaks of Druids almost in the same breath as Bards, but distinguishes between them. Irish tradition, too, strongly links Druids and Bards.

It seems as though the Bards had the responsibility of composing and reciting verses and the Druids of learning and teaching them. In any case, it is clear that the myths and tales about the past were considered valuable, to be committed to memory and taught as part of the Celtic heritage.

RELIGIOUS DOCTRINE

'The Druids … expound religious matters.'
Caesar, Gallic War VI, 13

Caesar's statement is tantalizing but neither he nor any other writer provides anything other than sketchy information about what the Druids believed or taught about the divine world. Caesar lists many topics upon which the Druids held long discussions and instructed their pupils, including 'the powers and spheres of action of the immortal gods'. Mela states that the Druids professed to know the will of the gods, and many authors (p. 88) speak of the divinatory and prognosticatory powers of the Druids, Diodorus remarks that they spoke the language of the gods and that their mediation with the supernatural world procured blessings for the devout. Lucan says almost exactly the same thing, namely that only the Druids had knowledge of the gods.

One specific detail of doctrinal Druidic teaching mentioned by Caesar concerns ancestor-worship: 'The Gauls all assert their descent from Dis Pater and say that it is the Druidic belief.' Dis Pater was a Roman god of night and the dead, but Caesar's comment implies that the Gauls had a similar god of their own.

(Left) Bronze figurine of a priest, from Cricklade, Romano-British date. This figure, with its draped head, represents a British priest, perhaps a Druid, at a religious ceremony.

(Right) Bronze figurine of the Celtic hammer-god Sucellus, with leaf crown, mallet and pot; second–third century AD; Glanum.

PHILOSOPHERS AND SCIENTISTS

*'They have also much
knowledge of the stars and
their motion, of the size of the
world and of the earth, of
natural philosophy, and of the
powers and spheres of action of
the immortal gods...'*
Caesar *Gallic War* VI, 14

*In the course of their studies of the
natural world, the Druids took a
great interest in the movements of
the heavens. Their astronomical
observations would have been
essential in making the calendrical
calculations which were needed to
establish the most auspicious dates
to perform special rituals and
ceremonies.*

*'Philosophers, as we may call them, and men
learned in religious affairs ... are called by them
Druids.'*
Diodorus Siculus, *Library of History* V, 31, 1

*'For it is by the moon that they measure their
months and years and also their 'ages' of thirty
years'*
Pliny, *Natural History* XVI, 95

A NUMBER OF CLASSICAL commentators
on the Druids, even those generally hostile to
them, remark on their role as philosophers or
learned thinkers. Pomponius Mela called the
Druids *'magistri sapientiae'* ('Masters of
Wisdom'). Ammianus (quoting the first-century
BC Timagenes) comments on their lofty intellect, saying that they investigated 'problems of
things secret and sublime'. His remarks convey
the impression that here were genuine thinkers,
who disdained the humdrum world of human
concerns.

The Alexandrian writers, who were – in the
main – respectful towards the Druids, accord
them a sophisticated intellect. Dio Chrysostom
compared Druidic philosophy with that of the
great civilizations of Egypt, Persia and India.
Clement of Alexandria went so far as to consider
that the study of philosophy had its genesis
among the Celts. The Alexandrians admired

what they perceived as the native wisdom of the
'Noble Savage'.

Astronomy and mathematics
One branch of science pursued by the Druids
was the study of the natural world, particularly
astronomy. Ammianus speaks of *euhages* (seers)
who 'strive to explain the high mysteries of
nature'. Cicero commented that the Druid Divitiacus had knowledge of natural phenomena.
Mela said that the Druids considered themselves
knowledgable about the size and shape of the
earth, the Universe and the motion of the stars.
Lucan mentions the Druids' claim to understand
astrology, as well as the secrets of divinity. This
link between Druids and astrology appears in
early Christian Irish texts: the Druid who reared
Saint Brigit (p. 135) used to study the stars.

The astronomical observations of the Druids
had one very practical purpose – that of math-
ematical calendrical calculation. Caesar and
Pliny both speak of the Druidic reckoning of
time by the moon. The Christian author Hippolytus says that the Druids were capable of fore-
telling certain events by means of Pythagorean
reckoning and calculation. It is quite reasonable
to suppose that they may, indeed, have used theories originating among the great Greek math-
ematicians like Pythagoras. There were Greeks in
southern Gaul from the seventh century BC, and
there is substantial archaeological evidence to
show close connections between Mediterranean
and Celtic Europe from the same period.

Mela's 'Masters of Wisdom'
It is difficult to know how to interpret state-
ments made by Classical observers about Druidic
philosophy. Some elements in their descriptions
undoubtedly crept in because of the background
of the commentators themselves. Posidonius was
a Stoic philosopher and Strabo's comment on
Druidic tenets concerning the periodic engulf-
ing of the Universe by fire and water comes
directly from Stoicism. However, it is, in my
opinion, perverse to ascribe all apparent Druidic
learning to a false and Classicized image imposed on them by their chroniclers. Druidic
thinkers were, perhaps, on the fringe of the great
philosophical debates which were centred in the
Mediterranean world. The most important
example of Druidic teaching, apparently influenced by Greek philosophy, was that of reincarnation, to which we now turn.

'They [the Druids] hold that the soul of a dead man does not descend to the silent, sunless world of Hades, but becomes reincarnate elsewhere; if they are right, death is merely a point of change in perpetual existence ...'
Lucan, *Pharsalia* I, 441ff

CLASSICAL AUTHORS specifically refer to the Druidic teaching that the soul was immortal and underwent an endless cycle of rebirth in different bodies. Some writers, like Hippolytus, link this belief to the Pythagorean philosophy of the Transmigration of Souls. The comparison is not entirely correct because Pythagoreanism taught that the human soul could migrate to any living body, whether human or animal, whereas Druidic thinking called for a transference between human bodies.

There is remarkable similarity, on this subject, between several of the chroniclers. Caesar says that the Druids attached great importance to the belief that after death the soul passed from one body to another. He comments that such teaching encouraged bravery because men did not fear death. Mela makes the same point and says: 'One of their dogmas ... is that souls are everlasting and that among the shades there is another life' (*De Chorographia* III, 2, 19).

Ammianus comments that the Druids were contemptuous of the mortal lot of humans and professed the immortality of the soul. Diodorus says that the Celts believed men's souls to be immortal and, at death, went into another body.

Both Diodorus and Valerius Flaccus (who wrote a work entitled *Factorum et Dictorum Memorabilium Libri Novem* in the early first century AD) speak of the Celts' belief in a literal immortality. Diodorus comments: 'we are told, at the funerals of their dead some cast letters upon the pyre which they have written to their deceased kinsmen, as if the dead would be able to read these letters.' In view of the apparent virtual illiteracy of the pre-Roman Celts, this is a curious remark. Flaccus comments that it was an old custom among the Gauls to lend money to each other, on the understanding that the loan would be repaid in the next world.

Although it is generally conceded by modern scholars that Pythagorean and Druidic ideas were different (although perhaps understandably conflated by some ancient writers), what needs also to be appreciated is that these authors were putting forward two conflicting and confused theories about Druidic teaching on immortality. One concerns the transference of the human soul between earthly bodies: this is the view of Caesar and Lucan. But what Mela and – by implication – Diodorus and Flaccus are describing is the perception of an Otherworld which is a copy or mirror-image of life on earth. The latter interpretation is the one enshrined in early Irish and Welsh mythology. It is the former theory – that of reincarnation – that led to the mistaken comparison between Druidism and Pythagoreanism.

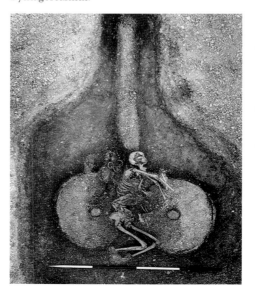

(Left) A Classical perception of Hades, a detail from a watercolour by William Blake, 'The Inscription over the Gate of Hell', an illustration for Dante's Divine Comedy, *1824–27. The Druids did not believe that their souls descended into hell, but underwent a continuous cycle of rebirth.*

Iron Age chariot burial of a young adult female, found with a large joint of pork and personal items of bronze, including a cylindrical box, perhaps once containing holy water or oil, from Wetwang, Yorkshire. The burial of grave goods with bodies implies a belief in an afterlife, in which the deceased will need sustenance and certain personal belongings.

DRUIDS AND ROMANS

IT IS POSSIBLE to detect a distinct change of tone in the attitudes to the Druids in the texts of the first century BC, and in those of the first century AD. The latter chroniclers are much more negative, combining hostility with contempt. Caesar, Diodorus and Strabo all reflect interest in Druidic practice and teaching, albeit tinged with disapproval of what they saw as outlandish behaviour, particularly human sacrifice. But Pliny, Suetonius, Tacitus and Lucan all speak with disgust about the Druids, referring to them as uncouth and savage. In his *Life of Claudius*, Suetonius alludes to the 'barbarous and inhuman religion of the Druids'. Lucan refers to their 'wicked religion'. Pliny hints darkly at such outrageous acts as ritual cannibalism.

The change of tone presented in the chronicles of the first century AD reflects both an internal decline in the Druids' prestige and the attitude of the Romans towards Gaul, as a newly conquered province. Druids were no longer perceived as an interesting curiosity, but as a threat to the civilized world, of which Gaul had become a part and which now had to be protected. But it is arguable that, even in the mid-first century BC, the influence of the Druids was already waning: Gaulish (and perhaps also British) society was already changing and moving closer to the Roman system; some polities had adopted a magistracy rather than a monarchical structure.

Notwithstanding the natural eclipse of Druidic power and the attempts by certain first-century emperors to get rid of them, it is clear from literary testimony that the Druids tended to pop up whenever and wherever rebellion against Rome was fomented. The implication is that, even if the Druids had largely withdrawn from the political arena by the mid-first century AD, they still maintained an active resistance movement which could spring back into life whenever disaffection burgeoned into revolt. They may, indeed, have been behind such uprisings.

One of the uprights of the stone 'skull-portico' at the shrine of Roquepertuse in southern Gaul. The skulls of adult men (probably vanquished warriors) were placed in niches as offerings to the victory gods of the local Saluvian tribe.

Fanciful picture of the Druids on Anglesey confronted by the Romans, who have come to smash their sacred stronghold. The attack on the sanctuary, in the mid-first century AD, was led by the Roman governor, Suetonius Paulinus, who wished to destroy the power of the Druids because they were a focus of British nationalism and anti-Roman activities.

One prominent rebellion against Roman dominion with possible Druidic involvement took place in Britain in AD 60/61, when Boudica, widow of King Prasutagus of the Iceni (in modern East Anglia) and the new leader of the tribe, led her own people and the neighbouring tribe of the Trinovantes against the Roman government. Boudica's army destroyed the three important Roman towns of Colchester, London and Verulamium (St Albans), while the Roman governor Suetonius Paulinus and most of his forces were, significantly, engaged upon the eradication of the Druidic stronghold on the island of Anglesey.

Confrontation on Anglesey

'The enemy lined the shore in a dense armed mass. Among them were black-robed women with dishevelled hair like furies, brandishing torches. Close by stood Druids, raising their hands to heaven and screaming dreadful curses.

'This weird spectacle awed the Roman soldiers into a sort of paralysis. They stood still and presented themselves as a target. But then they urged each other (and were urged by the general) not to fear a horde of fanatical women. Onward pressed their standards and they bore down on their opponents, enveloping them in the flames of their own torches. Suetonius garrisoned the conquered island. The groves devoted to Mona's barbarous superstitions he demolished. For it was their religion to drench their altars in the blood of prisoners and consult their gods by means of human entrails.'

Tacitus, Annals XIV, 30–31

To what extent were the two events of the Boudican rebellion and the Roman attack on Anglesey connected? Were they coincidentally coeval or is it possible that the Druids were still sufficiently influential to orchestrate a revolt in southeast Britain which was designed to deflect Paulinus before he could effect the utter destruction of the Druids' sacred island? My own view is that the Druids were – at least partly – responsible for fomenting the revolt.

ARCHAEOLOGY ENDORSES LITERATURE

Tacitus describes what must have been a (if not the) major British Druidic sanctuary, on Anglesey. It may be no coincidence that one of the most important Iron Age ritual deposits of votive objects from Britain also comes from this small, remote island off the northwest coast of Wales (p. 64). The hoard, which included large quantities of high-prestige metalwork, such as slave gang chains, weapons, shields and chariot ties, contains material made between the second century BC and the first century AD. However, the offerings could have been accumulated over a long period and then cast into the lake of Llyn Cerrig as a single gift to the gods by the Druids, in a desperate attempt to avert the Roman violation of their holy of holies.

More speculative, but still plausible, is a link between the Cheshire bog body, Lindow Man, and the Roman attack on Mona. It is generally agreed that the young man garotted and placed, naked, in the marsh at Lindow Moss (p. 81) was a victim of ritual murder. If, as appears to be the case, this sacrifice took place during the first century AD, and if human sacrifice was as rare as the general lack of archaeological evidence suggests, then the inference is that the killing was stimulated by a particular crisis. Cheshire is some distance from Mona, but one obvious route for the Roman army to north Wales, from several directions, was through this region. It is just possible that Lindow Man's death was intended to persuade the supernatural forces to halt the enemies of Druidism.

Bronze shield-boss, decorated with engraved Celtic motifs; Llyn Cerrig Bach, Anglesey. The shield was one of 150 prestige objects cast as votive gifts into the lake by British worshippers in the first century AD.

IV
DIGGING UP DRUIDS

'Nobody dared enter this grove except the priest; and even he
kept out at midday, and between dusk and dawn – for fear that
the gods might be abroad at such hours.'
Lucan, Pharsalia III, 372–417

THE FIRST-CENTURY AD Roman poet Lucan, writing
his commentary on the civil war between Pompey and
Caesar a hundred years after it took place in the mid-first
century BC, makes a direct link between sacred groves
and priests. Earlier in his book, he makes specific reference to the
Druids and associates them with human sacrifice. He reports on
the rituals of the Druids near Marseille which were enacted deep
in the woods that were dark and frightening and murmurous with
the bubbling of springs. Lucan even comments on the furnishings
of these Druidic groves, describing the images of the gods which
were 'stark, gloomy blocks of unworked timber, rotten with age,
whose ghastly pallor terrified their devotees' (p. 42).

While we cannot identify Lucan's sacred groves arch-
aeologically, we do have some evidence for his wooden effigies of
the gods: images like those from *Fontes Sequanae* (p. 99) may be
very similar to those described in Lucan's epic poem. Exploring
the archaeological evidence for priests – and especially for Druids
– presents a challenge, since it has to be largely circumstantial.

The archaeology of ancient religious officials can take a
number of forms: sacred sites may yield some clues; the evidence
of ritual behaviour, such as the offering of gifts to the gods; and
the rare survival of liturgical regalia, such as headdresses, sceptres
and the other insignia of religious office. But we need to be aware
of the presumed presence of objects and temple furnishings that
do not survive in the archaeological record: textiles, most wood,
food and wine. We have also to imagine the rituals themselves:
prayers, dancing, music and ceremony. Such evidence as the
dancing figures from Neuvy-en-Sullias in France and the
trumpets from Ireland (p. 62) allow us tantalizing glimpses of a
lively and complex ritual behaviour.

*Bronze Age 'sun chariot', a model wagon carrying a gilded sun disc. Found
deliberately deposited in a peat bog at Trundholm, Denmark, c. 1300–1200 BC.
The wagon pre-dates our earliest references to the Druids by nearly 1000 years
but is an example of organized ritual which must have involved specialist priests.*

PRIESTHOODS IN EUROPEAN PREHISTORY

(Above) Reconstruction of the main building at Navan Fort, County Armagh, Ireland, which dates to the early first century BC. This was probably a ceremonial building, used for religious events and festivals. Such a building suggests the presence of an organized priesthood, perhaps the Druids.

(Right) Navan Fort (identified as Emhain Macha, the ancient capital of Ulster) showing the outer enclosure and main internal circular structure.

Reconstruction of the early Bronze Age ritual timber circle at Sarn-y-Bryn-Caled, Welshpool, Wales. Inside was a central pit containing the cremated bones of young adults. The structure has been interpreted as a religious building.

THROUGHOUT MUCH OF the Bronze and Iron Ages, European society outside the Classical world appears to have been organized in a more or less hierarchical manner, with chiefs, noblemen and non-food-producing specialists, such as professional smiths and artists, at the top of the hierarchy. Large ceremonial structures, such as Stonehenge, were used and modified over centuries, from the earlier to later Bronze Age, and monuments like these are suggestive of an organized religion. The great stone and wooden circles of the early Bronze Age have their Iron Age counterparts, for instance at Navan Fort,

County Armagh, where a great multi-ring timber structure, 130 ft (40 m) in diameter, was erected, using oak which (so tree-ring dating tells us) had been felled at the beginning of the first century BC. The central focus of the building was an immense free-standing pole perhaps originally as high as 43 ft (13 m). The ritual activity here was curious: very soon after the circular timber structure was erected, its interior was deliberately filled with blocks of stone and then the outer wall was fired. It has been suggested that the whole monument was a gigantic fire-sacrifice. If this is so, then the ritual involved was sufficiently complex for us to envisage its orchestration by professional religious officials.

The solar priests of the Bronze Age

There is some archaeological evidence for an organized priesthood, associated with the specific cult of the sun, during the later Bronze Age of northern and central Europe. Certain curious, clearly ceremonial, gold objects are sometimes interpreted as sacred headgear: they consist of spectacular tall, hollow, sheet-gold 'hats', conical in shape, which are decorated with bands of 'solar' motifs, such as spoked wheels and concentric circles. They were probably made in about 1200 BC. The best-preserved cone is from Etzelsdorf in Bavaria: it is 37 in (95 cm) high, and its entire surface is decorated with repoussé and engraved designs. Another German example, from Schifferstadt, contained residues which indicate that its inner surface was once in contact with aromatic resins, a feature which suggests some kind of ritual association.

Gold and bronze were used for other ceremonial objects that may be linked to a solar cult and which may have been liturgical regalia. Most evocative is the Trundholm 'sun chariot' (p. 54), which was found, dismantled and buried in a Danish peat bog, by farmers ploughing in the area. The object consists of a bronze horse attached to a six-wheeled model wagon on which was a large disc made of bronze but gilded on one side. The entire piece is about 24 in (60 cm) long, and it was made c. 1300–1200 BC. That it was used in solar rituals can only be surmised, but the disc looks very sun-like and the horse itself wears a chamfrein (head-guard) with rayed decoration around the eyes.

The idea of the sun being conveyed across the sky in a horse-drawn chariot is an image common to many Indo-European peoples in antiquity, including Greeks, Romans and Persians. The Trundholm model may have been wheeled in ceremonial processions to coax the sun to reappear after winter, turned to face south to the meridian during the day, so that celebrants would see the gold solar image moving east to west, and turned back at sunset, the ungilded surface of the disc symbolizing the sun's nocturnal journey back from the west. It is not impossible that religious officials in such ceremonies wore or carried regalia, like the 'solar cones', though such an idea must remain speculative.

(Below) Bronze Age gold cone, decorated with solar wheels and circles, Etzelsdorf, Bavaria. Another similar cone contained aromatic gums. These objects were perhaps used in religious rituals.

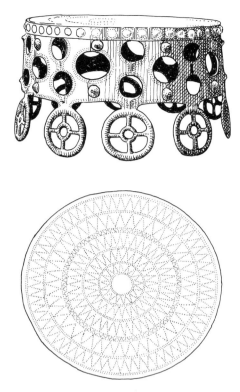

(Top and above) Side and top view of a Bronze Age 'sun drum', associated with solar ritual, found in a peat bog at Balkåkra in southern Sweden.

THE SACRED SITE OF LIBENICE

Sometime during the fourth century BC, a Celtic community at Libenice in Bohemia built a great open-air ritual enclosure, over 300 ft (90 m) long. The main activities seem to have taken place at one end, where there was a sunken area (right) containing the remains of two timber posts. The presence of two bronze torcs (neckrings) by the postholes suggests that the posts may have been fashioned into human images, adorned by the neck ornaments. The floor of this sanctuary was made up of a series of pits which could have been repeatedly dug to receive offerings (perhaps of food, or drink) and then filled in, over a period of years. That blood-sacrifices may have taken place is suggested by the presence of human and animal bones. Most significant of all is the burial of a woman in the centre of the enclosure. It is tempting to think of her as a cult official, perhaps a priestess, who presided over the sanctuary and its rituals. But she may, of course, have been a sacrificial victim.

IMAGES OF THE DRUIDS

Nearly life-size bronze boar, from the hoard of religious bronzes from Neuvy-en-Sullias, France; first century BC.

Bronze figure holding an egg-shaped object – possibly a 'Druid's Egg' – from Neuvy-en-Sullias; first century BC.

ON THE LEFT BANK of the River Loire, at Neuvy-en-Sullias, in France, a hoard of religious bronzes was buried just before, or at the time of, the Roman occupation of Gaul in the mid-first century BC. The bronzes may have come from the Gaulish sanctuary at Floriacum (Fleury) which is opposite the site of deposition. The cache contained figurines of animals, including a magnificent boar (nearly life-size), a stag and a horse dedicated to a native god called Rudiobus.

Even more interesting than the statuettes of animals are the human figurines, since they may be representations of temple clergy or cult participants. They include images of a musician, naked male and female dancers and a figure that has been interpreted as a Druid. This individual is male, with a short beard and curly hair: he wears a loose, long-sleeved robe to just below his knees and in his left hand he holds a small round object which, some scholars suggest, could represent the so-called 'Druid's Egg' referred to by Pliny (p. 46): in his *Natural History* he recounts that a Vocontian chief fell foul of the authorities at Rome during the reign of Claudius, because he tried to win a legal battle using the magical talisman called the 'serpent's egg': this amulet was claimed by the Druids to bring its possessor victory in the law courts, probably because it enhanced his rhetorical powers. We know that the Druids themselves were renowned for their verbal skills (p. 124).

Whilst no certain 'Druid's Eggs' have been discovered, there is a group of small egg-shaped stone amulets from Scotland, which appear (from their context) to be of Roman date. The most recent example, found casually on Bu Sands, Orkney, is of serpentine and, indeed, all five of the eggs recorded are made of unusual and visually interesting stones. At least two of the amulets, from Cairnhill, Aberdeenshire, come from what is arguably a ritual deposit, made in an earlier stone cairn.

People wearing torcs

Neckrings (torcs) of gold, silver or bronze were prominent items of jewellery during the European Iron Age, and seem generally to have been worn by people of high status. They were buried in the rich graves of central Europe from as early as the sixth century BC. Classical writers, like Polybius, speak of Celtic warriors wearing torcs (sometimes nothing but torcs) and, according to Dio Cassius, the great British female freedom fighter, Boudica, of the East Anglian Iceni tribe, went into battle wearing a great twisted gold neckring.

Torcs are frequently represented in Celtic religious iconography during the late Iron Age and Roman period. Some torc-wearing images probably represent gods, and the presence of the neckring makes sense in terms of its identification with high rank. The antlered god, known as Cernunnos, is usually depicted wearing a torc, and other Gaulish deities, such as Epona and Nantosuelta, also sometimes wear or carry neckrings. The link between torcs and the supernatural powers is also demonstrated by finds such as a gold torc at Mailly-le-Camp in Champagne, France, which bears an inscription in Greek characters declaring that it was part of an offering dedicated to the divine powers by the Nitrobriges, a tribe in southwest Gaul.

Given the clear association between torcs and gods and torcs and high rank, it is quite possible that the wearing of a torc could also sometimes signify membership of a priesthood and even – perhaps – sacred bondage to the divine powers. Tacitus discusses the symbolism of cords and binding in a passage describing ritual practices among the Germanic Suebi:

'In another way, too, reverence is paid to the [sacred] grove. No one may enter it unless he is bound with a cord. By this he acknowledges his

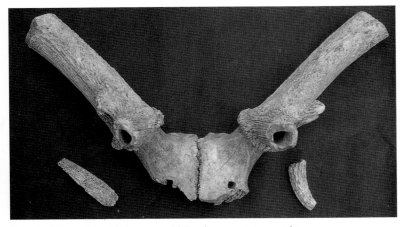

Pair of red deer antlers with the frontal bone pierced with square holes, as if for use as a headdress. The antlers were found associated *with fourth-century AD material in a Roman pit near a small Roman bath-suite near Hooks Cross, Hertfordshire.*

own inferiority to the power of the deity.'
Tacitus, *Germania*, 39

Stone head, possibly a deity, wearing a torc, from a sacred enclosure at Mšecké Žehrovice, Bohemia, third century BC.

So, for example, it may be that the torc-wearing images on the Danish Gundestrup cauldron represent priests and priestesses rather than divinities. It is even possible that images of an antlered, torc-bearing human being, who is usually identified as Cernunnos (the 'Horned One') do not represent a god but rather a shaman, dressed up in an antler headdress in order to communicate with the spirit world (p. 33). Indeed, a very recent British discovery may be relevant in this connection: archaeologists investigating a Roman bath house at Hooks Cross, near Stevenage in Hertfordshire, found a shallow pit next to the stoke-hole, which contained a pair of large antlers (probably of red deer) with the frontal bone pierced by two square holes, as if they had been fixed to something, perhaps a headdress. The accompanying Roman coins suggest a date in the early fourth century AD, but the 'headdress' has a marked similarity to that discovered at Star Carr in Yorkshire, which has been dated to 7500 BC.

Gold torc from a hoard of precious jewellery found at Snettisham, Norfolk, England, early first century BC.

PEOPLE WEARING MISTLETOE

A very distinctive group of human representations which occurs in early Celtic art consists of male heads adorned with huge crowns or headdresses in the form of two opposed comma-shaped leaves. This is a persistent motif, both in terms of time and space, and occurs both on large stone monuments and small decorative metal objects. In the fifth and fourth centuries BC, men wearing leaf-crowns appear on the stone carvings from Pfalzfeld and Heidelberg, in Germany: the former consists of a quadrangular pillar (p. 19), all four sides decorated with swirling foliage and a crowned human head; the latter is a freestanding head which may have once surmounted a stone pillar (above right). The heads at Pfalzfeld and Heidelberg are all also marked with an open lotus flower, carved on the forehead. Small objects with similar heads occur, for instance, on the gold appliqué faces at Schwarzenbach,

Germany, and on a bronze phalera at Hořovicky in the former Czechoslovakia, decorated with seven such heads. That the same tradition persisted through time is demonstrated by such items as the bucket from a cremation burial at Aylesford in Kent, which has escutcheons (handle fittings) in the form of leaf-crowned heads (below right), and which dates to the first century BC.

The leaves on these crowns have been tentatively identified as those of mistletoe. If that is so, given Pliny's statement about the sanctity of mistletoe and about its link with the Druids, it is possible that the leaf-crowns represent either divine beings or priests, perhaps even the Druids themselves. The lotus flowers carved on the stone heads may equally be symbolic: in the Classical world (whence much of the Celtic artists' inspiration came) the lotus was a motif associated with eternity and rebirth.

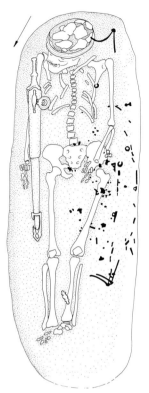

The body of a British warrior, buried with his coral-inlaid bronze brooch and sword with decorative scabbard, and wearing an ornamental headband or crown, from Deal, England, late second century BC. He may have combined the roles of warrior and priest, or he may have been a ceremonial leader, buried with a sword as a mark of honour rather than as a warrior's possession.

THE PRESENCE OF CELTIC priests in Britain wearing personal accoutrements which marked them out from the secular community is vividly demonstrated by numerous spectacular finds of ritual regalia, including crowns, diadems, headdresses, wands, sceptres and musical instruments.

Iron Age headdresses

Most of the headdresses are dated to the Roman period, but one notable exception is the decorated bronze headband found encircling the skull of an Iron Age man buried at Deal in Kent, England, in the second century BC. He has been identified as a warrior, for he had a sword in a finely ornamented bronze scabbard and a shield. But the headdress makes him special: apart from the decorative headband itself, there was a bronze cross-piece running over the top of the head. The traces of human hair found attached to the inside of the crown imply that it sat directly on the head. So this Iron Age Briton was interred wearing an item of non-functional headgear, which was certainly not a helmet and was not appropriate to a common soldier.

(Top) Bronze ritual headdress, from a Romano-Celtic temple at Hockwold-cum-Wilton, Norfolk, England.

(Below) Bronze crown or diadem, with adjustable headband, Roman period, from Cavenham, Suffolk, England.

Moreover, other grave goods are indicative of the man's high status: not only was his scabbard beautifully decorated with bird-head designs, and a ring for attaching the scabbard to his belt ornamented with coral mounts, but he was also buried with a pink-coral-inlaid bronze safety-pin brooch or *fibula*. The brooch was not by the shoulder, in the usual position for a cloak-fastener, but by the man's legs, which perhaps suggests that he was wearing a long flowing garment fastened below the knee, rather than a military cloak. So who was this man who was interred with war-gear but with a headdress and, perhaps, a long robe? He could have been a chieftain, someone who combined military office with high secular, and maybe ceremonial, status. He could also have been some kind of religious leader, who was buried with fine war-gear as a mark of prestige. We should bear in mind Caesar's categorical statement that the Druids were a separate class from the warrior-aristocracy and, moreover, that the Druids were exempt from military service. However, we also know that Caesar's Aeduan ally Divitiacus was both a member of the royal house and a Druid. The precise place of the Deal 'warrior' in British Iron Age society has to remain an enigma. But that the site of Deal had religious connotations is suggested by the presence of a curious subterranean shrine containing a chalk figurine.

The Deal find is not alone: another body wearing a crown was found in 1841 in a grave at Leckhampton, England, but has since been lost. Fragments of a similar band came from the same deposit as a number of late Iron Age religious bronzes, including three boar figurines and a solar wheel-model, at Hounslow near London.

Romano-Celtic ceremonial headgear

Most of the ceremonial diadems from Britain come from the tribal lands of the Iceni, in East Anglia. The Romano-Celtic temple at Hockwold-cum-Wilton in Norfolk was built in the second century AD. It had a rammed chalk floor in which six bronze crowns were found: each crown was fitted with an adjustable headband, so that it could be worn by different people. The most elaborate headdress was a diadem with a spiked top, decorated with silver plaques and with roundels depicting the heads of divinities.

In the same region, at Cavenham in Suffolk, a group of three crowns comes from the site of a possible shrine: no structure has survived, but roof tiles and pottery suggest its one time presence. Two of the headdresses were relatively massive pieces of sheet bronze, with high fronts, once ornamented with appliqué images, and narrowing to a band at the back. But the third consisted of chains formed of S-shaped links, joined by bronze discs; it must have been attached to a cap made of cloth or leather.

A set of three chain headdresses, similar in style to the Cavenham example, has recently been uncovered during excavations at the Wanborough shrine in Surrey: they are especially interesting because the tops of two of them were adorned with large cast-bronze wheel-symbols. Since the main attribute of the Celtic sungod was a spoked wheel, the decoration on the Wanborough headdresses may reflect the connection of their wearers to a solar cult.

Remains of chain headdresses, like those at Cavenham and Wanborough, formed part of a cache of religious material found buried in a pot at Stony Stratford in Buckinghamshire, along with sheet-silver and bronze plaques that may once have been attached to crowns, like the one from Cavenham.

One of the significant features of these headdresses is that they are generally found in groups rather than as single depositions. The implica-

Chalk figurine, found with second-century AD pottery, from a niche near the base of a pit (possibly an underground shrine) at Deal, Kent. The presence of this statuette indicates that the Deal site had religious associations.

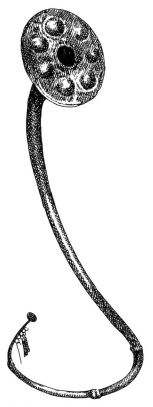

Late Iron Age bronze trumpet, one of four found in a lake at Loughnashade, County Armagh, Ireland.

THE PETRIE CROWN

*T*wo curious ceremonial Iron Age headdresses come from Ireland: one is from County Cork, but the more complete example is unprovenanced, and is known as the Petrie Crown (right). It consists of hollow bronze horns attached to decorative discs and mounted on an openwork bronze band. The Cork crown has three horns; fragments of leather adhering to them suggest that they were originally mounted on a leather headband. The ornament on the band, discs and horns of the Petrie Crown comprises delicate, sweeping curvilinear designs and birds' heads; the style of the art places the date of the headdress' manufacture in the first or early second century AD.

In the absence of context for the Irish crowns, it is impossible to tell whether they were worn by priests during religious ceremonies. They could, instead, have been badges of office worn by rulers. But it is difficult to dissociate such imposing, but unwieldy, pieces of regalia from some kind of ceremonial use, and it is tempting to imagine solemn rituals in which Irish Druids, wearing these tall horned crowns, presided over sacrifices or led processions.

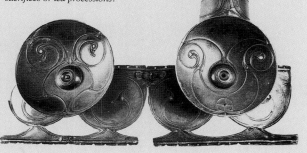

Bronze Romano-British sceptre-terminal, decorated with images of a dancing god, a wheel, an eagle, a dolphin and a triple-horned bull's head, from Willingham Fen, Cambridgeshire. The sceptre, found in what may be a shrine, was probably used by priests in cult processions.

Sheet-bronze sceptre-binding, with incised symbols, from a Romano-Celtic shrine at Farley Heath, Surrey, England. The binding was wound around an iron rod, which was used as a ceremonial wand by priests.

tion is that the shrines from which they came were served by several clergy, all, we have to assume, with different functions.

Wands and sceptres

Symbols of religious authority, in the form of wands of office, imply the presence of organized priesthoods. Plain bronze staffs have been found at such sanctuaries as Muntham Court, Sussex, England, but sometimes the sceptres are decorated with religious motifs. An elaborate sceptre-terminal comes from the site of a probable shrine at Willingham Fen in Cambridgeshire, England, together with other religious bronzes. The images on the Willingham piece show a youthful god, with his foot on the head of a monster, an eagle, a wheel, a dolphin and the head of a triple-horned bull.

A sheet-bronze strip, once the binding for a ceremonial staff, comes from a shrine at Farley Heath, Surrey, England. It bears densely packed but simply executed images and symbols, including animals and human figures. On both these objects, the iconography is sufficiently complex to argue for the representation of a mythological episode or narrative.

Various small bronze attachments, in the form of figurines, have been interpreted as sceptre-heads: an important example from Gaul is the little statuette of a solar god from Le Châtelet in Haute-Marne, France, which has rings at the back for suspension. Model horsemen, found in England, such as those from Brough in Yorkshire

THE WAVENDON TOTEM

Among recent finds of ceremonial regalia, none is more enigmatic than the wooden wheel-shaped object, 13 in (33 cm) long, from Wavendon Gate in Buckinghamshire, England. It comes from the bottom of a waterlogged pit, dated to the early Romano-British period. The wheel is carved of oak and has a tenon pierced with a hole: it may originally have been fastened to the tree trunk found with it in the pit. Such an item may have stood at the centre of a shrine, as a sacred emblem or 'totem', perhaps associated with a sun cult; it may even have been detached, on special occasions, for use in cult ceremonies.

The Wavendon wheel is a unique discovery; its suggested interpretation as a solar symbol is supported by the other finds from the site, including miniature bronze wheels. It is difficult to explain this material as anything other than the ritual furniture of a local shrine. The wheel was a recurrent symbol of the Celtic celestial god in Britain, Gaul and the Rhineland.

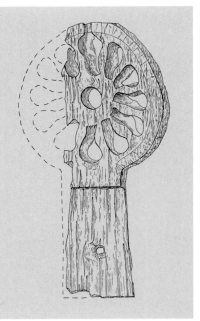

and Woodeaton in Oxfordshire, may also be the ends of ceremonial wands.

Music and the gods

Noise, chanting, singing, dancing and music must all have played a part in religious festivals and ritual. Rattles or *sistra* carried in processions are occasionally preserved in the archaeological record. These are bronze pole-tips or wands with rings for the suspension of tiny bells: six such 'jangles' come from a temple at Brigstock Northamptonshire, England. An object from a hoard of sacred bronzes, found in association with a coin dated AD 260 in a pot at Felmingham Hall in Norfolk, England, has been identified as a rattle.

Musical intruments are rarely identified on archaeological sites but, in Iron Age Ireland, the remains of several superbly crafted bronze trumpets bear testimony both to the skill of Insular bronzesmiths and to important ceremonial occasions. A group of four was discovered in 1798 in a lake at Loughnashade, County Armagh. The lake is at the foot of the hill on which stood the great Celtic stronghold of Navan Fort, the site of the Ulster royal seat of Emhain Macha which features so prominently in early Irish myth. The four trumpets, which are beautifully decorated with La Tène designs, were undoubtedly placed in the lake as a deliberate votive act. The alleged finding of human skulls here, too, implies that Loughnashade was a holy site of sacrifice. The trumpets represent the pinnacle of Irish Iron Age metal-smithing: they were each made of two tubes of sheet bronze joined in the middle, one cylindrical in shape, the other swelling out at one end to form the bell at the mouth. The seams of the tubes are sealed with narrow bronze strips inserted on the inside edge;

the join was then riveted together. Another trumpet, from Ardbrinn, County Down, is well preserved and contains more than 1,000 rivets. The incredible precision required to complete the final C-shaped instrument is eloquent testimony to the time, care and skill invested in the manufacture of these ceremonial pieces.

The Irish trumpets are distinctive (although Celtic war trumpets (*carnyxes*) were widely used), but they are strongly reminiscent of the great *lurer* of Scandinavia, which were manufactured in the late Bronze Age (between about 1200 and 700 BC). Fifty of these instruments are recorded; they could play about 12–15 notes, and images of people blowing the *lür* are depicted in Swedish rock art.

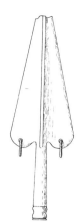

(Above) Bronze 'pole-tip' from a hoard of religious bronzes dating to the third century AD, at Felmingham Hall, Norfolk, England. The spear-shaped tip has rings for the suspension of bells or rattles, and was perhaps used by cult officials during religious ceremonies.

(Above) Late Bronze Age rock-carving from Bohuslän in Sweden, depicting lür- (trumpet-) players. Like the Irish Iron Age trumpets from Loughnashade, the Scandinavian lurer were probably associated with rituals and ceremonies.

Bronze figurine of a Romano-British female flute player, from Silchester, Hampshire. The statuette may represent a cult official in a religious ceremony playing her flute to accompany ritual dances or chants.

GIFTS TO THE DIVINE POWERS

Reconstructed Bronze Age buildings on an artificial island at Flag Fen, Cambridgeshire, England, the site of mass-deposition of prestige-goods and martial equipment as offerings to the gods, between 1200 and 200 BC.

PEOPLE LIVING IN Celtic communities, wishing to propitiate or give thanks to the gods, presented them with gifts: food, drink or material possessions, such as jewellery, coins or weapons. Such individual acts need not have been the concern of professional clergy, but represent private acts of devotion. On some occasions, however, the circumstance, character or amount of votive material lead us to envisage a more complex, formal arrangement which was perhaps orchestrated by the religious officials of the community or the tribe.

Flag Fen and Llyn Cerrig Bach

Recurrent ritual behaviour in later European prehistory includes the deposition of votive gifts in watery contexts: lakes, rivers or marshes. Two important sites in Britain in which such offerings took place are Flag Fen in Cambridgeshire and Llyn Cerrig Bach on Anglesey. Both involved large numbers of metal objects. Flag Fen is situated in the Fen wetlands: in about

1200 BC, an artificial island was constructed and a settlement built on it. A short time later, an alignment of large oak posts was erected linking the dry fen-edge with and beyond the island. Near the timber alignment, over 300 pieces – mostly military and high-status objects, such as swords and spears – were cast into the water, some having been first deliberately broken, presumably in an act of ritual separation from the profane world. Not only metalwork but items of pottery and shale were also thrown into the water, along with the bodies of dogs and at least one human being. People were active at the site over a long period, from about 1200 to 200 BC, thus spanning the later Bronze Age and the early Iron Age.

Llyn Cerrig Bach was a lake in which prestigious offerings (mainly of a martial and aristocratic nature) were cast over a period between the second century BC and first century AD. The deposit, discovered during the construction of a military airbase in 1943, comprises over 150 pieces, including chariot-fittings, swords, parts of shields, cauldrons, and two iron slave-chains. Once again, some of the offerings had been ritually smashed or bent before their deposition. The metalwork was not all locally made: some came from Ireland, and other pieces from southwest England. It is tempting to link Llyn Cerrig Bach with the Druids because we know from Tacitus' *Annals* that Suetonius Paulinus waged war upon sacred Druidic groves on the island of Anglesey in AD 60.

Gournay and Tayac

Jean-Louis Brunaux, excavator of the important Iron Age Gaulish sanctuary of Gournay-sur-Aronde, Oise, France, maintains that the ritual behaviour manifested here was so complex that it was almost certainly controlled by a profes-

The lake at Llyn Cerrig Bach, Anglesey, site of a possible Druidic sanctuary, into which high-status metalwork was cast as gifts to the divine powers in the first century AD.

sional priesthood, who probably lived on site. Gournay was situated on the boundary between three Gaulish tribes: the Bellovaci, Viromandui and Ambiani. Other temples were similarly built at the interface of tribal territories: Woodeaton in Oxfordshire, between the lands of the powerful tribes of the Catuvellauni and Dobunni, is a British example. Shrines like these may have had a political role: people may have gathered there to settle disputes about land, and other territorial matters. The Druids could have had a particular role in such temples. Caesar specifically refers to their function as arbitrators, commenting that during their annual assembly at a sacred place in the land of the Carnutes, the Druids settled any disputes that were brought before them.

The intense religious activity at Gournay – which lasted for at least four centuries, beginning in the fourth century BC – included large-scale animal sacrifice (pp. 85–87) and the deposition of more than 2,000 weapons, many ritually broken. The inference is that the arms may have belonged to a defeated enemy army and were collected as trophies for the gods. Caesar mentioned just such a custom among the Gauls: 'After deciding on battle they frequently vow to Mars whatever they may take in the war …' (VI, 17).

Tayac in western Gaul consisted of a very different kind of votive deposition but one which, nonetheless, may have been the result of a public rather than a private religious act. The offering at Tayac comprised a massive gold torc, buried with more than 500 Celtic coins; the neckring was deliberately broken into three pieces. The deposit was surely too valuable to have been the property of a single individual, unless he was of royal lineage. Another Gaulish torc, from Mailly-le-Camp in Champagne, actually bears a dedicatory inscription stating that it was part of a larger gift to the gods.

(Below) Bronze yoke-terminal (probably from a chariot), decorated with the religious symbol of the swastika (a solar and good-luck motif), from Llyn Cerrig Bach, Anglesey.

SNETTISHAM: A SACRED TREASURY?

The sheer size of the deposit of gold, silver and electrum torcs found at Snettisham in Norfolk, England, raises important questions as to the exact nature of the hoard. The site was first discovered in 1948, when three caches of torcs were unearthed by particularly deep ploughing. Thereafter, there were more sporadic finds in the 1960s and early 1970s. In 1990, a new set of deposits was discovered: one group of metalwork was buried in a bronze vessel; other hoards of torcs had been placed in 'nests' (right), packed tightly together in tiny pits, some with false bottoms to conceal the more valuable jewellery beneath. In all, nine hoards have been found: more than 75 complete torcs and fragments of 100 more, as well as remains of over 100 pieces of other jewellery and 170 coins made up this unique 'treasury' of precious metal buried in the earlier first century BC.

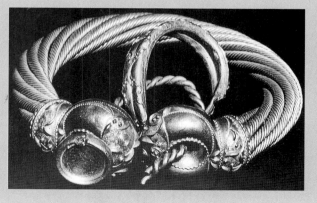

Snettisham has produced by far the largest collection of torcs and hoards anywhere in Iron Age Europe. The great debate is whether the deposits at Snettisham were votive offerings or the contents of a treasury: were they meant to remain concealed forever (because they were presents to the gods) or were they hidden for safe keeping, with a view to recovery? To my mind there is a sense in which both offering and treasury arguments may be valid. The jewellery buried at Snettisham is likely to have been under the protection of the gods even if it was not dedicated exclusively to them.

'These [Cimbrian holy] women would ... go up to the prisoners, crown them and lead them up to a bronze vessel which might hold some twenty measures. One of the women would mount a step and, leaning over the cauldron, cut the throat of a prisoner, who was held up over the vessel's rim.'

Strabo, *Geography* VII, 2, 3

FROM AS EARLY as the later Bronze Age in Europe, large sheet-bronze vessels were associated with funerary ritual, feasting and water. The archaeological record bears witness to the persistent practice, during the pre-Roman Iron Age, of placing cauldrons as ritual deposits in water, particularly in pools (sometimes the site of natural springs) or marshes. Such a custom is probably linked to the use of cauldrons in everyday life for boiling meat. In early Irish and Welsh myth, cauldrons possessed the dual symbolism of plenty, regeneration and rebirth, and water itself was sacred to the ancient Celts as a life-force and an agent of healing.

Some cult-cauldrons were extremely large: the Brå cauldron, found in 1952 in a pit near Horsens in eastern Jutland, had been deliberately broken into pieces before its deposition; complete, it had a capacity of 132 gallons (600 litres). The body of the cauldron was plain, but its ring-handles were ornamented with owls' heads, and around the rim were five cast-bronze bull-mounts. This great cauldron may well have belonged to a sanctuary rather than an individual household, and may even have functioned as a container for sacrificial blood, such as is mentioned by Strabo above.

Sacred vessels of Wales and Ireland

'I will give thee a cauldron, and the virtue of the cauldron is this: a man of thine slain today, cast him into the cauldron, and by tomorrow he will be as well as he was at the best, save that he will not have the power of speech.'

From the Second Branch of the *Mabinogi*

The *Mabinogion* is a collection of early medieval Welsh vernacular tales, which were compiled in written form probably in the tenth century AD and which survive in fourteenth-century manuscripts. Their essentially pagan character suggests that these tales contain resonances of pre-Christian myths and beliefs. The *Pedair Keinc y Mabinogi* comprise four separate but related stories. In the Second Branch, there is a description of a magical cauldron which comes from an Irish lake; it has the power to bring dead warriors to life, although their continued inability to speak indicates that they are still, in a sense, dead, and belong to the Otherworld.

Several Iron Age cauldrons come from Welsh and Irish watery contexts. Among the earliest are the bronze cauldrons which were thrown into a lake, along with other metalwork, at Llyn Fawr in south Wales, in about 600 BC. The vessels were already about a hundred years old when they were cast into the water, presumably as offerings to the gods.

Many Irish cauldrons have likewise been found in lakes or marshes. One oddity is a vessel carved from a solid block of poplar wood, which comes from a bog at Altartate Glebe, County Monaghan. A bronze cauldron from Ballyedmond, County Galway, had been frequently patched before its deposition in the first century BC or AD.

Duchcov and Gundestrup

The hoards of iron implements placed in cauldrons and deposited in Scottish lochs (see Box) have their counterpart on the other side of Celtic Europe, at Duchcov in Bohemia. The 'Giant's Springs' at Duchcov consisted of a natural spring which was the focus of religious activity during the third century BC. Here, a local community, perhaps directed by its priests, dedicated a great bronze cauldron filled with over 2,000 items of bronze jewellery – mainly armlets and brooches – to the local water-god. The presence of ornaments rather than military equipment has led some scholars to suggest that

Sheet-bronze cauldron (one of a pair) found deliberately deposited, with other metalwork, at Llyn Fawr, south Wales, in about 600 BC. The objects were votive offerings to the god of the lake. The cauldrons may have been particularly valuable, since they were antique when thrown in.

the offerings were those of women. This is certainly possible, but we should remember that both Celtic men and women wore jewellery.

The origins of the Gundestrup cauldron have long been the focus for debate. This great gilded silver vessel, its component plates covered with mythic iconography, was placed on a dry spot within a bog in Jutland, probably sometime in the first century BC. The imagery incorporates a wide variety of ethnic influences, some of them exotic and oriental, but many of the figural themes may be associated with the iconography of pre-Roman Celtic Europe: the images of deities wearing torcs; ram-horned snakes; a solar wheel-god and an antlered god are all motifs which may be closely matched by Gaulish imagery, particularly in the Roman period. Moreover, recent research has produced convincing arguments for connections between motifs on the Gundestrup cauldron and on finds from the La Tène *oppidum* (a large pre-Roman Iron Age defended site) and Roman *vicus* (a civil settlement attached to a Roman fort) at Titelberg in northeast Gaul. Moreover, those who would use the presence of elephants on the cauldron as a reason for ascribing oriental influence should be aware that Celtic coins minted at Titelberg also bear images of elephants. The commonly accepted thesis for the place of manufacture of the Gundestrup cauldron east of the Celtic world, in Thracian southeast Europe, has been recently questioned: silversmithing was a

The gilded silver Gundestrup cauldron from Raevemosen Bog, Jutland, Denmark; first century BC. This ceremonial vessel is made of thirteen plates each of which bear repoussé images of deities or mythological scenes. The cauldron possibly belonged to the Cimbri, a Germanic tribe, who may have acquired it from a Celtic community during a raid.

speciality of that region certainly, but the heyday for this skill in Thrace was in the fifth and fourth centuries BC, much earlier than the posited date for the cauldron.

Wherever the cauldron was made and whatever influences its imagery contains, the presence of such an object in a Danish peat-deposit must have religious significance. We cannot know how it came to be in Denmark, but a possible route was as loot belonging to a Cimbrian raiding party who plundered the bowl from a sanctuary and then offered it to their gods.

The Gundestrup cauldron, with its unique mythic narrative art, must have been a highly prized ritual vessel, perhaps used for holding sacrificial blood or a sacramental meal. It makes sense to think of it as part of the liturgical plate of an important shrine and the property of its priests.

SOME SCOTTISH CAULDRONS

At about the time of the Roman invasion of Scotland, in the later first century AD, two ritual deposits of cauldrons were made in lochs at Blackburn Mill, Berwickshire, and Carlingwark, Kirkudbright. Both contained caches of ironwork. The Blackburn deposit consisted of two hemispherical sheet-bronze vessels (below), one inverted over the other; the one at Carlingwark has a straight neck, carinated shoulder and circular belly: like the larger of the two Blackburn cauldrons, it was packed with iron objects. The watery deposition of the Scottish vessels matches occurrences in Wales and Ireland but, additionally, the presence of ironwork points to the ritual nature of the material. Hoards of iron objects are considered to have had some religious purpose simply because, at this period, iron would probably not have been thought sufficiently valuable to be hoarded for economic reasons, unless as scrap metal. Certainly, no one would place ironwork in water if it was intended for recovery and reuse.

DEATH, BURIAL AND THE AFTERLIFE

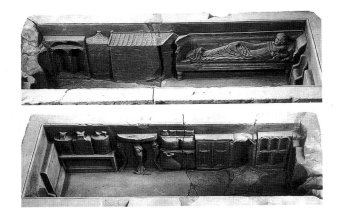

Two views of the interior of a stone sarcophagus of a high-ranking female of the Roman period, from Simpelveld, in the Netherlands. The dead woman is depicted reclining on a couch, surrounded by everything she might need in the Otherworld, including furniture, a bath house and pottery vessels.

'They [the Druids] are chiefly anxious to have men believe the following: that souls do not suffer death, but after death pass from one body to another; and they regard this as the strongest incentive to valour, since the fear of death is disregarded.'
Caesar, *Gallic War* VI, 14

'Funerals are on a large and expensive scale, considering the Gallic way of life; everything which they believe the dead man loved in life is given to the flames, even the animals; and it is only a short time since the slaves and clients who were known to have been loved by the dead man were cremated along with him …'
Caesar, *Gallic War* VI, 19

CAESAR, DIODORUS AND other Classical writers, including Strabo and Lucan, make specific reference to the Gaulish perception of life after death, a doctrine taught by the Druids. If we are seeking archaeological confirmation of such beliefs, the best place to look will be graves. Do the contents of Celtic tombs support the notion of a tangible life after death?

The meaning of grave goods

From the earliest Iron Age in temperate Europe (700 BC) until the Roman conquest and, indeed, beyond, certain individuals were buried with some of the possessions they had enjoyed during life. In prehistoric societies where such a custom pertained, it is tempting to interpret it as reflective of a belief that the dead needed their personal effects to accompany them to the next world. Such perceptions certainly existed, for example, in ancient Egypt, where not only the possessions but also the body of the deceased had to be preserved for use in the afterlife.

The placing of grave goods in tombs may have meanings other than belief in a tangible afterlife: for instance, it may be considered that a dead person's belongings have to die and be buried with the body because they are polluted by death and thus cannot be used by the living. Alternatively, rich items of gold or bronze may be placed with the dead as an act of conspicuous consumption, whereby kinsmen bury their dead relative with great ceremony, watched by the community, showing the wealth and status of the family by being seen to dispose of valuable objects. Grave goods may also be interpreted as gifts to the infernal powers, who may therefore be persuaded to keep the dead from returning to haunt the living, and to let the dead through the barrier separating this world and the next.

Because Classical writers emphasize the Celtic belief in an afterlife, it is at least highly likely that the goods placed in Iron Age tombs so reflect the acknowledgment of an Otherworld. The early vernacular myths of Ireland and Wales endorse this view. In these stories, the Otherworld is presented as a mirror-image of earthly existence: similar, but better and with no decay, illness or ageing.

Tombs of warriors and princes

The early Irish myths stress the notion of the Otherworld banquet, where enormous quantities of ever-replenishing meat and drink are consumed. Many Iron Age graves – both early and late – bear witness to the centrality of the funeral feast: drinking vessels, cooking pots and joints of meat were interred with the dead, either as tokens of the feasting which took place at the graveside, or as a kind of 'packed lunch' for the dead on the journey to the afterlife, or in payment to the gods for letting the dead soul through to eternity (rather as, for the Romans, the coin in the dead person's mouth was to pay Charon, the infernal ferryman, to take the deceased's soul across the River Styx).

Feasting is displayed very prominently in the famous tomb of the chieftain buried at Hochdorf in the late sixth century BC. He was interred beneath a great mound, within a chamber which contained his four-wheeled bier, a superb bronze couch, with engraved ornament, on which the dead man lay, and abundant evidence of the funerary banquet: nine drinking-horns were hung on the walls; a dinner-service for nine was stacked on the wagon, and a huge bronze cauldron (from the Mediterranean world), which had once held 88 gallons (400 litres) of mead, stood in one corner. The man went to his grave accompanied by evidence of the pastimes he took pleasure in during his life: hunting and fishing. The decoration of the couch bears witness, perhaps, to the kind of ceremonies which celebrated the man's life and mourned his passing – pairs of men can be seen dancing or sparring, in a graceful, ritualized manner, and images of wheeled vehicles drawn by horses closely resemble the hearse buried in the tomb itself.

Images of eternity

The symbolism of some early Celtic art lends credence to the perception of life beyond the

Detail of the gold armlet, decorated with a human face crowned with yew berries, from a chieftain's grave at Rodenbach, Germany, late fifth century BC. The dark evergreen foliage of the yew, with its contrasting bright red berries, may have symbolized blood, death and resurrection.

tomb. In the late fifth century BC, a chieftain was buried at Rodenbach in Germany. He wore a gold armlet on his right arm and a gold finger-ring. The motifs which decorated both pieces of jewellery may have possessed symbolic messages. The armlet is highly ornamental, but the central motif is a small male human face crowned with what look like yew berries. Yew is an evergeen and, moreover, is noted for its longevity. The berries are bright red and appear in winter, contrasting sharply with the sombre green foliage. The symbolism of this imagery may be quite deliberately evocative of death and rebirth: the foliage and the berries of the yew are poisonous, and the berries resemble drops of blood. But the death-symbolism is balanced, perhaps, by hopes of eternal life. The Rodenbach chief's finger-ring may also bear significant decoration: it takes the form of a janiform head, which gazes in two directions. Such a motif could represent the dead nobleman, at the threshold between earthly life and the Otherworld.

Reconstruction of a chieftain's tomb at Hochdorf, Germany, dating to c. 530 BC. The grave was sumptuously furnished with a great cauldron of mead, a funerary wagon, a dinner service for nine and nine drinking horns. The Hochdorf nobleman rested on a decorated bronze couch, with his gold-sheathed dagger and gold jewellery.

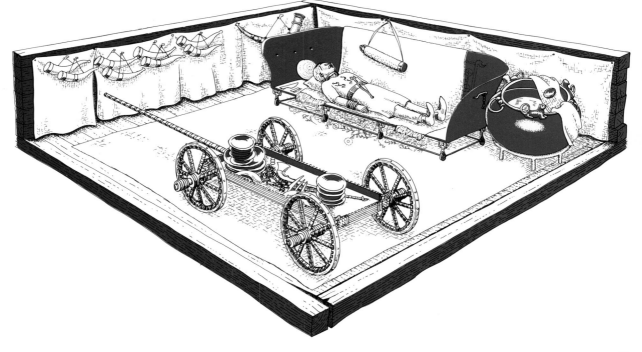

V
SACRIFICE AND PROPHECY

'But they would not sacrifice without the Druids. We are told of still other kinds of human sacrifices; for example, they would shoot victims to death with arrows, or impale them in the temples....'

Strabo, *Geography* IV, 4, 5

T O WHAT EXTENT can we believe Strabo's testimony? Is he, in common with other Classical writers, guilty of popular press sensationalism, or is he faithfully recording a genuinely observed religious practice? Strabo is not alone in making a direct correlation between human sacrifice and divination (the prediction of the future by observing and interpreting signs associated with the victim, and believed to be messages from the spirit world). In Strabo's description of various kinds of ritual murder, the use of archery is of particular interest: there is little evidence that the Celts used bows and arrows as weapons in warfare, and so their employment as instruments of sacrifice may represent the use of special weapons for special killing.

Strabo and other Classical commentators make specific reference to different methods of committing ritual murder. In addition to shooting and impalement, they record hanging, stabbing, drowning and burning. It is interesting to speculate as to whether these varied modes of dispatch reflect the invocation of different kinds of deity or different kinds of sacrifice, perhaps in respect of what was required from the divine powers. It may be that blood sacrifices (by shooting and stabbing) were efficacious for particular ceremonies, while burning or drowning were selected on other occasions.

The Wicker Man, as portrayed in the film of that name. Classical writers such as Caesar and Strabo describe a horrific ritual practice among the Gaulish Celts, in which humans and animals were burnt to death in a gigantic wickerwork image, as sacrificial gifts to the gods.

THE CONCEPT OF SACRIFICE

THE TERM 'SACRIFICE'

What do we mean by a 'sacrifice'? One definition is that a sacrifice is a once-living gift to the supernatural powers, which is of value to the donor and represents a genuine loss to that person or community. Two important concepts associated with ancient sacrifice are 'giving' and 'separation'. The sacrificial gift is ritually 'handed over' to the gods, and this may be demonstrated by killing it, perhaps in a distinctive way, by depositing it in a special place, and sometimes by doing something to it before death or deposition: such an act may take the form of torture, mutilation, the removal of certain bones, or the stripping and/or painting of a human victim.

Sculpture of a Roman sacrificial scene, showing the officiating priest, his head draped, and the sacrificial bull.

Altar to the Germanic goddess Vagdavercustis, from Cologne, Germany. Beneath the dedicatory inscription is a sacrificial scene, with the priest at the altar accompanied by other cult officials.

'*The Druids are concerned with the worship of the gods, look after public and private sacrifice, and expound religious matters.... When a private person ... disobeys their ruling they ban them from ... sacrifices. This is their harshest penalty.*'
Caesar, *Gallic War* VI, 13

MOST OF THE Graeco-Roman historians of the first centuries BC and AD mention sacrifice, particularly human sacrifice, among the Celts. Very frequently, they imply a link between sacrifice and the Druids, although their comments are sometimes ambiguous in terms of apportioning direct Druidic responsibility for ritual murder.

Caesar tells us that the Druids' powers of excommunication effectively made malefactors into outcasts, shut out of society and regarded as contaminated. To be excluded from religious affairs was perceived by the Gaulish Celts as worse than imprisonment or even death. Later in the same passage, Caesar makes a direct connection between the Druids and human sacrifice:

'... those who are suffering from serious illness or are in the midst of the dangers of battle, either put to death human beings as sacrificial victims or take a vow to do so, and the Druids take part in these sacrifices.... They believe that the immortal gods delight more in the slaughter of those taken in theft or brigandage or some crime, but when the supply of that kind runs short they descend even to the sacrifice of the innocent.'

There are strong similarities between the observations of Diodorus and Strabo, also writing in the first century BC. We have seen Strabo's comments at the beginning of this chapter. Diodorus says:

'In matters of great concern they devote to death a human being and plunge a dagger into him ... and when the stricken victim has fallen they read the future from the manner of his fall and from the twitching of his limbs, as well as from the gushing of his blood.'

Diodorus Siculus, *Library of History* V, 31, 3

Diodorus says that such acts are never performed without the Druids. Another comment he makes concerns the treatment of evil-doers who, he says, are kept in prison for five years before being impaled 'in honour of the gods'.

Pliny makes sinister allusions to ghastly sacrificial practices, which included killing and eating men in the name of religion. Lucan and Tacitus both make reference to the perpetration of human sacrifice in holy groves, under the auspices of the Druids. Lucan's *Pharsalia* (his commentary on the civil war between Pompey and Caesar) contains several such references to ritual murder, implying its connection with the Druids. One grove was deliberately destroyed by Caesar's soldiers: 'the barbaric gods worshipped here [in the grove] had their altars heaped with hideous offerings, and every tree was sprinkled with human blood.... Nobody dared enter this grove except the priest' (*Pharsalia* III, 372–417).

Tacitus describes an essentially similar scene in Britain, on the Island of Anglesey, when the Roman governor, Suetonius Paulinus, attacked the Druid stronghold there. He refers first to the imprecations screamed by the Druids against the Roman desecrators, and a few lines later: 'The groves devoted to Mona's barbarous superstitions he [Paulinus] demolished. For it was their religion to drench their altars in the blood of prisoners and consult their gods by means of human entrails' (*Annals* XIV, 30).

A SACRIFICIAL CURSE

'[Whoever] ... whether male slave or female slave, whether freedman or freedwoman, whether woman or man ... has committed the theft of an iron pan, he is sacrificed to the Lord Neptune with hazel.'

*T*his lead curse was found in silt dredged from the Little Ouse River at Brandon in Suffolk, near to the Hockwold Romano-British temple. It is remarkable for three reasons: first, it is an inscription mentioning sacrifice in connection with human beings; second, the Roman cursive script dates it to the fourth century AD, long after the demise of free Celtic society; third, it alludes to Neptune, a Roman water-god, in association with hazel, which has a strong symbolic significance in early Irish mythology. It is worth noting that hazel has been found in association with several Iron Age bog bodies, themselves probably sacrificial victims (p. 81).

A nineteenth-century engraving showing a naked and bound sacrificial victim being led through the forest near Carnac, France, to his death at the hands of the Druids. The procession is headed by a Druid harper, and a group of Gaulish soldiers look on.

SACRIFICE IN ACTION

Detail from the silver-gilt cult cauldron from Gundestrup, Denmark, with a sacrificial scene in which a god (or priest) drowns a human victim in a vat or bucket.

THE GREAT DECORATED silver cauldron found at Gundestrup (p. 67), deliberately deposited in a peat-bog in the first century BC, bears iconography that is highly relevant to sacrifice. One of the inner plates portrays an army on the march: infantry, cavalry and trumpet-players, in full war gear and with what appears to be a sacred tree. At one end of the plate is a huge individual, much bigger than the warriors, who holds a man upside down over a vat or bucket, perhaps in the act of drowning him. Close examination of this scene and the position of the hands of the larger figure show that he is definitely pushing the victim down towards the vessel, not pulling him out. We are reminded of the comment by Strabo, about human sacrifice among the Cimbri who sacrificed human victims by cutting their throats over a cauldron in which their blood was caught (p. 66).

Another of the inner plates and the base-plate appear to depict bull sacrifices: the latter is made from a reused *phalera* (a circular horse-trapping) and on it a great bull sinks to its knees after receiving a fatal sword stroke from a warrior, who is tiny in proportion to his victim. The other plate shows a similar scene: here three identical bulls are each threatened by a much smaller man with a sword. The iconography of both plates is ambiguous inasmuch as each 'warrior' is accompanied by a dog, so it may be that a ritual hunt is represented, with a wild aurochs rather than a domesticated bull as victim. Moreover, the huge size of each animal suggests that it is of supernatural origin, rather like – in Mithraism – the young Persian god Mithras who has to slay a divine bull in order to fertilize the earth. It may even be that a similar creation-myth is being enacted on the cauldron.

(Above) The base-plate from the Gundestrup cauldron depicting a great sacrificial bull, felled by a man with a sword.

THE WICKER MAN

'*Some tribes build enormous images with limbs of interwoven branches which they then fill with live men; the images are set alight and the men die in a sea of flame.*'
Caesar, Gallic War VI, 16, 4

'*... having devised a colossus of straw and wood, [they] throw into the colossus cattle and wild animals of all sorts and human beings, and then they make a burnt offering of the whole thing.*'
Strabo, Geography IV, 4, 5

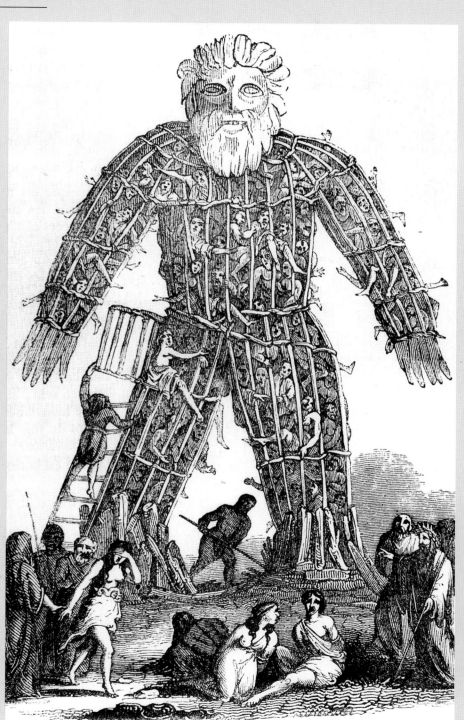

No less than three ancient sources make reference to a very specific type of ritual murder, a fire sacrifice in which victims were packed into a great hollow image of a man, made of wicker or straw, and burnt alive as an offering to the gods. The ceremony of the Wicker Man is recounted by both Caesar and Strabo; in addition, it appears in a ninth-century commentary on Lucan's Pharsalia.

It is probable that the very similar accounts of Caesar and Strabo both derive from a common source, Posidonius. Likewise, the commentator on Lucan's text had probably read one of the two earlier documents and then interwove the description with Lucan's own reference to the three savage Celtic gods he mentioned in the poem: these were Taranis, Esus and Teutates, whom the poet associates directly with human sacrifice (p. 78). The rite of burning straw men (happily without their live victims) was retained until quite recently in the spring festivals of post-pagan Europe. In Germany, images burned at Eastertime were known as Judas Men.

Nineteenth-century engraving of the Wicker Man being filled with human sacrifices. A Druid (bottom right) oversees the operation, as the victims bemoan their fate.

RITUAL MURDER

The skeleton of a man whose body was placed in a pit behind the rampart at the Iron Age hillfort of South Cadbury, Somerset. The position of the body suggests that he was bound; he may have been a victim of sacrifice, placed behind the defences in order that his spirit might magically protect the hillfort.

RITUAL DECAPITATION AT SAINT ALBANS

In 1995, a second-century AD pit outside a contemporary temple at Saint Albans in Hertfordshire, England, was found to contain the skull of a teenage boy which had been skinned at the time of death. Four large holes in the skull suggest that the boy had been battered to death before being beheaded and defleshed. Damage to the base of the skull and the missing lower jaw are consistent with the head's display on a pole. The lack of weathering indicates that it was kept indoors, perhaps in the temple. Only after its ritual usage was the skull disposed of in the pit.

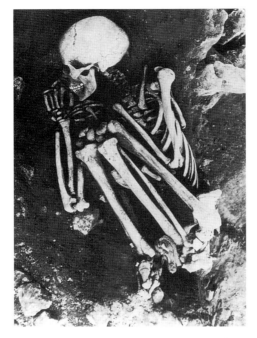

'It is in consonance with their savagery that they practise a unique impiety in their sacrifices.... They also use prisoners of war as sacrificial victims in paying honour to their gods.'
Diodorus Siculus, *Library of History* V, 32, 5

WE HAVE SEEN that the observers of the Celts from the Classical world made great play of the barbarism of their human sacrificial rituals. The observation of human victims in their death throes has given the Druids a bad press and caused them to be dismissed as barbaric and savage. 'They [the Gauls] used to strike a human being, whom they had devoted to death, in the back with a sword, and then divine from his death-struggles' (Strabo, *Geography* IV, 4, 5).

It is curious that Diodorus uses the term 'impiety', since the act of honouring the gods is generally deemed to be an act of piety. Here is an example of Classical censoriousness about a custom of which they did not approve and which they could not comprehend. For the Celts themselves, we must assume that such an act was, indeed, one of great piety. However, Diodorus' statement concerning the link between human sacrifices and war is interesting because it is endorsed by archaeological findings. The sanctuaries of Gournay and Ribemont in northern France contain the remains of several humans who may have died in battle, but who equally could have been sacrificed as captives of war. Gournay (p. 120), in particular, fits this picture in that thousands of weapons – arguably the result of plunder on the battlefield – were dedicated to the gods.

Archaeological evidence for human sacrifice will inevitably be circumstantial and equivocal. How can we tell whether someone whose remains we dig up died in battle, as a result of disease or as a ritual killing? Violent death will often leave its mark, but even then the death could be due to warfare, a hunting-accident, a quarrel or a punishment. Archaeologists have to be careful in interpreting the human remains they find on sacred sites as sacrificial victims. We also need to make a distinction between human sacrifice *sensu stricto* and the ritual treatment that bodies may have undergone after death. So, for example, the young man whose skeletal remains were found in a pit, dating to the early first century AD, behind the rampart at South Cadbury in southwest Britain may have been killed as a gift to the local gods, to ensure the defences would form a successful deterrent to raiders, but he could just as well have been a warrior killed in action, whose valorous spirit gave magical strength to the rampart in which he was interred. Likewise, the young men buried in pits at the Iron Age hillfort of Danebury in Hampshire, England, during the late first millennium BC, could represent thank-offerings consisting of the bodies of courageous soldiers.

Head hunting

Livy, Strabo and Diodorus all describe the – to them – outlandish practice of head hunting, which apparently sometimes occurred within the context of Celtic warfare. Not only were these heads cherished at home, but they were also offered up as votive gifts in shrines. Livy records the decapitation of a Roman general, Postumus, by the north Italian tribe of the Boii in 216 BC, who cleaned out the head, gilded it, and used it as a cult vessel. Such a practice seems to have been represented at Býčiskála in Bohemia (p. 84), where a human skull made into a cup formed part of the ritual deposition in the cave.

Roquepertuse and Entremont

Two pre-Roman sanctuaries in the Lower Rhône Valley in France, near Marseille, display clear

Iron Age rock-art scene at Camonica Valley, Italy, depicting what may be a sacrificial scene, with the victim flanked by priests with knives and perhaps wearing animal pelts, similar to shamans.

Group of carved severed heads from a shrine in the oppidum of the Saluvii at Entremont, southern France. Ritual head hunting went on in this region, and these carved heads may represent battle trophies offered to the gods of war.

evidence of ritual head hunting. One was at Roquepertuse, a cliff-top shrine the entrance to which consisted of a 'skull-portico' made of three stone pillars, linked by lintels, each containing carved niches for human heads. These skulls had once belonged to young men, probably war victims. A great stone janiform head guarded the doorway and on one lintel stood a large carved goose, a symbol of war. The temple contained other sculptures, including a frieze of horses' heads and statues of warrior-gods.

Entremont was an *oppidum*, the tribal centre of the Saluvii, which was sacked by the Romans in the late second century BC. On top of a hill inside the town was a stone shrine whose porticoes were decorated with carved stone heads and, like Roquepertuse, contained real skulls nailed into niches. That these were the heads of defeated warriors is strongly suggested by the javelin embedded in one of them. The sculptures from the sanctuary repeatedly emphasize the head-ritual. One image is that of a horseman, a head suspended from his saddle; another consists of a 'head-pillar', a tall stone incised with twelve severed heads, the absence of

mouths being suggestive of death. Warrior-gods are depicted here, some with carved human heads in their hands, as if to represent accepted offerings.

(Above) The 'head-pillar' from Entremont, France, depicting incised severed heads.

(Left) The body of a young man buried in a disused grain storage pit at the Iron Age hillfort of Danebury, Hampshire. He may have been a thank-offering to the infernal deities who looked after the seed-corn during the winter.

FLESH FOR THE GODS

'... and those Gauls who propitiate with human sacrifices the merciless gods Teutas, Esus and Taranis – at whose altars the visitant shudders because they are as awe-inspiring as those of Scythian Diana.'

Lucan, *Pharsalia* I, 422–465

LUCAN WAS WRITING in the mid-first century AD about deities allegedly encountered by Caesar's army in Gaul in the mid-first century BC (p. 23).

Lucan refers to human sacrifice in general terms, but a commentator on his poem, writing in Switzerland in the ninth century AD, clearly had access to early documents that have since been lost, for he elaborates on Lucan's comments in his description of the most appropriate human sacrifice for each of the three gods. Taranis, the thunder-god, was appeased by fire; the victims of Esus (the 'Lord') were stabbed and hanged from a tree until they bled to death; and those assigned to Teutates were drowned. The link between Taranis and fire has led to the assumption that the construction and burning of the Wicker Man (p. 75), described by Caesar and Strabo, were associated with the Thunderer. We cannot be sure about this, but the immolation of human victims by fire was a fitting rite for a god who was responsible for lightning.

Esus' name appears on a dedication which accompanies a stone sculpture found on the site of Nôtre Dame in Paris in 1711. The carving depicts a god chopping at a willow tree (p. 27); a similar image (though without the dedication) appears far away at Trier in Germany. So the link between Esus and trees, as presented in the literature, is corroborated by iconography. We have no definite images of Teutates (the 'God of the Tribe'), but the Gundestrup cauldron plate depicting a man held upside down over a bucket by a god (p. 74) may represent a drowning sacrifice. Taranis' name appears on seven inscriptions: in Britain, France, Germany and the former Yugoslavia. On some of the dedications he is equated with the Roman god Jupiter, presumably because both were celestial divinities and since one of Jupiter's roles was as Thunderer. If these three gods were as important as implied by Lucan, then their sacrificial rituals were surely presided over by professional clergy, quite possibly by the Druids themselves. Indeed Lucan mentions Druids by name just a few lines further down in the same passage.

Andraste and Boudica

'While they [the Britons] were doing all this [murdering and mutilating Roman women] in the grove of Andraste and other sacred places, they performed sacrifices, feasted and abandoned all restraint (Andraste was their name for Victory and she enjoyed their especial reverence).'

Dio Cassius, *Roman History* LXII, 7, 1–3

Dio Cassius, writing in the third century AD, was describing the activities of the infamous British freedom-fighter Boudica, queen of the Iceni after the death of her husband, the tribal chief Prasutagus. In AD 60/61, as we have seen (p. 53), Boudica led a confederation of rebel tribes, including the East Anglian Iceni and neighbouring Trinovantes, in an uprising against Roman domination. The revolt was triggered by the violent seizure of Icenian assets by Roman officials, and by the punitive flogging of Boudica and the rape of her daughters when she resisted.

Dedication to Taranis, the Thunder-God, in Greek characters, from Orgon, southern France. Taranis was one of the three Gaulish gods mentioned by Lucan as requiring propitiation by means of human sacrifice.

the deceased whose tomb it was. A later Iron Age chariot burial at Wetwang in northeast England, containing three bodies, a woman and two men, may reflect a similar practice.

Interestingly, Caesar specifically mentions the custom of suttee in Gaul, explaining that by the time he arrived in 58 BC the practice had become obsolete. 'it is only a short time since the slaves and clients … loved by the dead man were cremated along with him when the funeral was properly carried out' (*Gallic War* VI, 19).

(Left) Marble statue of Boudica and her daughters, in the City Hall, Cardiff, Wales. The sculpture was carved in 1913–15 by J. Howard Thomas. At the time of the Boudican rebellion, in AD 60/61, the Icenian queen invoked a goddess of victory, Andraste, and Roman women were murdered in her honour.

Although Dio does not specifically mention that Andraste was propitiated by human sacrifice, the implication is that the murdered Roman women were themselves sacrifices. Dio describes how these unfortunate victims were impaled on stakes and their severed breasts stuffed into their mouths, surely a violation which deliberately mirrored Boudica's own dishonour at Roman hands.

'Suttee' at Hoppstädten

Late in the La Tène Iron Age, a family was buried, all together, in a grave at Hoppstädten in the territory of the Treveri in the Moselle region of Germany. Unless all of them died at more or less the same time – as the result, perhaps, of an epidemic – then the implication is that a kind of 'suttee' is represented: this was a sacrificial rite in which, when the head of a family died, his wife and children were killed to go with him to the afterlife. A similar practice may be reflected in the much earlier double grave at Hohmichele in Germany, where a high-ranking man and woman were interred together under a mound in the sixth century BC. Since these two bodies were secondary burials within the grave-mound, they may both have been sacrificed in honour of

(Above) The man and woman buried together in a funeral mound at Hohmichele, Germany, in the sixth century BC. The couple may have died naturally at the same time, but it is possible that one was killed to accompany the other to the afterlife.

BODIES IN THE BOG

Lindow Man: the body of a young man ritually killed and submerged in a Cheshire bog, at the end of the Iron Age. He had been struck hard on the head, strangled and his throat cut. The discovery of mistletoe pollen in his stomach has led to conjecture about possible Druidic involvement in his death.

THE ARCHAEOLOGICAL RECORD does not generally reveal unequivocal evidence for human sacrifice, as we have seen. The strongest candidates for inclusion in such a category are the bog bodies, remains of human beings, often well preserved in the waterlogged marshes of northern and western Europe, which show signs of violence and ritual treatment. Some of these bodies have been dated to the Celtic Iron Age.

An Irish bog victim was discovered in 1821, 10 ft (3 m) down in a marsh at Gallagh in County Galway. Recent C14 analysis of the remains suggest that the body belongs to the Iron Age. According to reports written at the time of discovery, the individual was a young man with a beard and long black hair. He wore a knee-length deerskin garment, and he may have been killed with a garotte made of hazel (a band

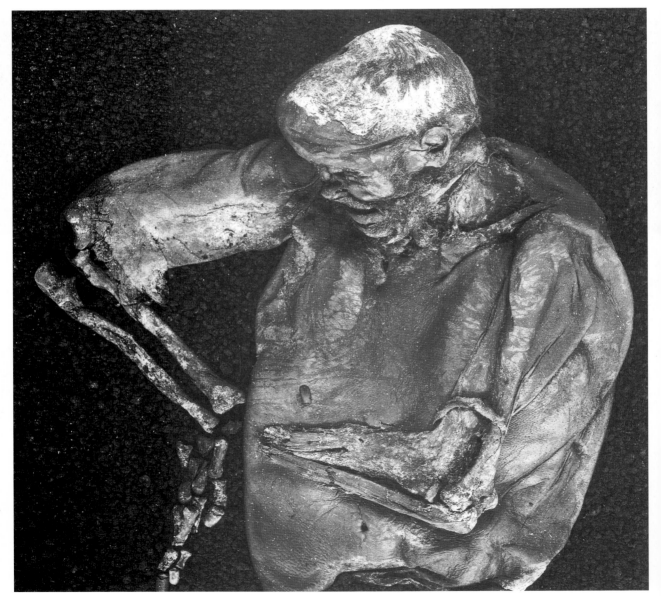

of thin hazel rods was found at his neck). Two wooden stakes flanking the body in the marsh also support the circumstantial evidence that the man was deliberately deposited.

Lindow Man

In August 1984 peat-cutters driving a mechanical digger at Lindow Moss in Cheshire, England, cut through part of a human body. On suspicion that they had come upon a modern murder victim, the police investigated the find, but the body was found to be ancient, and the remains were taken to the British Museum for analysis.

'Lindow Man' (or Pete Marsh, as he has been dubbed by some archaeologists and journalists) was a young, well-nourished man, about twenty-five years old, who had met a violent end and whose body was thrust face down in a shallow bog pool. He had sustained severe blows to the head which must have stunned him, though they did not cause his death. The murder weapon was a garotte of sinew which was passed round his neck, pulled tight and knotted at the back. Finally, his throat was cut. There has been controversy about the C14 dates for the body,

but current opinion is that Lindow Man died during the first century AD.

Although this young man may have been executed for a crime, certain aspects of his death point to some kind of ritual killing. He was naked but for an armlet of fox-fur, and his body was painted. Just before he died, he had consumed a specially prepared meal of bread baked on a griddle, containing a wide range of seeds and cereal grains, the remains of which were still in his stomach. Also in Lindow Man's gut was mistletoe pollen and, since Pliny makes reference to the association between mistletoe and the Druids (p. 18), this discovery has led to speculation about his possible link with the priesthood. Lindow Man was probably someone of reasonably high rank: this is suggested by his well-manicured finger nails and his neatly clipped moustache. The killing itself may have been carried out according to strictly prescribed rules, and it may be no accident that the victim had three 'deaths': injuries to the head, strangulation and throat slitting. There is an early Irish mythic episode in which a triple-fold killing of the sacral king is described.

A modern re-enactment of Lindow Man's death. Students at Darrenddeusant in south Wales play the part of Druids and their victim, in a film called 'Mysteries of the Unexplained'.

A second male victim has been found at Lindow Moss. He was probably killed about 100 years after Lindow Man. The circumstances and condition of the body were not dissimilar to those of the more famous find, but three features are of interest. First, he had been decapitated; second, he was found to have a vestigial thumb, this abnormality alone may have been sufficient to account for his selection as a sacred victim; and third, he had consumed a meal made substantially of crushed hazel nuts. Hazel was a sacred tree in early Irish myth, and the curse tablet from Brandon, which specifically mentions sacrifice associated with hazel, has already been noted (p. 73).

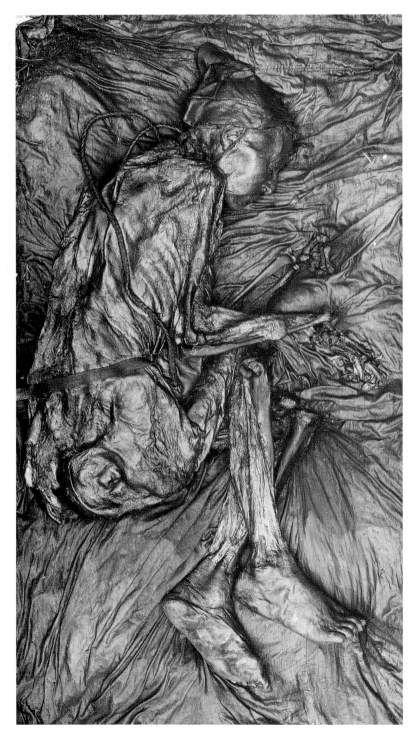

DENMARK WAS NEVER part of the Celtic world but there are, nevertheless, some marked similarities in terms of material culture between Celtic Europe and the Danish Iron Age. Denmark has produced an impressive array of bog bodies, some of whom quite definitely date to the later first millennium BC. One, Tollund Man, bears a strong resemblance to the British bog victim from Lindow Moss (p. 81). He too was strangled with a rope of sinew, and placed in the marsh naked, but for a leather girdle and cap. Like Lindow Man, the man found at Tollund had eaten a special meal of bread just before he was killed. Other men, too, were dispatched in a similar manner: the murdered man found at Borre Fen had been garotted; and another victim, Grauballe Man, had had his throat cut, again like the British victim.

It must be acknowledged that all these men may not have been gifts to the gods but criminals, executed with dishonour and cast into the marsh to symbolize the stigma of their end. In his treatise on Germany (which in antiquity included southern Denmark), Tacitus alludes to punitive killings in marshes:

'The punishment varies to suit the crime. The traitor and deserter are hanged on trees, the coward, the shirker and the unnaturally vicious are drowned in miry swamps under a cover of wattled hurdles.'
Tacitus, Germania XII

However, they may equally have been sacrificial victims: the specially prepared loaf, consumed immediately before death, suggests such an interpretation, as does the nakedness of the victims and the unnecessarily intricate knots with which the garottes had been fastened.

Burial alive
Two female Iron Age bog bodies appear to have died in a particularly horrific manner. A plump

Tollund Man: a Danish Iron Age bog victim, killed, like Lindow Man, by a garotte which can be clearly seen in the photograph. Like the British bog body, Tollund Man was placed in the bog virtually naked. Another link between the two victims is that both had eaten a special meal just before their deaths.

fifty-year-old lady, dressed in a skirt, cape and cap, was pinned firmly down in a peat bog at Juthe Fen in Jutland, probably while still alive. Wooden crooks were driven through the joints of her elbows and knees, and the swelling of one wound suggests she was still alive when it was inflicted. Great boughs were clamped across her body (exactly in the manner described by Tacitus), presumably to prevent her escape and, perhaps, to ensure that she could not return from the dead to haunt the living. Accounts written at the time of discovery refer to the look of terror and despair still visible on her face when she was taken from the marsh. The weekly magazine *Light Reading for the Danish Public* published an article on Friday 8 March 1839 describing the lady as a restless ghost who needed to be restrained.

When the Juthe Fen Woman was discovered, she was thought at first to be the notorious Norse Queen Gunhild, the cruel wife of King Erik Bloodaxe, who was murdered and sunk deep into a bog by the slaves of the medieval Danish King Harald. But in fact she can be firmly dated to the last few centuries BC, and we have no idea who she was.

As with the male bog bodies, the Danish women may have died as a result of punishment or sacrifice and, indeed, the two are not necessarily mutually exclusive. If they had offended the laws of their community, what are they likely to have done? The older woman could have been guilty of sorcery or Black Magic and may have been condemned as a witch. But it is difficult to imagine the very young girl found in the Windeby marsh as a criminal unless, of course, she was guilty of sacrilege. If, on the other hand, the women were the victims of ritual murder, they may have been selected because of some special circumstance, perhaps associated with their age, physical appearance or status within the community. We can speculate, for instance, as to whether the Windeby Girl might have been considered as an especially effective gift to the gods because she was at the threshold of adulthood, neither child nor woman, yet both. Alternatively, she could have been a high-born hostage, sacrificed to the local spirits after a treaty or alliance with a neighbouring tribe had broken down, although Tacitus does mention this manner of death for people caught in adultery. Both the Juthe Fen Woman and the Windeby Girl may have ended their lives as offerings to the divine powers because they were, in some way, marginalized within their social group: they may have belonged to a particular noble family, or have had unusual colouring, or

THE WINDEBY GIRL

A much younger female than the lady from Juthe Fen was the adolescent girl, twelve to fourteen years old, from Windeby in Schleswig-Holstein, north Germany. She had been subjected to a ritual or punitive act just before her death, for one side of her blonde head had been shaved with a razor. She was evidently led out into the bog alive, since a blindfold, made from a brightly coloured headband, had been placed around her eyes. She was stripped naked before her death, but for an ox-hide collar. There was no sign of how she was killed, but her body was pinned down in the marsh by birch branches and a great stone.

The Windeby Girl, an Iron Age bog victim from Schleswig-Holstein, north Germany. This young adolescent girl was led blindfolded to her death, and her body was weighted down with great birch boughs and a stone.

The horrific find of a fifty-year-old Iron Age woman buried alive in a bog at Juthe Fen, Denmark. When she was found, her discoverers noted the look of terror on her face. Like the Windeby Girl, she was probably sacrificed to the local gods. The swelling of her knee-joint confirms that she was pinned down by branches in the marsh before she died.

even a physical deformity or disfigurement that marked them out as special. That the Juthe Fen Woman was a sacrifice is strongly implied by the presence of a powerful natural spring exactly where she was buried.

There seems to have been a strong connection in Celtic religious tradition, between holy women and water. The Classical writers record the link between priestesses and sacred islands; and the association of female divinities with rivers and springs is very marked. So the Juthe Fen Woman might have been chosen to appease a goddess, perhaps the personification of the spring in the marsh, who was perceived as dwelling where the sacrificial victim was placed. The fact that both the Juthe Fen Woman and (probably) the Windeby Girl were pinned down while still alive may be significant: it may have been considered in some way appropriate that the bog itself – rather than the human agent – did the killing. Thus the spirit invoked by the sacrifice took an active part in the acquistion of the gift, which may therefore have been deemed of greater value.

THE HORRORS AT BÝČISKÁLA CAVE

In the sixth century BC, ritual events took place in a Bohemian cave, which appear to have included the sacrifice of both animals and humans. Parts of the cave seem to have been set aside for funerary ceremonies in which wagons, pots, corn and beasts were dedicated to the gods. The most grisly remains consisted of the bodies of forty people, most of them women, whose heads, hands or feet had been removed. A human skull had been placed inside a cauldron and a second skull had been fashioned into a drinking cup. Near the human bodies were the remains of two horses which had been quartered before their deposition on the floor of the cave.

(Below) The ritual activities at Býčiskála Cave, which included human and animal sacrifice, in the sixth century BC. The mutilated bodies of women and horses can be seen, and a participant in the ritual holds a cup made out of a skull.

'And some of them also slay even the animals captured in war as well as the human beings ...'
Diodorus Siculus, *Library of History* V, 32, 6

'After deciding on battle they frequently vow to Mars whatever they may take in the war; whatever captured animals remain over they sacrifice ...'
Caesar, *Gallic War* VI, 17

ALL OVER THE Celtic world, in shrines, graves and settlements, there is evidence for the sacrifice of animals to the spirit world. Of course, such a practice was widespread in antiquity and was as common in Classical as in 'barbarian' Europe. The sacrifice of a cow, sheep, pig or horse represents a serious economic loss to rural communities who might be living and farming at subsistence level. There were two kinds of sacrifice: in one, the entire animal was burnt or left to the gods; in the other, beasts were killed and butchered, some portions being left for the supernatural powers and the rest (usually the most palatable meat!) being consumed by the sacrificers or by the whole community.

There is overwhelming archaeological evidence that the Iron Age Celts preferred to sacrifice domestic animals rather than wild species. This may have been because domestic beasts were considered of greater value and because they were closely connected with the lives of humans.

In addition to the habitual sacrifice of the main farm animals, the Celts chose two creatures which were clearly of great significance to them: dogs and horses. Both animals enjoyed an especially close relationship with humans: dogs accompanied their masters in the hunt, guarded their homes and scavenged their rubbish; the possession of a horse was a mark of status, and horses were essential for transport, traction and warfare.

Nineteenth-century Italian coloured engraving of Druids sacrificing a bull for a Germanic chief and his followers.

A bronze plaque of a slain boar, perhaps a sacrificial victim, from a shrine of first-century AD date at Muntham Court, Sussex, England.

THE FUNERAL CORTÈGE AT SOISSONS

Occasionally, the intensity and special nature of sacrifice associated with graves lead to conjecture about the status of the dead. Only someone as important as an Iron Age warrior hero, tribal ruler or priest could have been interred at Soissons, where two men buried with four-wheeled carts were accompanied by an entire cortège of animals. In one, pairs of bulls, horses and goats were buried, along with a ram, a pig, and a dog. None of the carcasses had been butchered, all had been placed entire in the tomb.

The animals killed and buried with an Iron Age nobleman at Soissons, France.

Dogs and the spirits

In Celtic religion, dogs were symbols of both healing and death, the two roles coming together in perceptions of regeneration or rebirth after death. The infernal symbolism of dogs is demonstrated by their sacrifice and deposition deep underground, in pits or wells. The bodies of several dogs were placed in a 200-ft (60-m) deep shaft associated with a Romano-British temple, of first century AD date, at Muntham Court in Sussex; and the remains of five dogs were interred deep in a well at Caerwent in south Wales. Dogs were even sometimes eaten in sacrificial ceremonies: there is evidence that this occurred at the sanctuaries of Gournay and Ribemont-sur-Ancre in northern France. Dogs were occasionally killed to accompany their dead owners to the Otherworld: at Tartigny, France, a young dog had been skinned and eviscerated before being placed beside the body of his master.

Horse sacrifice

The sixth-century BC cave at Býčiskála (p. 84) contained the bodies of two horses which accompanied what may have been multiple human victims of ritual murder. The sacrificial use of horses continued sporadically throughout the Iron Age in temperate Europe: the sanctuary

Bronze figure of a horse from the late Iron Age religious hoard at Neuvy-en-Sullias, France. The horse was dedicated to a Gaulish god named Rudiobus.

of Ribemont contained a 'bone-house' constructed of the limb bones of horses and humans. Horses were occasionally placed with dead warriors in tombs, probably as the result of sacrifice. The King's Barrow chariot burial, in Yorkshire, England, of third century BC date, contained the corpse of a warrior with his horse team. Of the same date is the recently discovered burial of a man and his horse, placed together in a shallow grave at Stratford, east London. Horses interred as special deposits in pits at Danebury, Hampshire (below, p. 87), consisted of whole carcasses, partial bodies and skulls.

The death pit at Gournay

The shrine of Gournay was constructed in the fourth century BC, in an *oppidum* of the Bellovaci in Picardy, France (pp. 64, 76, 121). The first phase of religious activity took the form of the digging of a series of pits, some of which contained weapons. But the purpose of the great central pit was to receive the bodies of oxen, which were left there for six months or so, while their flesh decomposed (indeed, the first roofed building was erected in order to protect this pit). Then the bones were removed and placed in discrete groups, along with the remains of horses and other animals, in the enclosure ditch surrounding the sanctuary, with the ox skulls flanking the entrance way. The horses had probably died naturally and the young pigs, lambs and calves had been butchered for sacrificial feasting, but the cattle were treated in a more complex manner. All were elderly, and analysis of their bones revealed that when alive the animals had been put to work pulling ploughs or carts. Each ox was killed with a precise axe blow to the nape of the neck. After the decomposition process was complete, the body was removed from the grave pit, part of the skeleton was taken away from the shrine, and the rest remained within the precinct. The skulls were accorded particular attention: before their deposition by the entrance, the lower jaws were removed and the heads given a sword blow to slash off the muzzle.

Successive acts of sacrifice took place, each involving about ten beasts, at ten-year intervals. The sacrificial ritual at Gournay was so intense, complex and organized that, in the excavator Jean-Louis Brunaux's opinion, the presence of professional religious officials may be assumed. Bearing in mind Caesar's statement concerning the Druidic responsibility for sacrifice, Gournay is one of the best pieces of circumstantial archaeological evidence for the presence of Druids in sanctuaries.

Hayling Island

In about 50 BC, about 100 years before the Roman conquest, a circular timber shrine was built within a palisaded courtyard at Hayling Island, Hampshire, England. The focus of religious activity was this open-air area, which contained ritually broken weapons and substantial evidence for animal sacrifice, particularly of sheep and pigs. But most striking of all was the absence of cattle, which were such an important element in sacrifice on other sacred sites, both in Britain and elsewhere in the Celtic world. It is difficult to avoid the conclusion that there was some kind of 'taboo' on cattle-offerings associated with the cult at Hayling. Either cattle were repugnant to the local deity or, alternatively, they were very sacrosanct, just as in modern Hinduism cattle are holy and must not be killed.

The shrine at Hayling Island. The stone structure shown here is of early Roman date, and replaced a late Iron Age timber sanctuary.

(Left) The skeleton of a horse interred with a man in the first century BC, in London. The beast was perhaps killed to accompany his rider to the Otherworld.

ANIMAL RITUAL AT DANEBURY

*I*ntense ritual activity at the Iron Age hillfort of Danebury in Hampshire, England, was focused upon pits cut into the chalk; these had originally been dug for the storage of corn and then disused. Both humans and animals, or parts of their bodies, were interred in these silos. Several species of beast were present, but the most prominent participants in the Danebury ceremonies were horses and dogs, which were frequently deposited together.

Whilst we cannot be sure what was in the minds of these Iron Age celebrants, we can say with certainty that we are not witnessing mere rubbish disposal, but rather part of a complex ceremony, perhaps associated with the expression of gratitude to the infernal powers for keeping the

corn seed fresh, and thus ensuring the continued survival of the community.

The sacrificial burial of a horse and a dog in a disused grain silo at Danebury, Hampshire.

The skulls of oxen sacrificed in old age at the Iron Age shrine of Gournay, France. The ritual sword-slashes to the muzzles are clearly visible.

DIVINATION: TELLING THE FUTURE

> *'The Gauls likewise make use of diviners, accounting them worthy of high approbation, and these men foretell the future by means of the flight and cries of birds and of the slaughter of sacred animals, and they have all the multitude subservient to them.'*
> Diodorus Siculus, *Library of History* V, 31, 3

ONE OF THE MOST important roles of the Druids, so we are told by Classical writers, was to predict the future and the will of the gods, and to interpret whether omens were good or bad. This was done partly by the observation of natural phenomena, partly by the examination of the behaviour of animals and birds, and partly by means of human sacrifice. It was this last means of divination that so disgusted the Graeco-Roman commentators. The study of birds in flight (augury) and the scrutiny of the innards of animals were ritual customs common both to the Druids and to priests in the Mediterranean world.

Druidic prophecy appears to have had a close link with political propaganda. Cicero wrote that his Gaulish Druid friend, Divitiacus, told him that he was able to foretell the future both by augury and by inference (presumably meaning magical guesswork). In Tacitus' *Histories*, he says that in the time of Vespasian, Gaulish Druids prophesied that the burning of the Capitol in Rome was an omen of the destruction of the empire and of world domination by the 'tribes beyond the Alps'. Tacitus dismissed such claims as a combination of superstition and wishful thinking.

The reputation of the Druids as seers continued into the second and third century AD. Dio Chrysostom, writing his *Oratio* in the early second century, referred to their oracular powers, and the third-century AD author Hippolytus spoke of them as prophets and magicians, remarking that they predicted the future by means of ciphers and numbers, like the followers of the Greek philosopher Pythagoras. Chroniclers of third-century emperors, such as Severus Alexander and Diocletian, record the presence of Druidesses (p. 97) who foretold their fortunes.

'The Bard', 1774, an oil painting by Thomas Jones, which illustrates Thomas Gray's romantic poem of the same name. The last Welsh Bard, about to hurl himself into the river Conwy, curses the conquering English and their king Edward I, as he surveys his vanquished land. One might imagine that the Bard foretold his defeat by interpreting the flight of the birds above him.

The Coligny calendar

By its very nature, it is virtually impossible to identify any aspect of material culture – any monument or artifact – as associated with divination. But the bronze 'calendar' found in 1897 at the French town of Coligny, near Bourg-en-Bresse, appears to present a rare piece of corroborative evidence for the prediction of auspicious and inauspicious occasions, in the form of what is the longest Gaulish inscription that has yet been found (p. 37). The large but fragmentary tablet probably came from a sanctuary, and has been dated to the early first century AD. The bronze sheet is engraved with Latin characters with a list of the sixty-two months of a five-year period in the Gaulish calendar. The 2,021 lines of the inscription are divided into sixteen columns, each covering four months, except for the first and ninth columns each of which have an intercalary month and two normal ones. Each of the twelve months begins with its name and after it is either the word MAT(U) or ANM(ATU). These mean 'good' and 'bad' and the inclusion of these abbreviations has led scholars to conclude that such a calendar was used by Druids to predict the best or worst times for the community to undertake certain activities: warfare, sowing, harvesting, royal marriage and so on. But the terms can also mean 'complete' and 'incomplete', thus referring to whether a particular month had 30 or 29 days.

It is probable that the Coligny calendar was a Druidical device designed to help them in plotting predictions perhaps based upon astronomical observations. One interesting feature of the calendar is that it reckons by nights rather than by days, which may demonstrate a link with a comment made by Caesar: 'The Gauls all assert their descent from [the infernal god] Dis Pater and say that it is the Druidic belief. For this reason they count periods of time not by the number of days but by … nights' (*Gallic War* VI, 18).

William Stukeley's pen and ink drawing of 'The Midsummer Sacrifice of the Druids', 1759, showing a Druid sacrificing two birds in a 'winged temple' within a grove. The Druids were believed to be able to divine the future by observing birds in flight, and by examining the entrails of sacrificed animals.

Divination continued to be important in early Irish history and myth. The learned class particularly associated with such practices were the Filidh who, when Druidism declined after the adoption of Christianity, took over their oracular functions. Prophetic skill in Ireland was sometimes known as the 'Himbas Forosnai', the 'gift of foresight': a ninth-century commentator named Cormac describes a practice in which the flesh of pigs, dogs or cats was chewed in order to gain prognosticatory powers.

The ability to predict the future gave the Druids enormous influence in their communities, sometimes even greater than that of the secular rulers whom they advised. In the Ulster Cycle of prose mythic tales, the Druids attached to the royal households of Queen Medb of Connacht and King Conchobar of Ulster possessed the power to influence the decisions of their patrons, particularly in relation to warfare.

Detail of the Gaulish ritual calendar from Coligny, France, with the abbreviations MAT and ANM demarcating lucky and unlucky days of the month. Such calendars were probably used by the Druids in divinatory calculations.

PROPHETS AND ORACLES

THE IDENTITIES OF certain prophets, often directly linked with the Druids, have survived both in Classical documents and in Insular vernacular texts. We have already met the first-century BC Aeduan nobleman Divitiacus who, according to Cicero, practised augury to predict the future (p. 44). Augury (literally divination through the study of bird flight) was a ritual tradition that was equally familiar to Roman religious practitioners and contemporay Gaulish Druids.

In early Irish literature, a number of influential Druids are described. Perhaps most prominence is given to Cathbadh, the Druid of King Conchobar, whose activities are recounted in the Ulster Cycle. Cathbadh seems to have been rather like Samuel at the court of King David, constantly warning and advising his ruler (and altogether being rather a kill joy). Cathbadh was responsible for many important predictions which affected the fortunes of Ulster (p. 128). Cathbadh combined the roles of prophet, royal adviser and teacher of war craft, and he was clearly treated with considerable reverence because he was in tune with the forces of the Otherworld.

Oracles and shrines
In the Classical world, Apollo was one of the most important oracular gods, as well as being a divine healer. A Celtic version of Apollo was widely venerated in Gaul during the Roman period, and his sanctuaries – besides being curative establishments – were probably also associated with prophecy. Many ancient shrines were built around sacred springs, just as was the case in ancient Greece and Italy, and the murmuring spring water was perhaps perceived to be the speech of the gods. The temple of Apollo and his native consort Sirona at Hochscheid in Germany was built on the site of a holy spring, as were several sanctuaries to that god in the tribal territories of the Aedui and Lingones of Burgundy, France. Ravens and doves, with their distinctive 'voices', were part of the imagery of such shrines: in both Mediterranean and Celtic symbolism, ravens especially were closely linked with oracles. Ravens seem to have possessed a complex symbolism; their carrion-feeding habits and black plummage gave them an obvious association with death, but they could also be connected with healing, as at the curative shrine of Mavilly in France (p. 118), where a stone carving depicting an eye-healing ritual includes the image of a large raven.

The shrine at Beire-le-Châtel, France, was just one of several Burgundian healing-sanctuaries where multiple stone images of birds were offered as votive gifts. At Bolards, model pairs of eyes made of sheet bronze were dedicated as part of a healing ritual, in which the deity was invoked to replace the votive models with healthy organs, but they may also represent a desire for the pilgrim to become clear-sighted, able to gain knowledge or to see visions of the future. The shrine of Apollo Vindonnus at Essarois was dedicated to Apollo 'of Clear Light', and again model eyes were dedicated to him.

If such sanctuaries were associated with oracular powers, it is likely that the Druids, or some other professional clergy, had a role to play. Indeed, the poet Ausonius, specifically mentions the priest Phoebicius, who belonged to a Druidic family and who officiated at the temple of the healer-god Belenus (a native version of Apollo) at Bordeaux in France.

Sculpture of Roman date from Moux in Burgundy, France, depicting a god carrying fruit, accompanied by a dog and with two raven-like birds perched on his shoulders. The birds may reflect the god's oracular function.

(Opposite) Detail of a watercolour by William Blake, 'The Sun at his Eastern Gate'. In both Classical and Celtic religion the sun-god Apollo had oracular and healing abilities.

THE FEMALE DRUIDS

'The enemy [the British] lined the shore in a dense armed mass. Among them were black-robed women with dishevelled hair like furies, brandishing torches. Close by stood Druids, raising their hands to heaven and screaming dreadful curses.'

Tacitus, *Annals* XIV, 30

THUS WROTE THE Roman historian Tacitus of the reception committee encountered by the conquering general Suetonius Paulinus on the island of Anglesey in AD 60. Were the women he describes Druidesses or were they 'cheer leaders', supporting and encouraging their religious leaders?

The Classical writers provide us with tantalizing glimpses into a Celtic world where priestesses as well as priests took responsibility for communicating with the supernatural world. We learn of women – sometimes specifically called Druidesses – presiding over religious ceremonies, carrying out complex rituals and even telling the fortunes of Roman emperors.

The archaeological evidence is more challenging: how do we decide whether the body of a woman buried in the precincts of a sanctuary was that of its priestess? Can we infer the gender of the people who wore the headdresses or carried the sceptres found on archaeological sites? It is not always easy to make positive identification of female images as those of female religious officials, let alone Druidesses. But archaeological evidence does suggest that witchcraft – representing the dark aspect of religion, perhaps more properly termed superstition – may have been practised in Celtic Europe.

The vernacular mythic texts of Ireland make direct references to female Druids and seers, some of whom were poets. Both the early Irish and Welsh myths mention witches, who sometimes possessed the additional role of teachers of war craft to young heroes.

Bronze cult wagon, depicting a ritual stag hunt presided over by a goddess or priestess, holding up a sacred cauldron; from a warrior's grave dating to the seventh century BC at Strettweg, Austria.

WOMEN IN CELTIC SOCIETY

The grave of a high-born lady – perhaps a priestess – at Vix in Burgundy, c. 500 BC. The woman was interred with her four-wheeled bier, jewellery and drinking equipment, including an enormous bronze vessel imported from Greece or Italy.

THE IDENTIFICATION OF priestesses in pagan Celtic Europe needs to be viewed within the context of the social position of Celtic women in general. The employment of female religious officials by no means necessarily reflects the status of women in secular society: in Classical Athens of the fifth century BC, women were not even granted citizenship and almost their only contribution to public life was in the sphere of religious activity.

All three categories of evidence – the testimony of Classical authors, archaeology and the vernacular myths – suggest that some high-ranking Celtic women enjoyed a power which was at least comparable to that of their male peers. Both Mediterranean documentary sources and the archaeological evidence imply that extremely powerful and influential women could and did exist in pagan Celtic Europe between the fifth century BC and the first century AD. Such women may have been few in number but that they were acceptable within Celtic society is important: this was not the case in the contemporary worlds of Greece and Rome. Least unequivocal are the myths: Queen Medb of Connacht, a central figure in the Ulster Cycle, is often singled out as an example of a high status female in early historical Ireland. She is depicted as an independent ruler, with her own army, and is described as far more important than her consorts. But she is a figure of myth, a goddess rather than a queen, and there is no reference to her as an authentic historical figure in the early Irish king lists.

The ladies of Vix and Reinheim

One method of assessing the status of individuals in prehistory is by looking at the goods buried with them in their tombs. Clearly we need to be careful about making direct correlations between grave goods and the social position of the people whom they accompanied: it may be, for instance, that precious objects interred with a woman reflect the status of her husband or father rather than her own rank. But certain graves in Iron Age Europe appear to point to the presence of independent, high-ranking women, who may well have been dynastic rulers in their own right.

At the end of the sixth century BC, a thirty-five-year-old woman died and was entombed at Vix in Burgundy, France, at the foot of a hill on which stood the early Iron Age stronghold of Mont Lassois. She was laid in her grave with much ceremony; her body was borne to the tomb on a great four-wheeled bier, which was then dismantled and placed with the corpse in a wooden mortuary chamber, under a massive earth mound. The Vix lady was interred with sumptuous grave goods, including jewellery and vessels. She was buried with a huge gold torc, but the tomb's furnishings were dominated by an enormous bronze *krater* (wine-mixing vessel) which stood 5ft 6in (1.64 m) high. What is extraordinary about the presence of this vessel is that it was manufactured in Corinth or Etruria and, despite its size and weight, was transported (perhaps partially dismantled) all the long and arduous way over the Alps to northern Burgundy. Such a vessel argues for the extremely high rank of its possessor, not only because of the expense of the bronze and the craftsmanship involved in its making, but also because of its exotic character, implying that its owner had strong links with the Mediterranean world. It is possible that the krater came into the lady's possession through the mechanisms of gift exchange, whereby rulers gave presents to each other to symbolize alliances, patronage and relative rank. That the lady buried at Vix was probably an autonomous ruler is suggested by the lack of any commensurately wealthy male grave in the vicinity. The woman may well have reigned from the nearby centre at Mont Lassois.

Other early Iron Age women were buried with elaborate ritual and rich grave-furniture. In the fourth century BC, a lady was interred at Reinheim beside the River Blies in Germany. She took with her to the afterlife an exquisite set of gold ring-jewellery comprising a torc and armlets, all intricately decorated with engraving and repoussé. The torc and one arm-ring display images of a woman with her hands folded on her stomach, in the manner of a corpse, and with a great bird of prey perched above her head. Such iconography may represent a goddess, but it may equally depict the lady herself, the bird perhaps a reflection of her apotheosis. If this is so, then either the Reinheim princess was sufficiently influential to commission her own jewellery, or she was important enough in life for her corpse to be endowed with specially made ornaments.

Boudica and Cartimandua

The presence of high-ranking females wielding power in Celtic society is confirmed by Classical writers, particularly in late pre-Roman Britain. Two such women took centre-stage in British politics during the mid-first century AD and both came face to face with the Roman government, though in extremely different circumstances.

Boudica of the East Anglian tribe of the Iceni is referred to at some length both by Tacitus and by Dio Cassius (p. 78). She was the widow of the client-king Prasutagus, who had entered into a reciprocal contract with the Roman emperor Nero, whereby he retained his kingdom intact in exchange for keeping the peace and allowing his realm to act as a buffer state. After Prasutagus died, Boudica assumed power of the kingdom (illegally in Roman eyes). The subsequent confiscation of Icenian assets by Roman financial officials and the rough treatment meted out to Boudica and her two daughters caused the

The legendary Irish queen Medb of Connacht, a warrior ruler and central character in the Ulster Cycle tale the Táin Bó Cuailnge. Her animal familiars were a bird and a squirrel. Medb had magical powers of sorcery and prophecy.

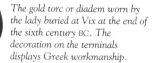

The gold torc or diadem worn by the lady buried at Vix at the end of the sixth century BC. The decoration on the terminals displays Greek workmanship.

Iron Age coin, first century BC, from Brittany, France, depicting an armed and naked horsewoman. The image may represent a goddess, but it may reflect instead the presence of female warriors in Celtic society.

Detail from a gold armlet belonging to an aristocratic woman buried in a grave at Reinheim, Germany, in the fourth century BC. The armlet and a gold necklet from the grave both bear the image of a woman, perhaps a goddess, or even the dead woman herself.

Cartimandua was the legitimate ruler of the huge northern British federation of the Brigantes. Tacitus records that she reigned for about twelve years and – interestingly – that her rank depended on her high birth, thus implying the presence of dynastic succession. Cartimandua was a client-ruler, like Prasutagus, and called upon the protection of Roman forces when challenged for the leadership by her jilted husband Venutius. Cartimandua was no home-rule heroine like Boudica but a quisling, a collaborator who betrayed the great freedom fighter Caratacus after he fled to her for sanctuary from the Romans. Cartimandua's activities demonstrate that, in the first century AD, British women were able to exert supreme authority, enter into treaties with foreign powers, lead their own armies and possess property, as well as being able to dispose of their unwanted husbands. On this occasion, Rome's dislike of powerful women was subordinated to expediency and the greater good of peace within the province.

Bronze figurine of a warrior-goddess, wearing a goose-crested helmet, from Dinéault, Brittany, France, first century BC. The goose was a Celtic symbol of war.

enraged queen to muster a huge force of British freedom fighters. The Iceni were joined by the neighbouring Trinovantes, who were disaffected after being pushed off their lands to make way for the settlement of legionary veterans. Boudica and her army sacked the three major Roman towns of Londinium, Camulodunum and Verulamium (London, Colchester and St Albans) and very nearly lost Rome her newest province. The Romans were particularly outraged by Boudica's victorious rampage through Britain because she was a woman. But, in the end, the discipline of the Roman legions overcame the British rabble-army; Boudica and her forces were defeated and she allegedly committed suicide.

A Cimbrian priestess, as described by Strabo, in the act of sacrificing a prisoner of war.

'They were grey with age, and wore white tunics and over these, cloaks of finest linen and girdles of bronze. Their feet were bare. These women would enter the [army] camp, sword in hand, and go up to the prisoners, crown them, and lead them up to a bronze vessel…. One woman would mount a step and, leaning over the cauldron, cut the throat of a prisoner [of war], who was held over the vessel's rim. Others cut open the body and, after inspecting the entrails, would foretell victory for their countrymen.'
Strabo, Geography VII, 2, 3

THE TEUTONIC TRIBE of the Cimbri were not Celts *sensu stricto* but they shared some of their religious customs, including head hunting, human sacrifice and the use of sacred cauldrons. Caesar, Strabo and Tacitus all comment on the presence of Germanic priestesses whose principal function was divinatory, their predictions often being associated with war.

Oracles to the emperors
There is a fascinating but questionable group of references to Druidesses in the late Roman literary sources known as the *Scriptores Historiae Augustae*. These consist of texts allegedly written in the fourth century AD by a number of authors, and their reliability as historical documents has been called into question: they may be wholly fictitious. The *Scriptores*, often referred to as the Augustan Histories, contain a series of *Lives* of the later Roman emperors.

One of the authors of the Augustan Histories was Vopiscus of Syracuse in Sicily. He speaks of two late-third-century emperors who had encounters with Druidesses: one was Diocletian, the other Aurelian. The encounter with Diocletian was apparently described to Vopiscus by his grandfather, and is said to have taken place when Diocletian was serving in the ranks of the Roman army. The Druidess came up to him when he was paying his bill in a tavern and chided him for being mean. He replied jocularly that when he was emperor he would be more open handed. She then scolded him for his flippancy but predicted (correctly, as it turned out) that he would indeed assume the imperial purple once he had slain 'the boar' (*aper* in Latin). This enigmatic statement was a riddle meaning that Diocletian would first have to kill the Prefect of the Praetorian Guard: his name was Aper.

Another author who contributed to the Augustan Histories was Aelius Lampridius, who recounts the prophecy of a Gaulish Druidess concerning the future of the third-century emperor Severus Alexander: 'Furthermore, as he went to war, a Druid prophetess cried out in the Gallic tongue 'Go, but do not hope for victory, and put no trust in your soldiers' (*Severus Alexander* LX, 6). Severus Alexander was, indeed, murdered by some of his troops: perhaps he did not understand Gaulish!

'On a certain occasion, Aurelian consulted the Druid priestesses in Gaul and enquired of them whether the imperial power would remain with his descendants, but they replied … that none would have a name more illustrious in the commonwealth than the descendants of Claudius.'
Scriptores Historiae Augustae: Aurelianus XLIII, 4, 5

Coin portrait of the emperor Diocletian. While he was still a Roman soldier, a Gaulish Druidess allegedly prophesied Diocletian's imperial destiny.

VELEDA THE PROPHETESS

'But any approach to Veleda or speech with her was forbidden. This refusal to permit the envoys to see her was intended to enhance the aura of veneration that surrounded the prophetess. She remained immured in a high tower, one of her relatives being deputed to transmit questions and answers as if he were mediating between a god and his worshippers.'
Tacitus, Histories IV, 65

*T*acitus makes reference to a belief among some German tribes that women were particularly blessed with divinatory powers. The most powerful one of all, Veleda, enjoyed almost divine status and was her tribe's political negotiator. Julius Caesar relates how the senior women in certain Germanic communities had the responsibility of deciding – by divination – whether or not to wage war (just as the Druids at the court of Queen Medb prevented her from engaging in battle when the omens were bad.

(Right) Stone statuette of a goddess found in a well at the Romano-British town of Caerwent, south Wales.

'The Three Witches' by Henry Fuseli (1741–1825), as described in Shakespeare's Macbeth; they bear a strong resemblance to the triple hags of battle – the Morrigán and the Badbh – who appear in Irish mythology.

SORCERY AND WITCHCRAFT belong to a kind of substratum of religious activity which exists beneath the mainstream belief systems of many societies. In early modern Europe, witches were perceived as operating in association with the occult – the dark side of the supernatural – rather than with God, and the same was probably true of the Celtic world. Traditionally, witchcraft has been closely linked with women, although present-day Neo-Pagan witches (pp. 162–165) can be of either sex and, indeed, by no means necessarily have anything to do with Black Magic. There is some evidence, too, that witches, or female magicians, were active on the margins of pagan Celtic religion. The testimony both of archaeology and the earliest myths point to the existence of such women. They were not

priests, in the accepted sense, but they dabbled in the supernatural and were deemed to possess spiritual powers which enabled them to exert some magical control over people and events.

The jawless old women of Britain

Witches cannot easily be identified by archaeological means, but the treatment of the bodies of some elderly British women of late Roman date suggests their presence. The Romano-British cemetery at Lankhills, Winchester, contained the burials of several old women, dating to the fourth century AD, who had been decapitated and their heads placed by their legs. This pattern of ritual behaviour occurs elsewhere in Britain, but a very specific rite took place around Kimmeridge in Dorset in the late third century

AD. Here, elderly women were decapitated and interred, their lower jaws removed and the heads positioned by the feet; each body was accompanied by a spindle-whorl.

Decapitation of bodies before or after death does not, in itself, point to the presence of witches: the bodies of men, women and children were sometimes treated in this manner. The placing of the head by the feet or knees may have been done simply to point the dead person's way to the Underworld and to ease the passage between earth and afterlife. But the removal of the lower jaw is more significant: such an action implies a desire to prevent speech, and it may be that such women were casters of spells and that there was a fear they would be able to do this even after death, unless steps were taken to stop them. The presence of the spindle-whorls may also be relevant: in both Classical and Celtic religion, spinning possessed the symbolism of fate and destiny. The Roman Fates and some Gaulish Mother-Goddesses were perceived to be able not only to predict the life and death of humans, but also to terminate life by snapping the thread. The spindle-whorls in the graves of the Dorset ladies may reflect the perception that they had also possessed such powers.

Peredur comes to the aid of the watchman at a castle as he is attacked by one of the Nine Witches of Gloucester, in the medieval Welsh tale Peredur.

THE LARZAC INSCRIPTION

Curses, condemning wrongdoers and invoking the punitive support of the gods, were frequently inscribed on sheets of lead or pewter and deposited in temples or springs. Lead seems to have been specially chosen, partly because it was cheap and soft, making it easy to inscribe, but also partly because it is a heavy, dark metal, which symbolized infernal and negative supernatural forces. Such curse tablets were known as defixiones, from the Latin verb 'to fix', and they were inscribed with magical formulae so that the curse would fix on the malefactor and not rebound on the curser.

An inscribed lead sheet of late Iron Age date was discovered in 1983 in a tomb at Larzac in southern France. It is not, strictly speaking, a curse, but it had a similar magical purpose. The tablet was found broken into two pieces which served to cover a pot containing the remains of a woman. The four sides were originally covered with a continuous text written, not in Latin, but in Gaulish (though using Latin script). Its 160 words make it one of the longest inscriptions in Gaulish to have been found so far. The tablet records the presence of two rival groups of female magicians (the inscription calls them 'women endowed with magic'). The text describes how one group had

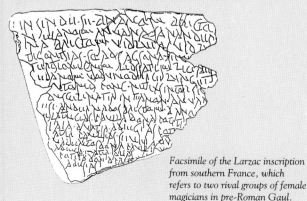

Facsimile of the Larzac inscription from southern France, which refers to two rival groups of female magicians in pre-Roman Gaul.

attempted to harm the other by magical means and how the wronged set of magicians had employed wise women to neutralize the evil charm. Such testimony provides a fascinating glimpse of a dark sub-world of superstition, in which witches were organized into guilds, and they could, on occasions, be driven to turn their magic on each other, perhaps because of competition for business. In this instance, the group commissioning the tablet did not simply employ a counter-spell on its ill-wishing sisters but summoned the services of other women, perhaps seers, to help them; they reinforced their defence by using lead to record the wrong done to them. It is tempting to make the assumption that the dead woman was the chief malefactor, hoist by her own petard.

The Irish battle-furies, known as the Morrigán or Badbh, who appear in the Ulster Cycle myths in triple or single form, and who shape-shift from the form of hag to raven. Here they pick over the bodies of the dead on the battlefield.

Welsh and Irish witches

One of the earliest mythic stories of Wales is that of *Peredur*. It belongs to the eleven tales which make up the *Mabinogion*, a collection of medieval texts which express a mythology that may relate to a much earlier pagan Celtic tradition.

An episode in *Peredur* describes how the eponymous hero encountered the Nine Witches of Gloucester, who had been busy laying waste the land round about. Peredur came upon one of the witches attacking the castle watchkeeper and he struck her on the head. She immediately addressed him by name and informed him that both their meeting and her injury at his hand were pre-ordained. She also told him that he must dwell with her for a while and that she would instruct him in war craft. Later in the story, Peredur met the magical women again; on hearing that they had killed and maimed members of his family, he, together with Arthur and other heroes, challenged the witches to combat: the women (rightly) predicted that Peredur would destroy them.

The role of these witches and their relationship with Peredur is curious and ambiguous: they were essentially destructive, but they had the responsibility of teaching Peredur the very skills that would kill them, and they prophesied their own downfall. The nine women possessed magical powers which they used for evil ends, but they could be overcome by humans (albeit with supernatural powers) and they were subject to a destiny that they could not themselves control.

Irish myths occasionally mention witches. The central tale in the Ulster Cycle is the *Táin Bó Cuailnge* (the *Cattle Raid of Cooley*), which tells of the conflict between the provinces of Ulster and Connacht, ostensibly over the possession of the great Brown Bull of Ulster. The main protagonists are Queen Medb of Connacht (p. 94) and the young Ulster hero Cú Chulainn. The *Táin* contains a reference to the death of Cú Chulainn who, because of his superhuman status, could only be destroyed by magic. To this end, Medb turned the six posthumous Children of Cailitín into witches and warlocks by means of their magical mutilation: each of them had to be deprived of an arm, a leg and an eye. Medb then sent them to learn the craft of sorcery and they returned armed with spears made by the god Vulcan, each destined to kill a king: Cú Chulainn perished at their hands.

Like Peredur's witches, these Irish ones were inherently evil but they were specifically created by Medb as instruments of her own wishes. The mutilation that they had to undergo is significant, in that the Irish battle-furies – the Morrigán and Badbh – themselves sometimes appeared to mortals in this mutilated guise.

The six Children of Cailitín, magically mutilated by Queen Medb to turn them into witches and warlocks who are destined to bring about the death of the Ulster hero Cú Chulainn.

PRIESTESS AND PROPHETESS IN IRISH MYTH

DRUIDESSES ARE NOT often mentioned in the medieval Irish mythic texts, but reference is occasionally made to such women. The Fenian Cycle of prose tales has as its focus the story of the great war leader Finn, a hero with a clear supernatural dimension. In describing the life of the young Finn, mention is made of his upbringing by a Druidess and a 'wise woman' (the term usually used for a female seer). These two women were given the boy to foster by his natural mother Muirna, whose bondswomen they were; at Muirna's request, they reared Finn in secret because of fears for his safety after a *coup* in which a usurper for the leadership of the Fianna (an élite royal war band) had killed Finn's father.

The Druidess and the wise woman taught Finn war craft, hunting and fishing (the survival arts), and also acted as guards and advisers, warning him of danger. The involvement of the two women is interesting since the function of Druid and prophet were normally combined. The Druids spoken of by Caesar and other Classical writers and most Irish Druids are described as having a divinatory role that is central to their religious functions. The apparently subservient position of these women in Finn's mother's household is also curious, since Druids were traditionally held in high esteem. One pos-

The Irish prophetess Fedelma, who warned Queen Medb of the prowess of her young adversary Cú Chulainn. Fedelma's speckled cloak and her multi-pupilled eyes show that she came from the Otherworld.

sible explanation is that Finn's family was of such high – quasi-divine – rank that the status of the bondswomen was also relatively elevated. Another solution to this anomaly may lie in the possibility that the two holy women deliberately kept their identity secret, in order to protect Finn's safety.

Other episodes in Irish myth concern holy women who may or may not have been Druidesses. Queen Medb of Connacht had a chief priestess called Erne who was attached to her royal court at Cruachain. She and her assistants were drowned in a lake, after being terrified by a monster called Olcai, and she gave her name to Loch Erne. One of the legends associated with Saint Brigit's monastery at Kildare concerns a group of pagan holy women who tended the sacred fire of a pre-Christian sanctuary on the site. Saint Brigit herself was transmuted from a pagan goddess and in both her identities she was associated with fire.

Irish warrior-prophetesses
In early Irish myth, a close link is made between war and prophecy. The warrior-goddesses, Morrigán, Macha and Badbh, all possessed the power to predict the future, particularly the outcome of battles and the destiny of individual war

Scáthach of Ulster, an Otherworld being who was both a prophetess and teacher of war craft to young heroes, such as Cú Chulainn.

heroes. This dual role extended to pagan holy women who, whilst not portrayed as goddesses, nonetheless had supernatural powers. Two such females are described in the *Táin*: Fedelma, who was both prophetess and poetess, and Scáthach, a warrior-teacher and seer.

Fedelma is described as 'the woman from the Fairy', the Otherworld. She attached herself to the court of Medb of Connacht, and she repeatedly warned the queen about the threat to her realm from Cú Chulainn. Fedelma first appeared to Medb as a beautiful young girl, armed and riding in a chariot. She was exquisitely dressed in a red, embroidered tunic, sandals with gold clasps and a speckled cloak; in both the Irish and Welsh mythic tradition, brindling (or speckling) signified Otherworld origins. Fedelma informed Medb that she had studied poetry and prophecy in Alba, a supernatural land belonging to Scáthach. Medb asked her whether she had the 'Himbas Forosnai' (the art of foresight) and Fedelma replied that she had. When asked to foretell the fortunes of the Connacht forces, Fedelma responded with a long, chilling poetic prophecy of doom, in which she repeatedly said of Medb's army 'I see it crimson, I see it red'. Fedelma predicted the crucial role of Cú Chulainn thus:

'I see a battle: a fair man
With much blood about his belt
And a hero-halo around his head
His brow is full of victories …'
From the *Táin*

Scáthach of Ulster was primarily a teacher of war craft to the young Ulstermen, and she was in charge of a battle academy. Her name means 'The Shadowy One' which suggests a link with the spirit world. Cú Chulainn came to her for training and he acquired his fearsome barbed spear, the *Gae Bulga* (a weapon whose wound was always fatal) as a gift from her. Like Fedelma, Scáthach was a war-prophet and she foretold the great conflict between Cú Chulainn and Medb and its culmination in his death.

Finn's foster-mothers and Fedelma and Scáthach all combined responsibilities for war and divination: all four warned of danger and doom and all were associated with the supernatural. Only one of Finn's mentors was specifically called a Druidess, but their functions suggest a strong similarity between those of the Druids. Cathbadh, Druid of King Conchobar, was linked with war, prophecy and warning, and the Druids commented on by Classical writers likewise predicted the future, often in relation to battle.

SOME OF THE most powerful religious functionaries in the Classical world were the Vestal Virgins, whose role it was to keep alight the sacred fire of the Roman goddess Vesta. They held office for thirty years, and the punishment for unchaste behaviour was burial alive. The Celtic world, too, had its virgin holy women. The importance of virginity among priestesses may have arisen from the perception that purity was desirable when in contact with the divine world, but also, perhaps, because virgins were regarded as especially potent symbols of fertility and regeneration: their sexual energy was intact and had not been squandered on mortals, preserving it for the gods.

Mela's island virgins

The Roman writer Pomponius Mela, writing in the early first century AD, speaks of the holy inhabitants of Sena, one of a group of islands called the Cassiterides which, from his description of their geographical location, were probably the Scilly Isles, off the southwest tip of England. On Sena there was, he relates, a Gaulish oracle attended by nine virgin priestesses who were able to predict the future, cure all illnesses and control the elements.

Pomponius' virgin holy women numbered nine, and this is interesting because three and multiples of three were sacred numbers for the Celts. In the iconography of pagan Celtic Europe, many deities were depicted with three heads or as three beings; and in the Irish and Welsh myths, three, nine and twenty-seven were among the special numbers that had particular significance.

The virgin cauldron-tenders of the Welsh Otherworld

Pomponius Mela's nine virgin priestesses belong to the pagan Celtic world of the first century BC. But the early Welsh mythic poem *Preiddu Annwfn* (the *Spoils of Annwn*) provides an interesting parallel. The poem survives in a thirteenth-century manuscript, and relates the journey of Arthur to Annwn to steal the magic cauldron of regeneration from the king of the Otherworld (Annwn). Such cauldrons are prominent in both Welsh and Irish tradition: they cooked ever-replenishing food and could raise the dead to life (p. 66). The cauldron of Annwn had a mind of its own and displayed a capriciousness that is common to many Celtic mythic beings. It was tended by nine virgins, and would only boil from the heat of their breath; another of the vessel's idiosyncracies was that it would never cook a coward's food.

The presence of nine virgins in this mythic

Bronze figurine of a priestess, her head draped for sacrifice, holding an offering plate and a circular object, which may be fruit or bread, from South Shields, northern England.

Aerial view of Bryher and Tresco, two of the Isles of Scilly. One of these islands may have been the home of the virgin priestesses mentioned by Pomponius Mela in the first century AD.

An earlier image that may well depict a priestess is on the seventh-century BC, bronze model cult wagon, found in a chieftain's tomb at Strettweg in Austria (p. 92). On the wheeled platform stand images of humans and animals, including two stags, horsemen and footsoldiers. At the centre, towering above them all, is a woman holding a great cauldron above her head. If the figure represents a goddess rather than a religious official, what could be represented here is the moving of a statue: the strut-like supports on the wagon suggest this interpretation.

Wooden figurine of a goddess or priestess, wearing a torc and with her head draped, as if to signify her participation in sacrificial ritual; first century AD, from the healing spring sanctuary of Chamalières, France.

tale and of nine virgin holy women on Mela's island may be mere coincidence, but the association of virginity and the number nine is suggestive of a link, and in both stories the sanctity of a number based on three and the importance of chastity may point to the existence of a common ancient tradition.

Images of Druidesses

Depictions of Celtic priestesses are uncommon in the archaeological record, and the few that appear to represent holy women are by no means certainly identifiable as Druidesses. One likely candidate is the lady from Chamalières in central France. Chamalières was a healing spring-sanctuary which was first patronized by pilgrims in the first century BC. The waterlogged site preserved thousands of wooden votive offerings, mainly models of parts of the human body that required a cure. Among these was an oaken image of a lady wearing a torc and with a veil over her head. Roman priests traditionally drew their robes over their heads whilst sacrificing, in deference to the gods. It may be that the Chamalières image represents the priestess of the shrine.

Side-panel of an altar dedicated to the Rhenish Mother-Goddesses, from a shrine near Bonn, Germany. The panel depicts a young woman, perhaps a priestess of the cult, with a garland of flowers and a platter of fruit, offerings to the goddesses.

THE MAENADS OF THE LOIRE

Strabo, writing in the late first century BC, provides a chilling account of an annual ceremony involving Celtic priestesses, of which he had read in Posidonius. Like Mela's holy virgins, these women – called the Samnitae – inhabited an island, near the mouth of the Loire. In Irish myth islands were often perceived as part of the Happy Otherworld, perhaps because they are cut off from the land-mass and thus seen as liminal places – gateways to the afterlife. Strabo relates how these priestesses did not allow men on their island but would travel to the mainland to have sex when they wished. So here is a variation on the theme of sacred virginity among Celtic holy women. The god worshipped here is called Dionysus by Strabo, but the Gaulish divinity probably had a local name, though his cult must have resembled that of the Greek god of wine and vegetation. When possessed by the spirit, the Loire women participated in a curious ritual which culminated in the sacrifice of one of their number:

'It is their custom once a year to remove the roof from their temple and to roof it again the same day before sunset, each woman carrying part of the burden; but the woman whose load falls from her is torn to bits by the others, and they carry the pieces around the temple crying out 'euoi', and

do not cease until their madness passes away; and it always happens that someone pushes against the woman who is destined to suffer this fate.'
Strabo, Geography IV, 4, 6

The behaviour of Strabo's women closely resembles that of the Dionysiac Maenads (above), whose savage rites are so graphically described in Euripides'

play The Bacchae. Strabo's passage is important because it makes a direct link between priestesses and built sanctuaries, and because of the very specific rite of re-roofing the shrine within a single day (as if it would be dangerous to leave it open to the spirits overnight). Most significant is the testimony to human sacrifice, which may have been particularly potent because the victim was herself sacred to the god.

(Below) The annual re-roofing ceremony at the temple near the Loire, at which the priestesses sacrificed one of their number to bless the refurbished sanctuary, while possessed by their god.

SACRED PLACES AND THEIR PRIESTS

'The axe-men came on an ancient and sacred grove. Its interlacing branches enclosed a cool central space into which the sun never shone, but where an abundance of water spouted from dark springs.'

Lucan, *Pharsalia* III, 400–404

LUCAN'S COMMENT ON a sacred grove encountered and destroyed by Julius Caesar's army near Marseille in the mid-first century BC clearly demonstrates that Celtic worship may often have taken place in naturally sacred places, including groves of oaks, lakes, river-crossings, the sites of springs or any feature of the landscape that, for some reason, was considered numinous (possessed by a spirit). The Gaulish word for a holy place, sometimes, but not always, meaning a sacred grove, was *nemeton* (*nemed* in Irish). The term is incorporated into the names of certain deities: Nemetona and Arnemetia are examples.

Natural sacred places, by their very character, seldom leave traces in the archaeological record, and we only know of their existence because Classical writers tell us so. Such commentators may have reported what they, or an eye-witness, had actually observed, or perhaps an element of barbarian stereotyping sometimes crept in. If writers from the 'civilized' world of Greece and Rome wanted to portray their Celtic neighbours as primitive, one way of doing this was to stress the ephemeral, unsophisticated character of their holy places, presenting a marked contrast with the great columns and pediments of Classical temples. Moreover, the sacred groves mentioned by Classical writers in the first centuries BC/AD may only have been used during the later Celtic Iron Age, and some Celts must have frequented other forms of holy place.

Graeco-Roman writers rarely allude specifically to Celtic religious buildings. But archaeological investigation is increasingly providing evidence for Iron Age sanctuaries, some of which underlie more substantial structures of Roman date.

A rag tree at Doonwell, Ireland. This tree is still a focus of local ritual, in which visitors hang personal belongings – handkerchiefs, scarves and bits of clothing – in order that they should benefit from the spirituality of the tree and its associated well.

SACRED GROVES AND POOLS

Rag tree outside Paphos, Cyprus. Local people still tie pieces of clothing, handkerchiefs etc. to the tree which is believed to have healing properties. Rag trees have a long and widespread tradition, from medieval Ireland to modern Turkey.

Bronze horned helmet, cast into the River Thames near Waterloo Bridge, London, as a votive offering, in the first century BC.

'According to local tradition, no birds ventured to perch upon the trees [of the sacred grove], and no wild beast made his lair beneath them; they were proof also against gales and lightning, and would shudder to themselves though no wind stirred ... superstitious natives believed that the ground often shook, that groans rose from hidden caverns below, that yews were uprooted and miraculously replanted, and that sometimes serpents coiled about the oaks, which blazed with fire but did not burn. Nobody dared enter this grove except the priest ...'
Lucan, Pharsalia III, 372–417

LUCAN'S ACCOUNT OF a sacred grove in southern France is strongly reminiscent of Virgil's description of the entrance to Hades (the Roman Underworld) in Book VI of his epic poem The Aeneid, and it is more than likely that Lucan was in fact influenced by Virgil's work. But several Classical observers comment upon the presence of sacred groves, not only in Gaul but in Britain (described by Tacitus on Anglesey) and even in Asia Minor: Strabo remarks on the re-unification of the three Galatian tribes which took place in a grove of sacred oaks at Drunemeton (this Celtic name means 'sacred oak grove' or 'sacred place of oaks'), where important matters of government were discussed.

Whilst it is virtually impossible for archaeologists to identify ancient sacred groves, there are indications that the Iron Age Celts sometimes erected wooden structures which copied these natural holy places. This may have been the thinking behind the construction of the great circular building, with its 'forest' of timbers, at Navan Fort, County Armagh, Ireland, at the beginning of the first century BC (p. 56). One possible epigraphic reference to a sacred grove consists of the Romano-Gaulish inscription from the French Pyrénées, dedicated to 'The God Six Trees'.

There is evidence that specific types of trees were considered sacred: altars in the Pyrénées were dedicated to Fagus ('Beech Tree'); the Gaulish tribal name Lemovices means the 'People of the Elm' and the Eburones were named after the yew tree. Pliny specifically associated oak trees with the Druids. Single large timbers found at British shrines such as Hayling Island in Hampshire and Ivy Chimneys in Essex suggest that the original cult focus of these sanctuaries was a tree or substitute tree. The same phenomenon has been recognized on the

LOWBURY HILL: AN ARTIFICIAL GROVE?

Lowbury Hill in Oxfordshire, England, has long been regarded as the site of a probable Romano-British temple. The summit of the hill is occupied by several earthworks, including a rectangular enclosure and a round barrow. The site was excavated in 1913–14, when the bank and interior were investigated. Further work has recently been carried out, including a geophysical survey and a limited excavation programme. One of the most interesting features discovered in this new investigation is the presence of a series of shallow, irregular scoops in the chalk, filled with dark, loamy soil, which have been interpreted as tree holes. These seem to have formed part of the primary demarcation of the sacred enclosure, and appear to represent deliberately planted trees. This activity perhaps took place in the first century AD. The inference is that the first construction was replaced in the second century AD by an enclosing wall: inside there was probably a simple temple building; associated with it were a group of spears (including a deliberately bent one), coins and other finds indicative of sacred use. But the first phase may have comprised a deliberately planted holy grove. One further discovery of possible relevance is the burial of a woman whose face had been mutilated, though it is uncertain to which phase this body belongs.

The excavation of Lowbury Hill, showing the pits in which the trees were planted, perhaps to create an artificial sacred grove.

LLYN FAWR

*I*n about 600 BC, the natural lake of Llyn Fawr in south Wales was the focus of religious activity which involved throwing precious metal objects into the sacred water. The offerings found in the peat-deposit in 1911 and 1912 included two locally made sheet-bronze cauldrons, which were already antiques when they were 'sacrificed': the more complete of the two vessels was a complex piece comprising five tiers of bronze fastened with 500 decorative rivets. Also in the hoard was exotic Hallstatt material, including part of an iron sword, one of the earliest iron objects known from Britain. Indeed, a

significant feature of the Llyn Fawr assemblage is that many of the pieces belong to types that were foreign to Wales. One reason for this could have been the reputation of the holy lake which may have been visited by people from far away. Alternatively, the exotic metalwork could represent loot from other communities, offered to the gods in thanksgiving for a successful raid.

(Right) Drama students re-enact a ritual, at the sacred lake at Llyn Fawr, south Wales, in which objects of iron and bronze were deliberately thrown into the lake as votive offerings, in about 600 BC.

Continent, for instance at Libenice in Bohemia (p. 57).

Certain cult objects were associated with sacred trees: a sanctuary at St Maur, Oise, France, produced bronze leaves; the remains of a gilded bronze tree were found in a third-century BC pit at Manching in Bavaria; and iron leaves with rings for suspension come from a French settlement at Villeneuve-St-Germain, Aisne.

In the pagan mythic texts of early historic Ireland, notably in the *Dinnschenchas* (the 'History of Places'), holy trees were particularly associated with sacral kingship, and the inauguration rites surrounding the election of a new king. Trees were venerated partly on account of their longevity, which symbolized wisdom, stability and sovereignty. The Old Irish word for a sacred tree is 'bile'. The oak, yew and ash were especially revered, as was hazel, which had a particular link with Druids and seers. In Ireland, hazel was associated with the acquisition of wisdom: Finn, hero of the Fenian Cycle, received knowledge from contact with the cooking flesh of the Salmon of Wisdom, who had itself gained its powers through consumption of the fruit of nine sacred hazels growing beneath the sea beside a well. A ritual shaft or well at Ashill in Norfolk, England, has produced evidence which could be related to the veneration of hazel: complete pots placed in layers and embedded in hazel leaves and nuts. Reference was made in chapter 5 (p. 73) to the lead curse mentioning hazel, found in a river near Brandon, in Suffolk.

Lakes, pools and springs

'the treasure found at Toulouse amounted to about fifteen thousand talents, part of it being laid up in the temple-enclosure and part in the sacred lakes ... the treasure there was unusually large since many made dedications and none would dare to profane them.'
Strabo, *Geography* IV, 1, 13

The general association between ritual practice and water has already been discussed in chapter 4. Strabo's comment concerning the deposition of treasure in sacred lakes is strikingly borne out by archaeological testimony. The great Swiss type-site of La Tène on the shore of Lake Neuchâtel, which has given its name to much of Celtic Iron Age material culture, seems to have been just such a focus of ritual activity. In 1857, the level of the lake dropped considerably, revealing wooden bridges and staging and more than 3,000 metal objects belonging to the Celtic aristocracy, which had probably been cast in as offerings to the gods: the bulk of the material dates to between the third and first centuries BC.

Gregory of Tours, who was Bishop of that city from AD 573–594, mentions (*In Gloria Confessorum*) an annual three-day festival at Lake Gévaudan in southern Gaul where peasants cast in sacrificial animals, food, drink and clothing as offerings to the gods. So this practice of casting votive objects into lakes and pools would appear to have continued long after the introduction of Christianity to Celtic lands.

The cult tree from Manching, Bavaria, third–second century BC. The stem is wood, the leaves are gilded bronze. It may have been carried in ceremonial processions or been furniture in a tribal shrine.

SHRINES AND TEMPLES

IRON AGE RITUAL structures do not conform to a standardized or formal religious architecture – unlike Greek or Roman temples or Christian churches – so that architecturally there is usually little to distinguish a shrine from a house or barn. Moreover, cult images are rare for this period, so we are unlikely to be able to use this criterion to identify the presence of sanctuaries. However, some sites have produced substantial evidence of ritual activity. The shrine of Gournay, with its abundant votive offerings of animals and weapons, has been discussed earlier (pp. 64, 76, 86). Other Iron Age sites have equally produced sufficient signs of cult activity to be classified as shrines.

Sanctuaries were sometimes sited in remote locations, sometimes in more densely populated areas. In either context, it is justifiable to think in terms of some priestly control over religious ceremonies, whether or not such clergy may actually have been resident at the shrine. It is interesting to speculate on the likely presence of local priests, independent of any overall religious authority, attached to specific shrines or cults, or of a network of centrally organized clergy. To what extent was being a priest a part-time or full-time job? Did communities share a priest

just as, in modern Britain, parish priests often have to divide their time between churches? We can only apply inference, but it may be that a variety of types of clergy operated in Celtic Europe.

Závist and Liptovska Mara

The Iron Age hillfort and sanctuary of Závist in Bohemia was established in the sixth century BC, on a rocky crag 650 ft (200 m) above the Moldau Valley. The holy place was situated on an 'acropolis' at the highest point of the site. The shrine or *nemeton* may always have been the focus of the settlement, which possessed a bronze workshop on the road leading to the holy place, for the sale of offerings to visiting pilgrims. The sanctuary, which was enclosed within the stronghold, underwent several building phases, but the most striking feature was the erection of large drystone walled structures, which may either have been great open-air altars or platforms for wooden buildings. The main temple was very large, about 1720 sq. ft (160 sq. m), and there was also a massive triangular open-air altar. Nearby was a sunken structure which has been interpreted as a sacrificial pit. The entire acropolis was abandoned in the early fourth century BC, probably as a result of destruction during warfare.

Liptovska Mara, in the same region, consisted of an *oppidum* with a great cult-portico, similar to that built at Roquepertuse in southern Gaul (p. 52), but of wood. Associated with this was a large pit containing pots, cereals, jewellery, ironwork, carved wood and human and animal remains.

Both shrines were contained within large proto-urban settlements, perhaps ruled by chiefs or oligarchs. The presence of cult sites in such contexts implies the existence of a centralized, politically controlled religion, which would undoubtedly have been supported by a priestly class.

Harlow

The cult site at Harlow in southeast England is an example of an increasingly recognized practice of building Iron Age shrines on sites with a long pre-existing history of ritual activity, particularly in Britain and Ireland. During the Bronze Age, people buried their dead on the hilltop; then, in the late pre-Roman Iron Age, a sanctuary was built: a penannular ditch probably marks

The hill-top sanctuary at Závist in Bohemia.

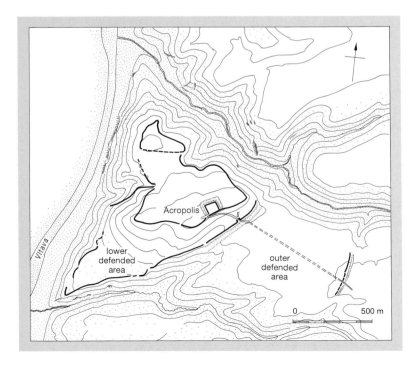

The Romano-British sanctuary at Harlow, Essex. In the foreground is an enclosed courtyard, with a monumental gateway. The temple replaced an earlier Iron Age shrine.

the site of a circular wooden shrine. During the Flavian dynasty of the Roman empire (AD 69–96), a rectangular temple was erected directly over the earlier cult building and over a late Iron Age deposit of gold coins. The Roman-period temple had an inner *cella* surrounded by a portico, with an open-air altar in front of the entrance; the religious buildings were set in a courtyard enclosed by a wall and with a monumental entrance. Along the two inner long walls were roofed buildings, which may have been shops, dormitories, treasuries or stores.

The Iron Age and Roman-period shrines at Harlow evince similarities in the use of animals for sacrifice and feasting: beasts were slaughtered and consumed here either as juveniles (six–nine months old) or as young adults (about eighteen months old). Whilst it is by no means clear to whom the Harlow sanctuary was dedicated, there are indications that a war-deity was venerated; a worn carving and a large helmeted stone head both depict warriors, and four model iron daggers (one in a bronze sheath) make sense as votive gifts to a military divinity.

Devotees made lavish presents of coins to the deity worshipped at the Harlow shrine. Some of the coins were of pre-Roman date, but it has recently been suggested that these may have been offered in the Roman period by suppliants who were deliberately and symbolically choosing archaic coin types, perhaps in acknowledgment of the longstanding sanctity of the site. Archaeologists found many coins in clumps, as if they had been suspended in nets or baskets in the roof and fallen in groups when the building collapsed.

Carved stone frieze of horse heads, from the pre-Roman Iron Age cliff-top sanctuary at Roquepertuse, southern France.

THE SACRED SPRING AT BATH

THE HOLY PLACE beside the River Avon in southwest England, called by the Romans *Aquae Sulis* (the Waters of Sulis), and today known as Bath, was venerated because of the hot springs which pump out water at a temperature of 46°C (115°F) at the rate of 250,000 gallons (1,136,500 litres) a day. It is not known how much use was made of the site prior to the Romans' arrival in this part of Britain, but it was probably Iron Age Celts who visited the springs and constructed a causeway across the marshy ground, leaving eighteen pre-Roman coins as votive offerings to the presiding goddess, Sulis. The hot water possesses genuine curative properties, being especially efficacious in the treatment of gout and arthritis. Early in the Roman period, perhaps only twenty years after the Claudian invasion of AD 43, engineering expertise was used to convert the simple native spring into a great religious complex consisting of a Classical-style temple, with a great altar outside, a set of baths and other associated buildings. The

(Below) Silver-gilt lunate pendant, from the sacred spring at Bath, possibly from a piece of liturgical regalia worn by a priest.

(Above) Gilded bronze head of the goddess Sulis Minerva, who presided over the thermal spring sanctuary at Bath. The head was hacked from a statue in antiquity, and the face also shows signs of deliberate damage.

(Right) Pewter mask, found in the culvert of the baths attached to the sanctuary of Sulis Minerva at Bath. The mask may represent a god or priest, or it may be the votive gift of a supplicant. Nail-holes along the edge of the mask suggest that it may have been attached to a door or a wall.

(Opposite) Reconstruction of the sacred spring and reservoir at Bath, as it may have looked in the third century AD.

A selection of lead curse tablets, or defixiones, *found in the sacred reservoir at Bath into which they had been thrown by pilgrims with grievances they wished the goddess Sulis to settle.*

The tombstone of Calpurnius Receptus, a priest of Sulis, who died at Bath aged seventy-five, set up by his wife, the freedwoman (ex-slave) Calpurnia Trifosa.

main spring was contained within a reservoir, and the resulting pool became the focus of intense ritual activity. Thrown into the water were more than 12,000 coins, personal objects, jewellery and – reflective of a sinister aspect to Sulis' cult – 130 curse tablets. These were small sheets of lead or pewter inscribed with messages invoking the vengeance of the deity for wrongs done to her dedicants. But the majority of the pilgrims who visited the great sanctuary came to be healed of physical or spiritual ills. They imbibed and bathed in the sacred water, the embodiment of the goddess herself. They set up altars to her, prayed to her and gave her presents in thanksgiving.

It is unthinkable that such an important religious precinct did not have its own professional clergy. Indeed, we know of one priest of Sulis, Calpurnius Receptus, who lived for seventy-five years and whose life is recorded on a tombstone set up by Calpurnia Trifosa, his widow who had been his freed slave. Another inscription records the dedication of one Memor, a *haruspex* (literally a 'gut-gazer'), a Roman cult official whose job it was, like that of the Druids, to divine the future by examining the liver and entrails of sacrificed beasts.

A pertinent question arises from the curse tablets, concerning the presence of religious officials at Bath. Were they written by professional scribes who knew the correct wording to use, or were they inscribed by temple priests? The curses are highly formulaic: magic was involved, so the invocation had to be absolutely correct.

Other objects from Bath hint at the presence of clergy; part of what may be a headdress was among the finds, together with a moon-shaped pendant, probably part of a sceptre. The moon-goddess Luna was venerated at Sulis' shrine, and the lunar symbol was traditionally associated with fertility. The life-size pewter mask found in the culvert of the baths depicts a male face with hair *en brosse*, in the manner of Celtic men described by Classical writers, and schematized Celtic features. The sheet metal of the mask is pierced along the edges with nail holes, as if it had originally been attached to a wooden board or post. The face could represent that of a pilgrim, a deity or – perhaps – a priest of Sulis.

The collection of pewter vessels from the sacred spring saw heavy-duty use after being inscribed, the inference being that they were used by religious officials for some time before being cast into the water as gifts to the goddess.

DRUIDS ARE NEVER mentioned as such on temple dedications. The Roman word *flamen* (priest) frequently occurs on inscriptions dedicating altars to Roman and native Celtic deities. At the shrine of the Romano-Celtic Mars Mullo at Rennes in France, an altar set up to the god in the reign of Hadrian mentions a *flamen perpetuus* (a priest elected for life). An individual called Priscus was a *flamen* at Lenus Mars' great sanctuary in Trier in Germany. A Gaulish name for a Celtic religious official was a *gutuater*: his function was to organize religious ceremonies. Two dedications to a local god, Anvallus, from Autun in Burgundy, France, have the word 'gutuater' inscribed on the base. The term has been interpreted as meaning 'Master of Voice', a reference – perhaps – to the oratorical skills often associated with the Druids. Book VIII of Caesar's *Gallic War* (which was written by Caesar's lieutenant Hirtius) mentions a Gaul from the tribe of the Carnutes called Gutuatrus: he was a freedom fighter, involved in a massacre of Roman citizens at Cenabum in 52 BC, and his name suggests that he was also a priest.

An important find comes from a shrine at Argentomagus, France, in the tribal territory of the Bituriges: on a pottery vessel were scratched the Gaulish words 'Vercobretos readdeas'. The pot had been deliberately deposited in a ditch within the cult precinct during the reign of the Roman emperor Tiberius; the inscription

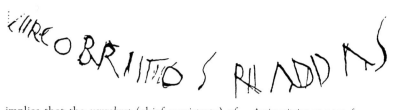

implies that the *vergobret* (chief magistrate) of the tribe presided over the votive ceremony. Other such magistrates are mentioned by Caesar; one was Liscus of the Aedui, who is described as having the power of life and death over his countrymen. The *vergobret* certainly appears to have had a number of functions in common with the Druids, as documented by the writings of Caesar, Diodorus, Strabo and their peers.

Other Gaulish priests are occasionally mentioned by different titles: a *curator* (keeper of the temple) was attached to the temple of a Celtic goddess Sirona at Wiesbaden, Germany. An official called an *antistes* occurs at several shrines, including that of Lenus Mars at Trier: his precise function is not known. The names of British priests have been found on inscriptions at Lydney and Bath. All of these different functionaries – *vergobret, curator, antistes, gutuater* – could have been Druids, but they are not so identified in the literature or in the epigraphy.

Although hard evidence for Celtic priests at sanctuaries is sparse, we can legitimately infer

An inscription on a pot, from Argentomagus, France; first century AD. The inscription refers to a vergobret, a Gaulish magistrate, who may have participated in rituals at the shrine.

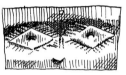

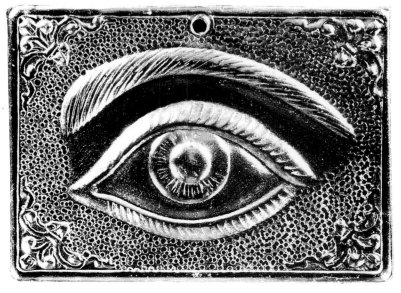

(Above) Three silver plaques depicting pairs of eyes, from the healing sanctuary of Sequana, at Fontes Sequanae near Dijon. Models of eyes and other organs were offered to curative deities in Roman Gaul and Britain by pilgrims, in the hope that such gifts would persuade the divine powers to reciprocate by healing the eyes and other ills suffered by their supplicants.

(Left) A modern eye-plaque made of aluminium, hung up in a church on the Greek island of Patmos. Model eyes, limbs, hearts and internal organs are still offered, though now to the Virgin Mary rather than a pagan divinity, in the Greek Orthodox and Roman Catholic traditions.

their presence, particularly at shrines where complex sacrificial ceremonies appear to have been carried out, as at Gournay and Ribemont. Regalia from British temples, such as the headdresses from Wanborough in Surrey and Cavenham in Suffolk, or the sceptres used at Brigstock, Northamptonshire, and Muntham Court, Sussex, imply the presence of clergy (pp. 60–64). Likewise the annexes or small separate buildings found in a number of temple precincts, such as those at Harlow, could be interpreted as the dwellings of cult officials, who may have been granted the pagan Celtic equivalent of vicarages close to the sanctuaries over which they presided.

(Right) Adjustable bronze diadem, found with other ritual headdresses at Cavenham, Suffolk, England, and similar to those from other sanctuaries such as Hockwold, Norfolk. Such headdresses once bore images of deities, and we can infer that they were worn by officiating priests during religious ceremonies.

(Above) Bronze openwork plate, probably part of a priest's headdress, from the sacred spring at Bath.

THE PRIEST-PHYSICIANS

*I*t is more than likely that priests who were also doctors were present at major curative sanctuaries in Gaul and Britain. At Bath, a stamp for an eye salve was discovered in the baths, and it has been suggested that an oculist, named on the stamp as Titus Janianus, may have held a regular clinic here.

There were doctors practising empirical medicine who were perhaps also cult officials at Gaulish healing shrines such as the sanctuary dedicated to the goddess Sequana at Fontes Sequanae. Once again, the evidence is in the form of metal stamps for eye ointment, and this is particularly interesting because the models of wood, stone and metal found here all emphasize the eye problems which beset some of Sequana's devotees. Indeed, the wooden models from Sequana's shrine speak so eloquently of the multifarious ailments from which her pilgrims suffered that it would not be surprising to find medical as well as spiritual help on hand. We are reminded of the situation in medieval British Christian religious foundations, where the monks and nuns were such diligent tenders of the sick.

The curing of illness by empirical means would have served to enhance the reputation of the healing divinities themselves, and the boundary between the healing effected by gods and doctors must always – perhaps deliberately – have been blurred. Chicanery must also have been rife: it is easy to envisage temple officials appearing in the guise of gods to sick pilgrims as they slept in the sacred dormitories, awaiting the visitation of the healing spirit. Nevertheless, the vision of the 'divinity' may have been of psychological benefit, particularly if a patient's disorder was linked with neuroses, depression or hypochondria.

Wooden image of a pilgrim, wearing a hooded cloak and suffering from a club-foot; from the goddess Sequana's sanctuary at Fontes Sequanae near Dijon. More than 200 of these oaken models were found in the vicinity of the sacred spring, and they may originally have been placed standing around the holy pool.

(Right) Bronze statuette of the healer-goddess Sequana, in her duck-prowed boat, which identifies her as a water-deity; from the shrine at Fontes Sequanae near Dijon.

(Below) View of Sequana's sacred pool at Fontes Sequanae, as it appears today.

(Below) Artist's impression of religious activity at the sacred pool of the goddess Sequana, near Dijon. Sick pilgrims offer wooden images of themselves and their afflictions to the goddess, setting them up around the water.

THE SACRED HEALERS

Stone carving of a healer-god, with a raven; behind him is a pilgrim wih his hands over his eyes, perhaps displaying his affliction with blindness or an eye disease; from a Gaulish curative sanctuary, specializing in eye-disorders, at Mavilly, Burgundy, France.

One of nine pairs of bronze tweezers from the healing shrine at Nettleton Shrub, Wiltshire, England. The temple was dedicated in the Roman period to Apollo Cunomaglus, and the tweezers may indicate the presence of physicians (who were perhaps also priests) at the sanctuary.

DURING THE ROMAN period, a number of important curative sanctuaries were established in Britain and Gaul. Some, if not all of these centres were pre-Roman in origin, but it was not until the Romanization of western Europe that the shrines were graced with monumental buildings and furnishings and began to attract other than a local clientèle of pilgrims. There was clearly a commercial aspect to these healing cult centres, just as there is at places like Lourdes today. Shops, fairs and markets would have crowded the religious precincts alongside the sacred buildings such as temples, baths and dormitories. But all the Celtic therapeutic sanctuaries had as their sacred focus the holy spring, which was both the source of healing and the personification of the deity.

The more sophisticated Romano-Celtic healing shrines had much in common with those of the Classical world: many curative cults were based upon the principle of reciprocity, inasmuch as sick pilgrims came to the temple of a healing divinity and offered models of themselves, or the parts of their bodies that required a cure, in the hope that the god or goddess would replace the ailing limb, eye, heart or liver with one that was whole and healthy. The votive model arms, legs, eyes and breasts discovered at such sanctuaries as *Fontes Sequanae* and Bolards in Burgundy bear an uncanny resemblance to those hung up in Catholic or Greek Orthodox Christian churches in the Mediterranean world today.

Chamalières and Lydney

The shrines at the Source des Roches de Chamalières, in central France, and Lydney, on the River Severn in Gloucestershire, England, represent opposite ends of the spectrum in terms of the sophistication of healing cult centres in the Celtic world. Chamalières was perceived as holy because it was a place where two springs, each containing beneficial minerals, gushed from the earth. Archaeologists investigating the site found no temple buildings: the shrine appears to have consisted merely of a sacred pool, enclosed by a wall, where the spring water welled up. The coins dropped or offered at this sacred spot suggest that it was only in active use for about 100 years from the first century BC to the first century AD. What makes Chamalières of exceptional interest are the 2,000 wooden images of devotees and their afflictions which were found buried in waterlogged ground by the springs and which may originally have been set up around the holy pool.

By contrast, the great third-century AD temple precinct at Lydney is evidence of a sophisticated and wealthy cult clientèle, which showed its appreciation for the healing powers of its deity by erecting an imposing, Classical-style temple building, a guest-house, a suite of baths and a long building, which has been interpreted as a dormitory for sick pilgrims to sleep and experience a vision of the divine presence. The site, overlooking the great River Severn, was probably deliberately chosen because it offered a clear view of the massive Severn Bore (a tidal wave which, under certain conditions, rises near Gloucester), and its position within an earlier Iron Age hillfort must also be relevant. Whilst the presiding spirit of Chamalières remains anonymous, inscriptions at Lydney indicate that the shrine was dedicated to the British god Nodens. That he was a healer is suggested by the bronze model arm and hand which shows signs of disease, and the oculists' stamps – used by physicians to mark their cakes of eye ointment – found at the site. But the most idiosyncratic group of offerings are the nine model dogs – one of which has a human face – dedicated by the worshippers: dogs were symbols of healing throughout the Classical and Celtic worlds

because they were observed to heal their own wounds by licking them. Images of pilgrims and deities holding dogs occur at many Gaulish spring sanctuaries; and live sacred dogs were kept at the great temple of the Greek healer-god Asklepios at Epidaurus in the Peloponnese.

The cult establishment at Lydney was powerful and well endowed, attracting wealthy patronage. Most interesting, for the present study, is the unequivocal evidence for at least one temple priest. In the fourth century AD a mosaic floor, decorated with an aquatic scene, was dedicated to the temple of Nodens by one Titus Flavius Senilis. The mosaic was paid for by temple worshippers and its inscription also records the profession of Senilis – he calls himself the 'superintendent of religious rites'. He may have been the individual who wore the bronze diadem, depicting the sun-god riding in a chariot, which was found at the site.

Mosaic floor from the Romano-British healing shrine dedicated to Nodens at Lydney, Gloucestershire. The inscribed mosaic was the gift of Titus Flavius Senilis, a religious official, part of whose name can be seen in the mosaic floor.

Bronze figurine of a deerhound, one of nine images of dogs which were dedicated to Nodens by pilgrims at Lydney. Dogs were symbols of healing in both Classical and Celtic religion.

(Above) Carved wooden head of a blind pilgrim; from the curative shrine of the goddess Sequana at Fontes Sequanae near Dijon; first century BC.

ENCLOSING HOLY SPACE

The great Iron Age cliff-top fort of Dun Aengus on the isle of Inishmore, County Galway, Ireland. The fortifications may have demarcated an area for defensive purposes, but they may have also served as a religious boundary, enclosing sacred space.

AN ASPECT OF sacred space which is receiving particular attention in current study is the concept of ritual enclosure, not simply the sanctity of the space enclosed but of the boundary-ditches themselves. The sanctuary of Gournay-sur-Aronde in the Oise region of France was contained within a rectilinear enclosure, defined by a ditch and bank, which was constructed in the fourth century BC and later embellished with a wooden palisade. The shrine is of especial interest because of its evidence for intense ritual activity, involving the offering of more than 2,000 ritually broken weapons, and complex behaviour associated with animal (and possibly also human) sacrifice (p. 86). There was clearly a close relationship between the shrine at Gournay and surrounding settlements: the presence only of selected bones of many animals suggests that animal sacrifices were often conducted some distance away from the sanctuary. The enclosure ditch was of particular significance, for it was there that the military equipment and the bones were finally and carefully deposited. The roofed wooden building at Gournay was not erected until the late third century BC, and the boundary ditch evidently remained the main focus of religious activity until about 30 BC. The site was deliberately closed at the time of the Roman conquest but its sanctity remained; a small Romano-Celtic temple was erected there in the fourth century AD.

Gournay was by no means unique, the ditches of other sacred sites in the Oise region contained similar depositions. Throughout Iron Age Europe, holy places were demarcated by boundary ditches and banks, which served to separate the sacred from the profane, but which may also have had specific sanctity in their own right. Boundaries and thresholds have importance in many religious traditions, including those recorded in the Old Testament and in early Celtic vernacular myths. Indeed, the significance of boundaries may well account for the prominence given to sacred islands, both in Celtic mythic texts and in Classical references to holy islands off the coasts of Gaul and Britain. Islands remained important as places of sanctity in the early western Christian tradition. Many late pre-Roman Iron Age shrines were placed in boundary-locations: Harlow, for instance, was on the boundary between the tribes of the Catuvellauni and Trinovantes; and Gournay, though in Bellovacian territory, was close to the boundaries of three other tribes – the Ambiani, Viromandui and Suessiones.

Boundaries may have been significant because they separated and belonged to two worlds – those of earth and the supernatural. Just as priests could be viewed as mediators between spirits and humans, so physical boundaries may have been seen as facilitating contact with the divine powers. Indeed, it may be that priests dwelt in boundary-positions, as did members of the learned class in medieval Ireland. The ritual importance of bogs, lakes and rivers during the Iron Age may also be associated with liminal space and, perhaps, boundaries between worlds.

Wells and shafts

Continental Europe has produced the most promising body of evidence for pre-Roman ritual shafts: the rectilinear enclosures known as *Viereckschanzen*, which are often considered as sanctuaries, sometimes contain or overlie deep shafts. Some *Viereckschanzen* may have had a ritual purpose, but the evidence is far from clear, and serious doubt has been cast on the original interpretation of the classic type-site of Holzhausen in Bavaria, which allegedly contained a shaft with traces of human sacrificial remains at the bottom. However, the *Viereckschanze* at Fellbach Schmiden near Stuttgart did contain a well which, although perhaps functional, produced wooden figurines, including a fine stag carving, which undoubtedly had a religious purpose: dendrochronology (dating by tree-rings) indicates that the oak was felled in 123 BC, well before the Roman period.

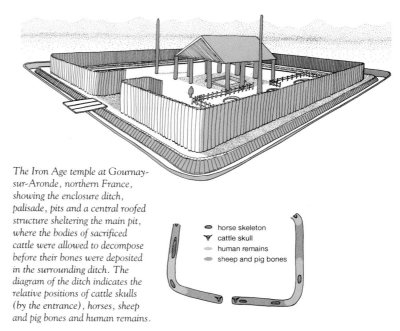

The Iron Age temple at Gournay-sur-Aronde, northern France, showing the enclosure ditch, palisade, pits and a central roofed structure sheltering the main pit, where the bodies of sacrificed cattle were allowed to decompose before their bones were deposited in the surrounding ditch. The diagram indicates the relative positions of cattle skulls (by the entrance), horses, sheep and pig bones and human remains.

- ⬤ horse skeleton
- ⩒ cattle skull
- — human remains
- ⬤ sheep and pig bones

The La Tène site of Bliesbrück, Germany, contained more than 100 deep shafts, filled with votive objects and planted either with tree trunks or living trees (reminiscent of the artificial grove referred to earlier at Lowbury Hill, p. 108).

In Britain, most 'ritual' shafts or wells are of Roman date, although they may well have been associated with native cult activity. Many of them were associated with shrines: the circular sanctuary at Muntham Court in Sussex, which has been dated to the first century AD, was juxtaposed with a 200-ft (60-m) deep well in which were numerous dog skeletons. The temple at Jordan Hill, Weymouth, was associated with a well containing a very curious deposit, including sixteen pairs of tiles between each of which was the skeleton of a crow.

The idea of using shafts sunk deep into the ground as cult foci is not confined to Iron Age temperate Europe – the Classical world had its *mundi* (Roman) and *bothroi* (Greek) which were perceived as links with the spirit world. Since the landscape was – to the Celts – full of supernatural power, it would have been natural to imagine that chthonic spirits dwelled beneath the earth, and needed to be propitiated in order that humans living in their territory should prosper and be safe from harm. The British deposits of dogs and crows may be intrinsically significant in that, in Celtic myth, both were symbols of the Underworld.

Fragmentary wooden image of a stag, dating to the late second century BC; found in a well at the Viereckschanze (rectangular enclosure) at Fellbach Schmiden, near Stuttgart in Germany. The stag was originally part of a more complex carving which represented the offering of the animal by a human figure.

VIII
DRUIDS IN IRISH MYTH

'Then Medb sent the Druids and satirists and harsh bards for Fer Diad, that they might make against him three satires to stay him and three lampoons, and that they might raise on his face three blisters, shame, blemish and disgrace, so that he might die before the end of nine days if he did not succumb at once.'

From the *Táin Bó Cuailnge*

HE EVIDENCE FOR the Druids in Ireland appears in two main types of early literature: one consists of the vernacular (written in Irish) mythic texts, such as are contained within the Ulster Cycle, the Mythological Cycle and the Fenian Cycle; the other comprises the *Lives* of early Irish saints, such as Patrick and Brigit. Both sets of documents were compiled in written form during the period from the seventh to the twelfth centuries AD and each was composed within a Christian monastic context. The mythic texts present us with a picture of a pagan Druidic system that is essentially similar to that described by Classical authors like Caesar. Many scholars are of the opinion that these sources contain genuine accounts of pre-Christian beliefs and practices, even though by the time the myths were written down, if not composed, Ireland was thoroughly Christian. But others present the (to me unconvincing) counter-argument that medieval monastic literature cannot be regarded as presenting a reliable record of pre-Christian Druidism but is, instead, largely invention.

As is often the case with strongly polarized arguments, the truth probably lies somewhere between the two. The myths have to be regarded as heavily anachronistic but, at the same time, they may well contain echoes or resonances of pre-Christian paganism, which were woven into the literature because they were already present within oral tradition.

Aerial view of the royal site of Tara, Ireland. Tara features in the medieval Dinnschenchas as a sacred site associated with the initiation of the high kings of Ireland. Investigation has revealed the sanctity of Tara from as early as Neolithic times; it continued to be of ritual significance into the early historical period.

THE LEARNED CLASS

By the seventh century AD, many Druidic functions in Ireland had been taken over by the Filidh. Moreover, during the medieval period, the Filidh assumed many of the functions previously carried out by the Bards.

Iron Age bronze bowl from Keshcarrigan, Ireland. The vessel, found in the River Shannon, has a handle shaped as a bird's head, and was a high-status piece, perhaps with a ceremonial function.

'Among all the tribes, generally speaking, there are three classes of men held in special honour: the Bards, the Vates [seers] and the Druids.'
Strabo, *Geography* IV, 4, 4

THE IRISH LITERARY sources describe a learned class divided into three sub-classes, members of each having different but sometimes interrelated functions and responsibilities. These were the Druids, Bards and Seers (Druí, Baird and Filidh). This tripartite division reflects exactly the same system as that described by Classical writers such as Strabo (above).

Druids, Bards and Filidh in Irish society

In Ireland the three groups – Druids, Bards and Filidh – appear to have shared certain duties and activities: thus the Bards were primarily singers, praise poets and satirists, but the last two respon-sibilities also fell to the Filidh. Likewise the Druids and the Filidh shared certain duties, notably prophecy, divination and teaching. Both the Filidh and the Druids trained for many years before gaining full proficiency in their crafts. Caesar tells us that the Druids trained for a lengthy twenty years, and Insular sources inform us that the Filidh's apprenticeship lasted for twelve.

The Druids seem to have been the most politically influential of the three groups of learned men. They had the ear of the rulers and their divinatory powers meant that their advice was sought before any important activity was undertaken. They were mediators between kings and the spirit world. They also controlled the kings by means of *gessa* – divine injunctions or prohibitions with which they bound rulers to keep their power in check.

What appears to have happened in Christian Ireland is that when the old pagan system began to lose its hold, so the influence of the Druids also gradually disappeared. But the Filidh remained strong, and they took over many of the old Druidic functions, especially the role of prophesying the future. Indeed, the Filidh's political power did not finally disinte-grate until British rule prevailed in Ireland in the seventeenth century.

THE POWER OF WORDS

A strong theme running through Irish literature – and illustrated by the opening quotation to this chapter – is the power engendered by speech, whether praise poetry, satire or prophecy. The Bards and the Filidh had magic in their voices and utterances, and the poets of later medieval Ireland saw themselves as successors of the Druids and poets of early legends. One such mythic character was Amairgin, who is described in the Mythological Cycle as one of the Gaels or Celts who colonized Ireland in the last of a series of mythic invasions, after they had deposed the divine race called the Tuatha Dé Danann.

Amairgin's name means 'Wonderful Mouth', and he is said to have chanted a poem called the 'Invocation of Ireland', as he set foot on the land. In the poem, Amairgin extolled the knowledge and wisdom that enabled the Celts to overcome Ireland's previous inhabitants.

Words had the power to wound as well as to bless. There are many descriptions of the physical disfigurement that could be caused by the lashing tongue of the satirist, whose blight was in many ways as effective a sanction

(Above) The power of satire: an Irish Bard blasts the face of his victim with satirical poetry.

or control as excommunication in medieval Ireland. The following passage is part of an early fifteenth-century poem by the chief poet of Ireland, who was angry because his corn had been burnt:

'Before the wave of my fury surges up to burn the level cropland of your cheek I will speak out to warn against myself although I do myself an injury …

'Even though the scorching of your handsome face might well have been the outcome of the deed, it is not right to redden people's faces for the grain glowing dreadful in the fields …'

IN IRISH MYTHIC literature the Druids are portrayed as wielding immense power and influence, both in religious and political affairs. Descriptions of their activities indicate their close relationship with the kings, and they appear to have been just as important as their rulers, if not more so. Time and again, the Druids are depicted as advisers to the royal household, warning their kings against particular actions and curbing immoderate behaviour. They were mediators between the gods and terrestrial power, and their ability to predict the future course of events meant that kings were dependent on the Druids for guidance in correct political action.

If we look a little more closely at the character of these Irish Druids, we can discern an uncanny resemblance to the fierce prophets of the Old Testament, notably Samuel and Nathan, through whom God sought – not always successfully – to control the actions of King Saul and King David. Both Samuel and Nathan used divination to learn the will of God. The negative, somewhat gloomy attitude held by these prophets towards their rulers is reminiscent of Irish Druids, such as Cathbadh of Ulster.

Finn and the Druids: good and evil

The hero of the twelfth-century Fenian Cycle of mythic tales is Finn, leader of the Fianna, a war-band dedicated to the king's protection. The stories told about Finn are interesting in the present context because in them the Druids are presented as both beneficent and harmful.

When Finn was an infant, his mother Muirna entrusted him to two bondswomen, a Druidess and a wise woman, who brought him up as their foster-son. Both acted as guardians, advisers and teachers of war craft (p. 101).

In an episode relating to the young hero's growing supernatural powers, Finn went to learn the craft of poetry from Finnegas the Bard, and it was through him that Finn acquired the gifts of prophecy and wisdom. When the two initially met, Finnegas had just caught the Salmon of Knowledge, for whom he had been fishing for seven years in a pool. Finnegas put Finn in charge of cooking the salmon and, as he did so, the youth burnt his thumb on the hot flesh. He sucked his burnt thumb and thereby ingested all the salmon's knowledge. Although Finnegas is described as a Bard rather than a Druid, it is clear that he enjoyed many

---

KING CONAIRE'S PROHIBITIONS

'For he [Conaire] took sovereignty after his father and Ninión the Druid said that these were the injunctions of his reign:
(1) He should not go out from Tara every ninth night
(2) He should not approve theft in his reign
(3) He should not allow marauding
(4) He should not restrain the quarrel of the two servants from Túathmaugain, and
(5) He should not spend the night in a house out of which light would be visible after sunset.'
From The Story of Da Derga's Hostel

(Above) Mog Ruith, a Druid who wore a bird-costume and used a bull's hide to foretell the future.

The main recension (coming together) of the mythic tale Togail Bruiden Da Derga (The Story of Da Derga's Hostel) dates to the eleventh century, and originates from two earlier, ninth-century versions. The prohibitions or injunctions (Irish gessa) were common 'taboos' laid upon Irish kings or heroes. Their negativity is strongly reminiscent of most of the Ten Commandments. The geis was in part a convention of the storyteller, a means of anticipating the almost inevitable taboo breaking and consequent disaster. But such prohibitions were also bound up with divinatory prediction, destiny, and the preservation of the sacred order. The actions of the king were intimately connected to the fortunes of Ireland; if he behaved incorrectly, the land would suffer. Conaire infringed several of his gessa and perished as a result.

In one version of the tale, the gessa were laid upon Conaire by one Nemglan, who is described as a 'bird-man', perhaps because birds – particularly ravens – were believed to have oracular gifts, or because some kind of shamanistic metamorphosis had taken place. Interestingly, another Irish tale – The Siege of Druim Damhghaire – links Druids and birds. A Druid called Mog Ruith, who could conjure storms at will, wore a speckled bird-dress and used a bull's hide in his magical rituals.

---

characteristics commonly associated with Druidism.

One of the central stories about Finn concerns a malevolent individual known as the Black Druid. One day, while hunting, Finn encountered a young woman in the form of a deer; her name was Sava. She had been metamorphosed by the evil magic of the Druid because she had spurned his attentions. Finn was able – at least temporarily – to reverse the spell, and he married her. Sava produced a son Oisin (Little Deer), who had a close affinity with stags

Bronze figurine of a doe, third century BC, from Rákos Csongrád, Hungary. Sava the wife of the Irish hero Finn was changed by a Druid into a deer.

*Finn and the Salmon of
Knowledge, the taste of whose
flesh, cooked by Finnegas the
Bard, gave the boy infinite
wisdom. Finn was brought up
by a Druidess and a female seer.*

and may himself have been a skin-changer. Finn
found the boy abandoned in the wilderness, after
his mother had been reclaimed by her unwanted
Druid suitor.

Partholón and the invaders of Ireland

References to the wisdom and fortune-telling
powers of the Druids are frequently found in
the Insular myths. The *Book of Invasions*, an
account of a series of mythic colonizations of
Ireland, describes Partholón, the leader of the
first invasion after the Flood. He was accompanied by his family and his entire retinue, which
included three Druids – Fiss, Tath and Fochmarc
– whose names 'Intelligence', Knowledge' and
'Enquiry' refer directly to their role as learned
men.

A further group of invaders, the divine
Tuatha Dé Danann ('People of the Goddess
Danu'), were closely associated with Druidic
magic: in an account of their journey to Ireland,
they came borne in dark clouds, to preserve their
secrecy from the demon Fomorians who already
occupied the land. When the next and final
invaders, the Gaels, arrived, the Druids of the
Tuatha Dé Danann conjured storms in an
attempt to repel them, but in vain – the magic of
the invaders was stronger.

The Gaels (Celts) brought their own Druids
with them to Ireland, and the Irish myths record
tensions between the newly arrived Druids and
those belonging to the previous colonists. One
of the newcomers, a Druid called Mide, lit the
first Druidical fire in Ireland, at Uisneach in
County Meath. The fire burnt for a lengthy
seven years and all other fires in Ireland were lit
from it. Mide and his successors demanded their
entitlement to a pig and a sack of corn from
every household. When the indigenous Druids
protested, Mide cut out the Druids' tongues and
burnt them. This cruel punishment presumably
fitted the crime, in that all Druidic power and
influence lay in their capacity for speech.
Deprived of the ability to teach, use rhetoric to
warn, advise or persuade, or to predict the
future, Mide's Druid victims were as good as
dead.

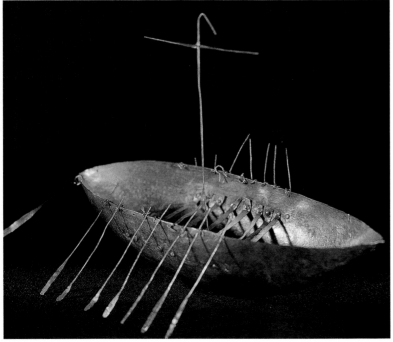

*Gold model of a boat, complete
with benches, oars and mast, part
of a hoard of goldwork from
Broighter, County Derry, Ireland,
dating to the late first century BC.
According to Irish myth, the
earliest Celts allegedly sailed to
Ireland from Spain.*

DRUID SHAPE-SHIFTERS

One of the episodes of the Táin, which describes the epic conflict between the provinces of Ulster and Connacht, contains a specific reference to the ability of Irish Druids to change their shape at will:

'Then the magical sweet-mouthed harpers of Cáin Bile came out from the red cataract at Es Ruaid, to charm the host. But the people thought that these were spies from Ulster among them, and they gave chase after them until they ran in the shape of deer far ahead of them to the north among the stones at Liac Mór, they being Druids of great knowledge.'
From the Táin

(Right) 'Grania questions the Druid', from The Pursuit of Diarmid, a tale told by Andrew Lang. Hand-coloured illustration by Henry Justice Ford, c. 1902. According to Irish legend, Grania (or Grainne) was betrothed to the ageing war hero Finn, when she fell in love with Diarmid on the eve of her wedding day. The lovers fled from Finn's wrath, and engaged the help of Oenghus, god of love, who tricked the pursuing Finn by using his ability to shape-shift and changed into Diarmid's shape. The couple were eventually pardoned by Finn, but his desire for vengeance remained, and he finally brought about his rival's death. Finn invited Diarmid to take part in a hunt for an enchanted boar. Through Finn's trickery, Diarmid was fatally wounded by the boar's poisonous bristles.

CATHBADH OF ULSTER

*'The boy Conchobar was reared by Cathbad
and was known as Cathbad's son.'*
From the *Táin*

THE CENTRAL STORY of the early medieval Ulster Cycle is the *Táin Bó Cuailnge* (the *Cattle Raid of Cooley*). One of the main characters is the Druid Cathbadh, a man of enormous influence, who was not only the court Druid of King Conchobar of Ulster, but also his father or foster-father. Cathbadh is a complex character and we are told that before he became Conchobar's Druid he led a war-band (or Fiana) of roving warriors. An episode in the *Táin*, where he was involved in the arming of young heroes (see below), demonstrates his continued interest in war craft.

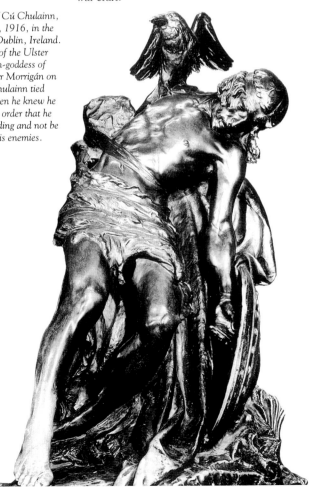

Bronze sculpture of Cú Chulainn, by Oliver Shepherd, 1916, in the main Post Office, Dublin, Ireland. It depicts the death of the Ulster hero, with the raven-goddess of Death, the Badbh or Morrigán on his shoulder. Cú Chulainn tied himself to a tree when he knew he was going to die, in order that he should remain standing and not be seen to fall before his enemies.

Cathbadh was a teacher as well as Conchobar's adviser. The *Táin* describes how he ran a school near the royal stronghold of Emhain Macha, where he instructed noble youths in such Druidic lore as the interpretation of omens and portents.

The doom of Cú Chulainn

'Cathbad the Druid was staying with his son, Conchobar mac Nessa. He had one hundred studious men learning Druid lore from him – this was always the number that Cathbad taught. One day a pupil asked him what that day would be lucky for. Cathbad said that if a warrior took up arms for the first time that day his name would endure in Ireland as a word signifying mighty acts, and stories about him would last forever …'

But Cathbadh continued ominously:

'He who arms for the first time today will achieve fame and greatness. But his life is short.'

One of the witnesses to Cathbadh's proclamation was the young Cú Chulainn, a small boy at the time but destined to become Ulster's greatest hero. On hearing the Druid, Cú Chulainn immediately demanded weapons from King Conchobar.

'"What do you ask for little lad?" said Conchobar.
"I wish to take arms", said the little boy.
"Who advised you, lad?" said Conchobar.
"Cathbad the Druid", said the little boy.
"He would not deceive you lad", said Conchobar.'
From the *Táin*

Cú Chulainn proceeded to break all the weapons offered him, until finally accepting the king's own equipment.
Cú Chulainn fulfilled Cathbadh's prophecy: he had superhuman strength, courage and beauty, and gained many victories over Ulster's enemies. But he died by the trickery and magic of Medb, the warrior-queen of Connacht and Cú Chulainn's bitterest foe. Cathbadh and the other royal Druids tried in vain to turn aside Cú Chulainn's doom, but Medb's power was stronger: she engaged the Children of

Cailitín (p. 100), whom she trained in witch-craft, to lure the hero to his death. The witches and warlocks conjured up illusions of desperate battles which Cú Chulainn yearned to join. The Druids and the Ulstermen uttered howls to drown the tempting sounds of fighting but, in the end, Cú Chulainn was deceived.

The hero's end is closely linked with Druid magic: as his enemies approached, he encoun-tered three Druids, each of whom asked for one of Cú Chulainn's three spears. It was unlucky to refuse a Druid and, in any case, they threatened to bring dishonour on him and on Ulster by lam-pooning him. Cú Chulainn hurled a spear twice and each time killed one of the Druids. The third spear was recovered by the warrior Lugaid, who threw it back at Cú Chulainn and killed him.

THE STORY OF DEIRDRE AND CONCHOBAR

*T*he tale of 'Deirdre of the Sorrows' appears in a text dated to the ninth century AD; it was later absorbed into the Ulster Cycle, as a foretale to the Táin. In the story, Cathbadh is described as having such power that he could predict Deirdre's identity and her future while she was yet unborn.

At a gathering at which Fedlimid – the chief storyteller at the royal court – Conchobar, Cathbadh and other noble Ulstermen were present, Fedlimid's pregnant wife was serving food and wine. As the men conversed, the unborn child suddenly gave a loud shriek. Confused and frightened, the woman turned to the Druid to explain this extraordinary phenomenon:

'She turned distracted to the seer Cathbad: "Fair-faced Cathbad, hear me – prince, pure, precious crown, grown huge in Druid spells …"'

Cathbadh placed his hand on the woman's stomach and prophesied that the child would be a girl named Deirdre, and that she would be exceedingly beautiful but would bring about the ruin of Ulster:

'Then the daughter was born and Cathbad said: "Much damage, Deirdriu, will follow your high fame and fair visage: Ulster in your time tormented, demure daughter of Fedlimid…"'

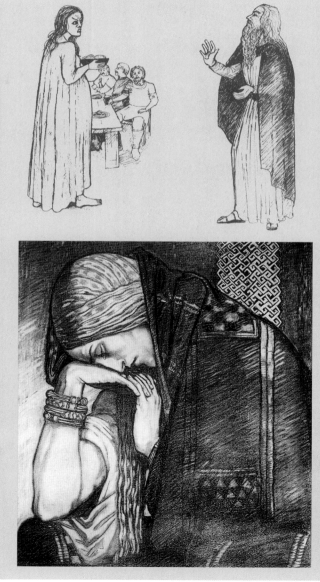

The Druid was right. Despite the demands of Conchobar's noblemen that the baby be destroyed, the king allowed her to be reared in secret, vowing to marry the lovely girl as soon as she came of age. But Deirdre had other ideas: she fell in love with a handsome youth named Naoise, and fled with him to Scotland. Conchobar sent them a pardon, but his forgiveness was treacherous and, once the lovers returned to Emhain Macha, he destroyed them. The dishonour of this deed led to the defection of three great Ulster warriors – Cormac, Ferghus and Conall Cernach – to the enemy province of Connacht. In the long and bitter fighting which followed between the two provinces, with Ulster sorely weakened by the heroes' desertion, both Connacht and Ulster suffered such heavy losses that they were nearly obliterated.

(Above left) The Druid Cathbadh accurately prophesies that the unborn child carried by Fedlimid's wife will bring doom upon the men of Ulster.

(Left) Drawing of 'Deirdre of the Sorrows', c. 1900, by John Duncan (1866–1945). The drawing shows the young Deirdre grieving for the death of her lover Naoise and his two brothers.

> *"'It seems wonderful to me", said Bres to his Druids, "that the sun should rise in the west today and in the east every other day". "It would be better for us if it were so", replied the Druids. "What else can it be, then?", asked Bres. "It is the radiance of the face of Lugh of the Long Arm", said they.'*
>
> From *The Fate of the Children of Tuirenn*

THE PASSAGE QUOTED above comes from an account of the mythical battle between the divine race of Ireland, the Tuatha Dé Danann, and an indigenous group of demons, the Fomorians. King Bres was a Fomorian, and his Druids warned him of the approach of Lugh, the new champion of the Tuatha Dé Danann, who would vanquish him and assert the authority of the gods.

A strong thread which runs through the Insular myths is the link between kingship and the spirit world, with the Druids acting as mediators between them. Divine advice had to be sought in the selection of a new king, and the divinatory powers of the Druids were crucial in the interpretation of omens.

The sacred trust of kingship

Once a likely candidate for the kingship had been selected, he had to undergo a series of tests or ordeals to ensure that the rightful ruler had

Gold torc from a hoard of gold objects of first-century BC date, found at Broighter, County Derry, Ireland. Torcs were probably symbols of high status, perhaps worn only by the king himself.

THE BULL SLEEP

A prophetic ritual described in several myths is the Tarbhfhess, which means 'bull sleep' or 'bull feast'. A bull was sacrificed and a man was selected to feast on the meat and drink the broth. After he had consumed all he could, he went to sleep to the chanting of four Druids, and the next rightful king to rule in Tara was revealed to him in a dream. When he awoke, he recounted his vision to the Druids. It was apparently possible for them to tell whether or not the sleeper spoke the truth.

One account of the Tarbhfhess appears in The Story of Da Derga's Hostel. As in other texts describing this rite, the imperfect tense is used, suggesting that this ceremony already belonged to the past when the story was constructed.

The Tarbhfhess is significant not simply because of its association with sacral kingship but also because of the bull itself. Cattle were important indicators of wealth and status in early Ireland and the Táin revolves around two great supernatural bulls, the Donn ('Brown') bull of Ulster and the Findbennach ('White-horned') bull of Connacht.

There is substantial evidence for bull sacrifice in pagan Celtic Europe. The Iron Age sanctuary of Gournay in Picardy, for instance, was the focus of very elaborate ritual (p. 121) involving the slaughter of elderly bulls and oxen, their decomposition and the subsequent deposition of the bones in the enclosure ditch.

The Tarbhfhess or 'bull sleep': Irish myth contains a description of a ritual presided over by four Druids, involving bull sacrifice, performed to predict the identity of the rightful new king.

The Stone of Fál, a sacred standing stone at Tara, which allegedly cried out when touched by the rightful king-elect.

been chosen. The applicant had to put on the royal mantle, which would be too big if he was not suitable. The royal chariot actively rejected the unworthy; and two great stones, with only a handsbreadth between them, opened to admit the chariot of the legitimate king. Finally, the Stone of Fál, brought to Tara as one of four magical talismans of the Tuatha Dé Danann, shrieked when touched by the correct king-elect. The High King Conn of the Hundred Battles stepped onto the stone and it uttered several howls. These cries were interpreted by the Druids as symbolic of the number of Conn's descendants who would rule as kings of Ireland.

Irish kingship was inheritable within an extended family group, the *derbhfhine*, which consisted of four generations. Because kingship was sacred, the inauguration of a new ruler was hedged about with ritual behaviour. Newly elected kings attended the *Feis Temhra* (the Feast of Tara), which was held to validate the new régime.

The Goddess of Sovereignty

The inauguration of the king was sometimes known as the *banais ríghi*, the wedding feast of kingship. This was because the king's position was a sacred gift, and sacral kingship involved the ritual marriage between the king and his kingdom. This union between the ruler and the land was perceived as a symbolic marriage between a mortal king and the Goddess of Sovereignty, the personification of Ireland itself. The bond was so strong that the behaviour of the king had a direct effect upon the prosperity of the land. If the king were just and generous, his kingdom flourished, but if he were mean or dishonourable, Ireland's fortunes waned.

This link between the king's character and his domain is clearly illustrated in the mythic

THE LEGEND OF THE WHITE MARE

*A*n inauguration ritual which symbolized the union between the Ulster king and the Goddess of Sovereignty was chronicled by Gerald of Wales (Giraldus Cambrensis) in 1185, in his Topographica Hibernica. The account is especially interesting because here the goddess is represented by a horse. During the ritual, the king played the part of a stallion and pretended to mate with a white mare. She was then slaughtered and the flesh cooked in a cauldron. The king-elect sat in the vessel, surrounded by the meat and broth, and he ate and drank his fill.

The symbolism of the ritual is complex but appears to reflect the perception of the mare as representative of the land of Ireland, which united with the king in a ritual marriage. The identification of Ireland with a mare is significant: Macha was an Irish sovereignty-goddess who was closely linked with horse symbolism. One of the most popular goddesses represented in the pagan Celtic iconography of the Roman period was Epona, a horse-deity who was associated with fertility and prosperity.

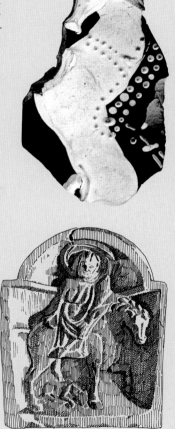

(Above) Fragment of pottery depicting a white horse; (below) stone relief of the Celtic horse-goddess Epona.

131

Stone relief of a goddess with a spear and vat; from Lemington, England. The stone is dedicated to Dea Riigina (the Queen Goddess); she may represent the Goddess of Sovereignty who plays a prominent role in Irish myth.

**'No meat on the plates,
No milk of the cows;
No shelter for the belated;
No money for the minstrels:
May Bres' cheer be what he gives to others!'**
From the Book of Invasions

(Above) View inside Newgrange, Ireland, a megalithic passage grave, dated to about 3100 BC. Neolithic tombs became woven into the later Irish myths, in which they were preceived as sídhe – Otherworld dwellings of the gods.

LUGH AND THE DRUIDS

When the supernatural young hero Lugh arrived at King Nuadu's royal capital of Tara, he presented himself at the gate and gave a long list of his accomplishments, in the hope of gaining admittance to the court of the Tuatha Dé Danann. One of Lugh's claims is interesting:

"'I am a sorcerer", said Lugh. "We do not want one. We have numberless sorcerers and Druids."'
From the Book of Invasions

Later Lugh was accepted by the Tuatha Dé Danann as their champion warrior against the demonic Fomorians, indigenous inhabitants of Ireland. Once the Tuatha Dé Danann had defeated the Fomorians and had captured their king Bres, the latter begged for his life:

"'What ransom will you pay for it?" asked Lugh. "I will guarantee that the cows of Ireland shall always be in milk", promised Bres. But before accepting, Lugh took counsel with his Druids: "What good will that be", they decided, "If Bres does not also lengthen the lives of the cows?"'

(Right) Bronze head of a celestial deity; from a hoard of bronzes found in Norfolk. Lugh's name proclaims him as a god of light.

account of the niggardly reign of King Bres, in the *Book of Invasions*. Cairpré, the Bard or Druid of the Tuatha Dé Danann, subjected him to a magical satire, the very first to be uttered in Ireland. Its words were so powerful that they caused the king's face to erupt into red blotches. One rule of kingship was that the ruler must be unblemished, and so Bres was deposed.

The Druids and the kings
The story of Cathbadh of Ulster (p. 128) illustrates the close connection between kings and Druids in Irish myth. The royal Druid was the king's political and religious adviser, and he was on hand to interpret the divine will, as presented in omens and magical events. The power of the Druids was very great: it is reported in one tale that King Conchobar could only speak on official occasions if first spoken to by one of his

Cormac's Dream, a medieval Irish tale in which the Ulster king accurately foretold the beheading of the women of Ulster by the men of Connacht.

OGAM AND DRUIDISM

A unique system of writing, called ogam, was developed in Ireland by the third century AD and probably went out of use by the eighth century. It was a system whereby twenty letters were represented by inscribing grooves or strokes either crossing or set at different angles to a vertical line. The ogam alphabet was based phonetically on groups of consonants and vowels, and was inspired by Latin writing. Ogam-inscribed stones have been found all over Ireland, with dense clusters in the south; they also occur in Wales, Devon and Cornwall and in areas of Scotland. Many ogam stones are tombstones.

Ogam inscriptions on wood are mentioned in Irish myths, and some are associated with the Druids. In the Mythological Cycle tale of the mortal girl Etáin and her divine lover Midhir, the god took her from the court of her spouse, King Eochaid of Ireland, and the pair eloped, transformed into swans. The king learned of Etáin's hiding place, in Midhir's underground palace of Brí Leith, by means of Druidic magic: a Druid named Dalan consulted ogam letters inscribed on wands of yew, and they gave him the answer.

three Druids. There is perhaps some monastic exaggeration at work here, but the story probably arose from the important role played by the Druids. The king would frequently ask his Druid such questions as how certain dreams should be understood, what the ruler's future fortunes would be, or who would inherit the throne.

In a tale entitled *Cormac's Dream*, King Cormac of Ulster had a terrifying dream, in which he saw the adultery of his wife, and the men of Connacht beheading the women of Ulster. When he awoke, he sent for his Druid, Melchend, to interpret the dream. The Druid confirmed that the predictions of Cormac's vision would come to pass.

When the kingship of Ulster was offered to Cormac (in a story called the *Bruiden Da Choca*) and he had accepted, the new king was told of a list of *gessa* which had been imposed upon him by the Druid Cathbadh. Like the injunctions laid upon King Conaire (p. 125), these were broken, thus causing Cormac's premature death.

An origin myth, constructed to explain the circumstances of the dynasty of King Niall, is contained within a tale which is dated as early as the fifth century AD. In one episode, Niall's nephew Dáithi, king of Ireland, consulted the Druids as to his future, at the festival of Samhain. The chief Druid, Dogra, took Dáithi to Rath Achaill in County Sligo, where the Druids' altars were. At sunrise, the Druid entered the room where Dáithi was sleeping, and pronounced his fate: he told Dáithi to return to Tara, call a gathering of the provincial kings and make preparations for an expedition to Scotland, Britain and France. The most interesting statement in the tale is Dogra's announcement that he had consulted 'the Clouds of the Men of Erinn'. This enigmatic comment could mean that Dogra had spoken to the Tuatha Dé Danann, who dwelt in the spirit world after their dispossession by the Celts: one account of the invasion of Ireland by the Tuatha Dé Danann refers to their travelling in clouds.

In another kingship story, the *Cóir Anmann*, King Dáire of Ireland was told that a son of his called Lugaid would succeed him as king. Dáire promptly gave all five of his sons that name. He then asked his Druid to predict which of them would be the next king, and the Druid replied that a fawn would enter the assembly, and the son who caught it would be king after Dáire.

DRUIDISM AND CHRISTIANITY

'This is the penitance of a Druid or a cruel man vowed to evil, or a satirist or a cohabiter or a heretic or an adulterer, namely seven years on bread and water.'

From a seventh-century Irish Penitential

THERE IS A SUBTLE shift in the treatment of the Druids from the mythic literature, which allegedly describes a pre-Christian Ireland, to the overtly Christian texts, which chronicle the conversion of the Irish by Saint Patrick and other early saints. Yet the same Christian monks were responsible for both sets of documents, and it was probably the case that the two different images of Druids presented a deliberate contrast. So, in the myths, Druids like Cathbadh enjoyed considerable *gravitas* and *dignitas*, whilst the Druids encountered by Saint Patrick are presented as devious, spiteful and sometimes faintly ridiculous.

Many of the tales set in early Christian Ireland describe episodes in which kings who clung to Druidic influence met their downfall because of their persistent paganism. Some of the stories illustrate the direct challenge of Christianity to paganism by reference to Druidic prophecy and ineffectual Druidic magic. What is quite clear is that the monastic redactors were neither ecumenical nor tolerant of paganism or Druidism. For the early Christian missionaries in Ireland, Druids, rather than the kings themselves, were the targets for attack. Early eighth-century Irish Canons declare that the justice of a just king included the injunction not to heed the superstition of Druids, sorceresses and Augurs.

On occasions, the Druids themselves are presented as prophets of the new faith. A story about King Conchobar, called the *Aided Conchobar*, tells of the king's injury by a brain-

THE STRUGGLE OF SAINT BERACH

*T*here is a seventh-century Life of Saint Berach, *which describes a long and bitter conflict between a saint and a powerful local Druid, who was determined neither to be supplanted nor to be deprived of his lands by a Christian cleric. The saint condemned the Druid thus: 'Your father, Satan, having been cast out of heavenly inheritance ... sought the depths of hell. You, therefore, like your father, are not fit to possess this land dedicated to God ...'*

The Druid sought the help of young warriors from the local Fianna, but they were rendered incapable of fighting. At this sign from God, the king was converted and begged Berach's forgiveness. But even when confronted by further miracles, the Druids remained implacable, 'full of treachery and malice'.

Engraving showing a clash between the Druids and the newly arrived followers of Christianity.

ball (a charming custom described in Insular myth involving the decapitation of an enemy and the removal of his brain, which was then mixed with lime and allowed to set hard; it thus became a trophy or a formidable weapon). When Conchobar was wounded, his physician informed him that he would recover if the ball was left in his head, but that he must on no account become agitated. Conchobar's Druid then told the king that a great earthquake had been caused by Christ's crucifixion; on hearing this challenge to the pagan order, Conchobar flew into a great rage and died of apoplexy.

Druids and Saints

The chronicled lives of two famous early Irish Christian saints illustrate two very different aspects of the interface between paganism and Christianity. In the two *Lives* of Saint Brigit, a Druid is involved in the rearing of the holy

woman, and he is presented as humble in the face of the new faith. By contrast, two *Lives* of Saint Patrick present a picture of total hostility between Patrick and the Druids of the king of Ireland.

Brigit: a Druid's foster-child

The earliest account of Saint Brigit's life is the seventh-century Latin *Vita Brigitae* by Cogitosus. The first version written in Irish is the *Bethu Brigte* which presents Brigit as a contemporary of Patrick, who allegedly converted Ireland in the mid-fifth century, although other evidence suggests that Brigit belonged to the late fifth to early sixth century AD.

The first link between Brigit and the Druids concerns Druidic prophecies about the birth of a wonderful and heroic girl. A nobleman of Leinster, named Dubthach, had a sexual relationship with his slavewoman, Broicseth, and

Painting by William Holman Hunt (1827–1910) – 'A Converted British Family Sheltering a Christian Missionary from the Druids', 1850. The missionary hides with the family, while, in the background, the Druids perform their pagan ceremonies within a stone circle and pursue another Christian across a field.

BRIGIT AND THE DRUID'S FOOD

'I am unclean but that girl is full of the Holy Spirit. However, she does not take my food.'

The Christian sanctity of Brigit was fully revealed by her rejection of the food prepared for her in the Druid's household. The Druid realized that his food was making the child ill because it was contaminated by his paganism, and so he selected a special white cow, milked by a devout virgin, Christiana (the symbolism of the name is clear) to provide pure nourishment for Brigit.

Wooden figure from Ireland, dating to the early first millennium BC, a product of paganism more than 1,000 years before St Brigit.

she became pregnant. One day, Dubthach and Broicseth were riding past a Druid's house in a chariot. On hearing the rumble of the wheels, the Druid emerged and said to Dubthach 'Take great care of the woman, for what she has conceived is marvellous'. He went on to predict that 'the seed of your wife will serve the seed of your slavewoman to the end of time' and that Broicseth would produce 'a radiant daughter who would shine in the world like the sun in the zenith of heaven'.

More Druidic portents surrounded the unborn saint. Two British Christian bishops, Mel and Melchu, visited Dubthach's wife and prophesied that the descendants of Broicseth's child would do hers good. Nonetheless, the woman demanded of Dubthach that Broicseth be sold and sent away. He reluctantly agreed.

Broicseth was bought by a Druid; on the night he brought her home, a Christian holy man came to stay. He prayed all night to God and frequently saw a ball of fire on the spot where Broicseth lay asleep. In the morning, he told the Druid of his vision. This is only the first of many fire-portents associated with Brigit. The predictions continued: when Broicseth was ready to give birth, the Druid invited his king and queen to supper. The queen was also close to confinement, and the royal servants asked the Druid to predict the most auspicious time for a baby to be born. The Druid said 'if at sunrise tomorrow morning, the child will have no equal on earth'. The queen was delivered too soon, but Broicseth gave birth to her daughter at the break of dawn.

Once the child was born, the miracles and omens were just as prominent. Her Druid foster-father was visited in a dream by two white-clad priests who baptized her and anointed her with holy oil. One of them said 'You are to name this virgin Brigit'. Other incidents served to remind Brigit's guardian of his holy charge. Fire is a particularly important omen: the Druid repeatedly witnessed the child apparently threatened by fire, which left her unscathed. On one occasion, he saw a ribbon around the child's head burst into flames, but the fire disappeared as he and her mother rushed to put it out. Another incident occurred when the Druid was star-gazing at night, as was his custom: he saw a pillar of fire rising from the hut where the child and her mother lay asleep. Again, the fire left Brigit unharmed.

The story of Brigit is clearly constructed to show Christianity as dominant over paganism. But the child's foster-father is consistently benign, and there is no hint of conflict between the old and new religions. Instead, the subservience and humility of the Druid is emphasized. The *Lives* of Patrick present a very different picture.

Patrick and the Druids: a clash of faiths

'There shall arrive shaven-headed
With his stick bent in the head
From his house with a hole in its head
He will chant impiety;
From his table
In the front of his house.
All his people will answer,
'Be it thus, be it thus!''

From Muirchú's *Life of Saint Patrick*

The passage quoted above is a prediction of Patrick's coming by two Druids, Lochru and Lucat Mael, attached to the court of King Loegaire of Ireland. They prophesied that a foreign way of life, with a burdensome doctrine, would appear from abroad, overthrowing the old order, seducing the people and annihilating the old gods.

Patrick allegedly converted Ireland to Roman Christianity in AD 432. The conflict he stirred up with the pagan Druids is chronicled in two seventh-century *Lives* of the saint, that of Tírechán, Bishop of Tirawley, and Muirchú Mocciu Machtheni. The conflict centred around Patrick's appearance at Loegaire's court and the attempts of the royal Druids to stop the

king's conversion. Loegaire was very dependent on his Druids and had entrusted to them the education of his daughters. It was a Druid called Matha who first turned Loegaire against Patrick by prophesying that the newcomer would steal from him the living and the dead. When Patrick first met Loegaire, the Druid Lochru insulted the saint and his religion and Patrick countered this by praying (successfully) for Lochru's death.

The focus of the power struggle was a great pagan feast at Tara, when the Druid Lucat Mael attempted to poison Patrick's wine. The saint removed the drop of venom from the cup. Lucat then challenged Patrick to a contest of miracles. He caused snow to fall over the plain of Tara, and Patrick melted it. Loegaire then suggested a trial by ordeal; Lucat became uneasy and tried to extricate himself. But the trial went ahead: a hut with two rooms was built, one entered by the Druid, wearing Patrick's cloak, the other by Patrick's boy, Benignus, wearing the Druid's mantle. The hut was set on fire: Lucat perished, but Patrick's cloak was untouched; Benignus survived but the Druid's garment was burnt away.

Some scholars see a close parallel between the Tara incident and certain Old Testament episodes: the great feast of Nebuchadnezzar of Babylon, described in the Book of Daniel, may be the model for the Tara festival, and the fire miracle is analogous to the struggle between Elijah and the prophets of Baal in the Book of Kings.

(Right) Nineteenth-century stained glass window, from Ballylynan, County Laois, Ireland, depicting Saint Patrick. Unlike Saint Brigit's experiences, Patrick's encounters with Druids were far from cordial: when he came to convert Ireland to Christianity (allegedly in AD 432), he met hostility from the royal Druids, who feared the loss of their influence over their kings in the face of the new faith. In tests of the efficacy of Christianity versus paganism, Patrick was always victorious, and he became Ireland's patron saint.

(Left) Nineteenth-century stained glass window, from Ballylynan, County Laois, Ireland, depicting Saint Brigit. Brigit was allegedly reared by a Druid, and indeed her conception and birth were hedged about with Druidic prophecies. Despite her early upbringing, Brigit's Christian faith was acknowledged and respected by her pagan foster-father. The holy child grew up to become Ireland's most important female saint, founding her monastery in Kildare in the late fifth or early sixth century AD.

FIRE, DRUIDS AND THE HILL OF SLANE

Just as fire is a recurrent motif in the story of Saint Brigit, so an episode in Muirchú's Life of Saint Patrick is also concerned with fire symbolism. Patrick lit his paschal fire on the Hill of Slane, a site sacred to pagan belief, in direct defiance of a Druidic custom that no fire be lit there until one had been kindled at Tara. When Loegaire's Druids saw Patrick's fire they were filled with foreboding:

'Unless this fire, which we see and which has been lit before one could be kindled in your house, is extinguished on this same night that it has been lit, it will never be extinguished forever ... and he who has kindled it ... will on this night overcome us all.... And all kingdoms will fall to him.'

DRUIDS RESURRECTED

'*Though time with silver locks adorn'd his head*
Erect his gesture yet, and firm his tread....
His seemly beard, to grace his form bestow'd
Descending decent, on his bosom flow'd;
His robe of purest white, though rudely join'ed
Yet show'd an emblem of the purest mind'.

From John Ogilvie's poem, *The Fane of the Druids*, 1787

THE REVEREND DR JOHN OGILVIE was an Aberdeenshire vicar with antiquarian interests. In common with many of his eighteenth-century peers, Ogilvie erroneously associated the Druids with megalithic monuments. His description of an Archdruid, in the quoted extract, typifies the romanticism with which Druids were regarded by antiquarians of this period.

Ogilvie's portrait contains an amalgam of material from the Classical writers, overlain with eighteenth-century idealism. We have a venerable sage, a Noble Savage with an unsullied mind, clothed in a dazzling white garment and adorned with a long flowing beard.

Between the sixteenth and nineteenth centuries, there existed – both in Britain and on the Continent – a lively interest in antiquarian matters. The prehistoric past, Celts and Druids were the subjects of much debate and guesswork. Antiquarians used the perfunctory references in the Classical literature as a nucleus around which they wove a fantasy of Druidic attributes and functions. At their extreme, these Druid-seekers assigned them all manner of virtues, together with most ancient monuments. Inevitably, in the absence of a scientific system of classification to construct a chronological framework for the past, enquirers compressed the material remains of the ancient inhabitants of Europe, so that anything demonstrably pre-Roman belonged to the same cultural horizon. So Stonehenge, the Celts and the Druids became inextricably (and erroneously) intertwined; for some, they remain so to the present day.

A nineteenth-century Italian engraving of three Druids, showing the romanticized view of Druids and their appearance that was common in the eighteenth and nineteenth centuries.

THE DRUIDIC REVIVAL OF THE RENAISSANCE

'Let us imagine what kind of a countrie this was in the time of the ancient Britons ... a shady dismal wood: and the inhabitants almost as savage as the beasts whose skins were their only raiment....
Their religion is at large described by Caesar. Their priests were Druids. Some of their temples I pretend to have restored, as Avebury, Stonehenge etc.... They were two or three degrees I suppose less savage than the Americans.... The Romans subdued and civilized them.'

John Aubrey, Introduction to *Essay Towards the Description of the North Division of Wiltshire*, 1649

Portrait of John Aubrey from J. Britton, Memoirs of John Aubrey, *1845. Aubrey was a seventeenth-century antiquarian who was the first to connect the Druids to Stonehenge. His most famous work on this subject was* Monumenta Britannica, *which he finished in the 1670s.*

APART FROM THEIR appearance in the mythic texts, particularly those of Ireland, there seems to have been little serious interest in the Druids in the medieval period, especially in Britain. But at the beginning of the Renaissance, the rediscovery and circulation of Classical literature led to a new absorption with the prehistoric past and with the Druids to whom references were made in these ancient documents.

The sixteenth-century antiquarians of Britain and Europe could have no scientific perspective on the past, because they lacked the means to classify and date antiquities. The Celtic and Druidic past mentioned by the Graeco-Roman authors had, therefore, to fit into the framework of the Biblical past: seventeenth-century clerics, of whom the most notable was Archbishop James Ussher of Armagh, calculated the exact age of the world, based upon the number of 'begats' in the Bible; thus, the world and its human inhabitants began in 4004 BC. The picture painted in the sixteenth century is of a past consisting of Adam and Eve, Noah, the Flood and the repopulation of the earth by Noah's sons Ham, Shem and Japhet. All Europeans were perceived as descendants of Japhet.

On the Continent, the interest in Druidism was closely tied to national pride. For the French, the Druids symbolized their glorious Gaulish past: in 1532, Jean le Fèvre wrote *Les Fleurs et Antiquitez des Gaules, où il est traité des anciens Philosophes Gaulois appellez Druides* ('The Flowers and Antiquities of the Gauls, wherein the ancient Gaulish Philosophers called Druids are discussed'). The Germans nurtured similar feelings (an irony since Caesar firmly stated that there were no Druids in Germany): one German author, Esaias Pufendorf, wrote a *Dissertatio de Druidibus* in 1650. Although the Druids were thus now extolled in several Continental tracts, the image projected there was ambiguous, just as it was in the ancient sources: they were at the same time savages, who carried out human sacrifice, and high-minded philosophers.

Just as the Classical authors were divided into pro- and anti-Druid camps, so were some early antiquarians. Michael Drayton called the Druids 'sacred Bards' and profound thinkers in his *Polyolbion*, published in 1622; in the poem, Drayton describes the Druids as being drawn through the air by dragons. Jon Fletcher's *Bonduca* ('Boudica') of 1618 described the Druids as patriotic champions of freedom against Roman tyranny. The poet Andrew Marvell identified himself with the Druids, likening himself to 'some great Prelate of the Grove'. But Aylett Sammes, in his *Britannia Antiqua Illustrata* of 1676, stressed the barbarity of Druidic human sacrifice, and his illustrations hammered home the point.

Aubrey the antiquarian (1626–1697)

John Aubrey was perhaps the most influential of the seventeenth-century British antiquaries. He is most famous now for his *Brief Lives*, which he began in 1680. This book consists of a series of brilliant vignettes of his contemporaries, often written around horoscopes, thus displaying Aubrey's deep interest in astrology. *Brief Lives* was not substantially published until 1813.

Aubrey was the first to link the Druids and Stonehenge, and thus began a trend which has persisted until today. Aubrey did not idealize or romanticize the Druids, but, in the absence of a long prehistoric perspective, he argued that since Stonehenge and Avebury were not Roman, they must be pre-Roman, and because they were clearly temples, they must therefore be Druidic. He was by no means alone in his assumption, as we shall see, and his views about the association between Druids and megalithic

monuments were widely proclaimed by his eighteenth-century antiquarian successors.

Aubrey made a systematic archaeological survey of Stonehenge and Avebury. He wrote a long treatise on megaliths which he originally called *Templa Druidum*, but later re-named *Monumenta Britannica* (with 'Templa Druidum' remaining as the title of the opening section). The work was completed in the 1670s but remained unpublished until the 1980s. Aubrey realized that his claims for the Druidic affiliation of Stonehenge and its sister monuments were speculative and that he had 'gonne further in this Essay than anyone'.

But the madness about Druids which was to grip later antiquarians, notably William Stukeley, shows itself already in Aubrey: on being shown a strigil from Roman Reculver, he cried: 'Behold the golden sickle with which the Druids used to cut mistletoe'.

'John Aubrey, Esq ... was the only person I ever then met, who had a right notion of the temples of the Druids ...'
From a letter written by John Toland to Viscount Molesworth

John Aubrey's survey of Avebury; from his Monumenta Britannica. *Aubrey linked the Druids with megalithic stone circles, which he called the Temples of the Druids.*

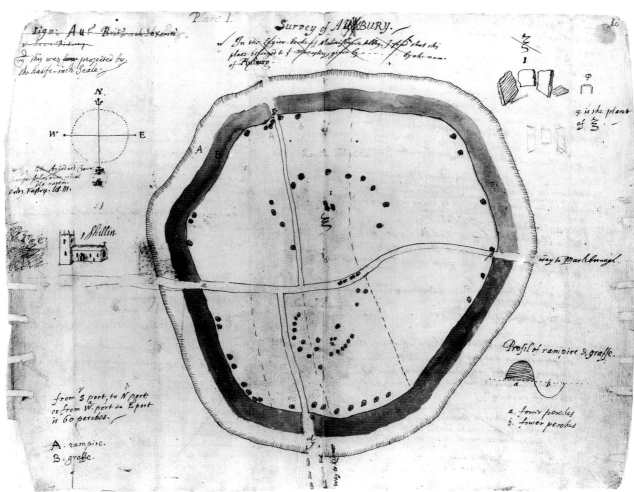

STUKELEY AND HIS PEERS

A self-portrait of William Stukeley. Like Aubrey before him, William Stukeley was convinced that megalithic monuments such as Stonehenge and Avebury were the holy places of the Druids. In his later years, Stukeley saw himself as a Druid called 'Chyndonax'.

'My intent is (besides preserving the memory of these extraordinary monuments, so much to the honour of our country, now in great danger of ruin) to promote, as much as I am able, the knowledge and practice of ancient and true Religion; to revive in the minds of the learned the spirit of Christianity'.

William Stukeley, Preface to *Stonehenge*, 1740

WILLIAM STUKELEY, a Lincolnshire doctor, was born in 1687, and, in 1729, took holy Orders and became the Vicar of Stamford. He was influenced by Aubrey's work and he, likewise, made a connection between the Druids and megalithic monuments that – with the benefit of modern scholarship, we now know – properly belonged to a period more than two millennia earlier than the Celtic priesthood. In 1724, he published his *Itinerarium Curiosum*, the result of his tours of Britain over four to five years, in which he claimed Celtic or Druidic affiliations for Neolithic and Bronze Age burial mounds. Stukeley's interest in megaliths was bolstered by an equal passion for ancient religion. Moreover, he sought to establish a link between the Old Testament Patriarchs, the Druids and Christianity.

Stukeley the Archdruid

In 1623, an inscription found near Dijon was published. It allegedly mentioned a Druid called Chyndonax, and Stukeley adopted the name for himself: indeed, it appeared on the frontispiece of his *Stonehenge*, published in 1740. From that time onwards, Stukeley identified himself increasingly with Druidism. He even had his garden laid out in the form of a Druidic grove, in which he conducted a pagan burial ceremony for his miscarried child.

In 1753, a hoard of pre-Roman bronzes turned up during the landscaping of Kew Gardens. Kew was the home of the Princess Dowager Augusta; Stukeley wrote up what he termed the 'Druid celts' (which were in fact Late Bronze Age

'The Druid sacrifice of the autumnal equinox' by William Stukeley, 1759.

bronze axes), and presented her with the manuscript at an audience granted to him at which the two enthusiastically discussed Stukeley's work, Druids and sacred oaks. The Druid-smitten antiquarian returned home carrying an oak branch laden with acorns which he presented to his friend Mrs Miriam Peirson, 'a present from the royal Archdruidess, to her sister Druidess'.

Stukeley's sermons became more and more steeped in Druid lore. In 1763, he dedicated a volume of sermons to the Princess Dowager, entitled *Palaeographia Sacra* ('Discussions on Sacred Subjects'). The dedication was to Princess Augusta as Veleda, Archdruidess of Kew (Veleda was the name of an ancient German prophetess mentioned by Tacitus (p. 97)) and was signed 'Chyndonax of Mount Haemus (Hampstead), Druid'. It is little wonder that the modern Order of Bards, Ovates and Druids claim Stukeley as chief among the revived eighteenth-century Druids.

ABRAHAM, DRUIDS AND CHRISTIANS

In attempting to reconcile Christianity with the existence of the Druids, Stukeley constructed an elaborate pedigree for both Druids and Christians. According to him, the Druids first arrived in Britain with the Phoenicians, shortly after the Flood. He described the Druids as being 'of Abraham's Religion', and thus considered them to be associated with both the Old Testament and the Christian Faith. The origins of such a notion were not peculiar to Stukeley but echoed eighteenth-century perceptions in which Christianity went back to the time of the Creation, and the 'Natural Religion', as practised by the Druids, was akin to Christianity.

By 1726, Stukeley was coming to the view that the beliefs of the Druids were 'near to the Christian doctrin'. In the 1760s, when a clergyman in London, he preached and published the 'Vegetable Sermons' in which Druids, vegetables (made for the glory of God) and Natural Religion were all intermingled. For Stukeley, the Druids were 'Noble Savages', thinking profound thoughts and practising Natural Religion in their sacred groves. Their closeness to Christianity was proved, he said, by their consciousness of the sanctity of the number 3 and thus their recognition of the Trinity: 'As once of old in groves, so here in their representative fabrics, we adore the three sacred persons of the Trinity'.

Stukeley's portrait of a Druid. He stands beneath an oak, with a bottle and staff; an early Bronze Age axe-blade is at his belt.

THE STONEHENGE CONNECTION

Prince Bladud, the mythical founder of Bath, was believed by the architect John Wood to have been a Druid. Wood's obsession with all things Druidic may be reflected in his work. The Circus of Bath is thought by some to mirror the most readily available plan of Stonehenge at the time Wood was planning the Circus. The plan, by Inigo Jones, showed Stonehenge to be a circle 980 ft (300 m) in diameter with three entrances that Jones believed to have originally existed. The diameter and entrances are almost exactly copied in the Circus' design.

(Opposite page) William Danby's nineteenth-century folly, complete with trilithons, which he called a Druid Temple, at Swinton Hall, Ilton, West Yorkshire. The folly was originally surrounded by oak trees.

'So it is clear, that all the monuments which I have here recounted, were Temples; Now my presumption is, that the Druids being the most eminent priests among the Britaines …'
John Aubrey, *Monumenta Britannica*

AUBREY'S WORK WAS the catalyst that triggered a Stonehenge-Druid fever among eighteenth-century antiquarians, particularly in Britain. The architect John Wood, a native of Bath, was obsessed with Druids and, like John Aubrey and William Stukeley, combined systematic planning of Stonehenge with fanciful notions about its Druid affiliations. According to Wood, Stonehenge was one of four constituent Druid colleges (along with Avebury, Exmoor and Mendip) of the main Druidic University at the Stanton Drew stone circles. He also allocated the Druids a centre at Bath, where they worshipped Apollo.

During the mid-eighteenth century, there appeared a spate of pamphlets on Stonehenge, all steeped in Druidism and generally built upon a Stukeleian foundation. People did not stop at writing: in the 1820s, William Danby built a folly in the grounds of his home at Swinton Hall in Yorkshire, modelled on Stonehenge, which he called a Druid Temple. Antiquaries such as William Borlase, who carried out fieldwork in Cornwall and produced the book *Antiquities of Cornwall* in 1754, claimed most Cornish megaliths as the Druids' work. But some learned men were far from enraptured by Druids and megaliths. On encountering a Scottish 'Druid Temple' near Inverness, Dr Samuel Johnson remarked:

'To go and see one druidical temple is only to see that it is nothing, for there is neither art nor power in it: and seeing one is quite enough.'

STUKELEY AND STONEHENGE

In 1710, Stukeley visited the megalithic stone circle known as the Rollright Stones near Chipping Norton, and commented: 'I cannot but suppose 'em to have been an heathen temple of our Ancestors, perhaps in the Druids' time'. Stukeley was especially taken with Aubrey's connection between the Druids and Stonehenge. His fieldwork on megalithic monuments was impeccable, but his reasoning about its origins, especially in his later writings, was fuelled by his Druid mania. When he surveyed Stonehenge, Stukeley hit upon the 'Druid's Cubit', a unit of linear measurement 20.8 ft (6.3 m) which he thought had been used in the circles' construction.

In 1723, Stukeley began to write The History of the Temples of the Ancient Celts, the title of which he changed, c. 1733, to The History of the Religion and Temples of the Druids (right, see top right-hand corner). In 1740, his

Stonehenge, a Temple restor'd to the British Druids *appeared, to be followed by a companion volume on Avebury in 1743. In the mid-eighteenth century, Stukeley gave a lecture on the*

Druidic associations of Stonehenge to the Society of Antiquaries in London, *wherein he recounted a dinner he and his friends enjoyed at the monument, using one of the trilithons as a dining table.*

REALISTS AND ROMANTICS

'The Bard' – detail of a painting by John Martin, 1817, which illustrates the poem by Thomas Grey also called The Bard, *about the last surviving Welsh Druid, perched on a cliff over the River Conwy in Wales, cursing the English conqueror, Edward I, for ordering the slaughter of his comrades.*

Stukeley's drawing of a Druidical sacrifice, with the serpent temple of Avebury in the background and Silbury Hill in front.

THIS WAS HOW many eighteenth-century antiquarians wished to present the past. In this period, antiquarians approached Druids from widely differing perspectives. Some British scholars in the earlier part of the century, such as Henry Rowlands, were unsympathetic. Others, like Stukeley, were besotted with romantic ideas of the Druids as simple but noble mystics, which clouded their academic judgment and which gradually forced serious scholarship into the background. But whatever their persuasion, these antiquaries were convinced that Druids and megaliths belonged to the same cultural and chronological continuum.

John Toland, Covent Garden and Primrose Hill

Toland was born in Londonderry in 1670; he was a friend of Aubrey and espoused many of his views. Toland was an important influence on eighteenth-century Druidism, and in a letter to his friend Viscount Molesworth, he wrote: 'no heathen priesthood ever came up to the perfection of the Druidical'. He planned and began a *History of the Druids* but died in 1722 before its completion.

John Toland was a Christian, but one who rebelled against the elaborate ritual of the Church. Tradition has it that in 1717 a meeting was held at the Apple Tree Tavern at Covent Garden, attended by delegates from Druidic and Bardic circles from all over Britain, Ireland and Brittany. This gathering allegedly formed the modern Druidic Order by founding the 'Mother Grove'. Toland was reported as having been elected Chief Druid at an inauguration ceremo-

ny which took place on Primrose Hill at the autumn equinox in 1717. Both these events may be apocryphal, but the British Circle of the Church of the Universal Bond claims direct descent from Toland's Primrose Hill gathering.

A contemporary of Toland's was the Reverend Henry Rowlands, an Anglesey vicar who, using Tacitus' account, quite correctly linked the Druids with the island of Mona. In 1723, he published his *Mona Antiqua Restaurata*. For Rowlands, as for Stukeley, the Druids were descended from Noah, and he allotted them both the sacred groves referred to by the Classical authors and megalithic tombs, interpreted by him as Druidic altars.

THE ANCIENT ORDER OF DRUIDS

*I*n 1781, Henry Hurle founded a secret society in London, which he called the Ancient Order of Druids. The Order was inaugurated on 29 November 1781. Its members first used The Kings Arms in Poland Street (near Oxford Street in the heart of London) as a meeting place: the tavern is still there and bears a plaque recording the revival of the AOD in 1781. The Order was organized on lines very similar to

Freemasonry, being arcane, exclusive and masculine, and its foundation owed much to the activities and influence of William Stukeley. Its early members were cultivated gentlemen, who enjoyed good conversation, music and poetry. But by 1810, certain lodges of the Order were admitting people of the lower classes, and their superior brothers took violent exception to their membership, taking steps to establish a black-

balling mechanism to exclude such riff-raff from their lodges. In 1833, a breakaway movement of the poorer members, seeking to make the Order into a source of financial relief, re-established itself as a Benefit Society, calling itself 'The United Ancient Order of Druids', whilst the remaining part retained its exclusivity.

Another remnant of Hurle's original Order, 'The Church of the Universal Bond' (which claimed

both Stukeley and Blake among its founding luminaries), survived until 1963, when it was displaced by the modern Order of Bards, Ovates and Druids. The OBOD is only one of a large number of modern Druid Orders.

'The March of the Druids' by the Ancient Order of the Druids at Stonehenge in August 1905. During the ceremony, 256 new members were initiated.

'La Druidesse' – a nineteenth-century painting by La Roche, of a Druidess, with a sickle and mistletoe (inspired by Pliny's account), in front of a megalithic monument.

Druids and poets
'All Things Begin and End in
Albion's Ancient Druid Rocky Shore'
William Blake, *Jerusalem*, 1804–20

An abundance of eccentric literature on the Druids appeared in the eighteenth and nineteenth centuries. These include William Cooke's *An Enquiry into the Druidical and Patriarchal Religion* (1754); and the *Neodruidic Heresy in Britannia*, written by the Reverend Algernon Herbert, Dean of Merton College, Oxford, in 1838. Herbert was concerned to sniff out heretical Druids in the early Christian Church.

Some of the literary giants were infected with Druidic romanticism: Thomas Grey wrote a poem called *The Bard*, which described the last surviving Welsh Druid, perched on a cliff over the River Conwy in north Wales, cursing the English conqueror, Edward I, for ordering the slaughter of his comrades (pp. 88, 146). William Wordsworth was fascinated by the Druids and, like Marvell before him, identified himself closely with the ancient priesthood.

By the later eighteenth century, the Druids were becoming increasingly mixed up with what Stuart Piggott has termed a curious, irrational mysticism. This is exemplified by the work of the poet and artist William Blake, who frequently refers to the Druids in his *Prophetic Books*, published between 1797 and 1804, which were illustrated with engravings of Stonehenge and Avebury. Blake saw the Druids as priests, philosophers and law-givers, who originated in Britain and whose teachings had a wide influence in antiquity. Indeed Noah, Abraham and Shem were all Druids and Druid temples were built all over the world. Blake held the view that the Celtic Druids represented the flame of freedom against the brute force of Rome.

That Blake, like Stukeley and Wordsworth, identified himself as a Druid is demonstrated very clearly by his refusal to take the Oath at the Chichester Assizes, on account of his Druid faith.

In France, too, the mania was spreading and was, arguably, even more extreme than in Britain. In France, stone circles were rarer but megalithic tombs and alignments, such as those at Carnac in Brittany, were all eagerly claimed as Druidic. In 1729, Jean Martin published his *Religion des Gaulois*, which discussed Patriarchal Druids and linked them with stone alignments. In 1805, Jacques Cambry published his *Monumens Celtiques*, in which he described Breton megaliths as Druidic and associated them with astronomy. In the nineteenth century, perhaps the most bizarre character was a literary forger named Vrain Lucas, who, in the 1860s, fabricated letters purporting to be the work of ancient Gaulish noblemen. The maddest of these was a letter from Lazarus (the same man whom Jesus raised from the dead) to Saint Peter, which alluded to the Druids.

WORDSWORTH AND THE DRUIDS

'A youthful Druid taught in
shady groves
Primaeval mysteries, a bard elect
To celebrate in sympathetic verse
Magnanimous exploits'

And hark! the ringing harp I hear
And lo! her druid sons appear
Why roll on me your glaring eyes?
Why fix on me for sacrifice?'
Juvenalia 'Vale of Esthwaite' c. 1805

So Wordsworth (right) dramatized himself in The Prelude, *an autobiographical poem written between 1799 and 1805. Wordsworth was a deeply emotional poet, who found delight in Nature and, through Nature, humankind. Elsewhere, he dwells on the dark aspect of the Druids and on their sacrificial rites:*

'At noon I hied to gloomy shades
Religious woods and midnight
glades …

The Voice of the
Ancient Bard.

Youth of delight come hither.
And see the opening morn.
Image of truth new born.
Doubt is fled & clouds of reason
Dark disputes & artful teazing.
Folly is an endless maze,
Tangled roots perplex her ways.
How many have fallen there!
They stumble all night over bones of the dead,
And feel they know not what but care;
And wish to lead others when they should be led.

Detail of 'The Voice of the Ancient Bard', by William Blake, plate 54 from Songs of Innocence and Experience *by Blake c. 1815–1826, relief etching, finished in ink and watercolour, 11.5 x 7 cm (magnification 1.8x original size). Blake was fascinated by Druids and regarded them as profound philosophers and religious thinkers. He mentions them frequently in his Prophetic Books, and identified himself as a Druid.*

DRUIDS AS ILLUSTRATED

THE TITLE PAGE of Elias Schedius' *De Dis Germanis*, published in 1648, bears a picture of a Druid within a grove filled with headless corpses. He wears a long robe over a knee-length tunic, with voluminous sleeves, a fringed border and a sash at the waist. His brow is wreathed with oak leaves; he wields a knife stained with sacrificial blood, and his drum is beaten with drumsticks made from human thigh bones.

In Aylett Sammes' book, *Britannia Antiqua Illustrata*, published in 1676, the archetypal

Druid is portrayed with a long beard, bare feet, a short tunic and a hooded cloak. He wears a purse at his waist and carries a book and staff. Stukeley's Druid, published in 1723 (p. 143), was a modified version of Sammes' image: the beard is shorter and much less wild; a bottle has replaced the money-bag; and an early Bronze Age axe-head adorns his belt. In Henry Rowlands' treatise on ancient Anglesey *Mona Antiqua Restaurata* (also 1723), Sammes' book is replaced by an oak branch.

(Left) Aylett Sammes' portrait of a Druid, published in his Britannia Antiqua Illustrata *of 1676.*

(Above) The Reverend Henry Rowlands' Druid, published in his Mona Antiqua Restaurata *of 1723.*

The title page of Elias Schedius'
De Dis Germanis, *published in*
1648, showing a Druid in his
sacred grove, with a heap of
decapitated corpses at his feet. He
holds a wine goblet and a sacrificial
knife, and is accompanied by a
woman with a drum and a human
skull at her belt.

ELIÆ SCHEDII
De
DIS GERMANIS,
Sive
Veteri GERMANORVM, GALLO-
RVM, BRITANNORVM, VAN
DALORVM *Religione*
Syngrammata Quatuor.

Amſterodami,
Apud Ludovicum Elzevirium. Anno 1648.

William Price: A Welsh Druid

In 1884, Dr William Price of Llantrisant, south Wales, was tried at the Cardiff Assizes for illegally cremating his five-month-old son Iesu Grist (Jesus Christ). The ceremony, like that earlier funeral conducted by Stukeley (p. 142), was a Druidic affair, with Price dressed up in the long white robe of an Archdruid. He was acquitted and was himself cremated in 1893.

William Price was born in Monmouthshire in 1800, the son of an academic, the Reverend William Price, Fellow of Jesus College, Oxford. Price père went mad at the age of thirty and went naked round the south Wales countryside cutting down trees (on both public and private land) with a saw. Price fils, who became a doctor, evidently inherited some of his father's eccentricity: most notably, he was a Druid. He went about clad in a bizarre costume consisting of a white tunic, bright red waistcoat and green trousers, a foxskin draped – Davy Crockett fashion – over his head and shoulders (right). He could be observed engaged in such activities as chanting 'a song of the Primitive Bard to the Moon' at a local rocking-stone.

Like Caesar's Druids before him, Price was a political animal; he became involved in the Chartist movement (a nationwide protest movement aimed at achieving the vote for all adult men rather than simply landowners), which sometimes erupted into violence, notably at Newport, south Wales, in 1839.

Price was not alone: several eccentric Bards were active in the area of Mid Glamorgan at about this time. A Pontypridd watchmaker, Myfyr Morgannwg, claimed the title of Archdruid; he appeared at the Llangollen Eisteddfod of 1858 with a 'Druid's Egg' round his neck. Another local Bard, Owen Morgan, who died as late as 1921, published a series of mad books on Druidry, and equated the early Welsh poet Taliesin with Jesus Christ.

'This [September 23] being the day on which the autumnal Equinox occurred, some Welsh Bards, resident in London, assembled in Congress on Primrose Hill, according to ancient usage…. The wonted ceremonies were observed. A circle of stones formed, in the middle of which was the Maen Gorsedd, an Altar, on which a naked sword being placed, all the Bards assisted to sheath it.'
Gentleman's Magazine, October 1792

DURING THE LATTER part of the eighteenth century, a strong interest in early Celtic literature, particularly poetry, resulted in the gathering together of verse and music by a number of Welshmen. One such researcher was the harper Edward Jones, who published two important collections: The Musical and Poetical Relics of the Welsh Bards in 1784, and The Bardic Museum of Primitive British Literature in 1802. One of Jones' pieces was 'A Druidical Song', set for the harp, with the following verses and chorus:

'When infant science first began
To shed its influence on Man,
And on the Fathers of our Isle,
With look benignant deign'd to smile;

'Chorus: Hail, all hail, to the Mistletoe,
Hail, hail, all hail, to the Mistletoe, hail….

'The enlighten'd Crowd with grateful raptures glow,
And crown his head with Sacred Mistletoe,
With Mistletoe, the leaves of Oak they bind,
And hail him Druid, Friend of Human kind,
And hail him, Druid, Friend of Human kind….'

To be able to claim Welsh ancestry became fashionable among the English upper classes during the eighteenth century. When speaking of this, the Welsh historian Emyr Humphreys commented: 'Welsh pedigrees went up in value when druids became fashionable…. The druids were very well connected'. (The Taliesin Tradition, 1983)

It was against this backdrop of increasing Welsh interest in Celtic roots that Iolo Morgannwg created a myth in which Druids, Wales, stone circles and the National Eisteddfod all melded together in one rich, if doubtful, brew.

Iolo Morgannwg: forgery and fantasy

'Iolo, old Iolo, he who knows
The virtues of all herbs of mount and vale ...
Whatever lore of science or of song
Sages and bards of old have handed down!'

From a poem by Robert Southey, 1820s

Edward Williams was born in Glamorgan, south Wales, in 1747. From the early 1770s he worked as a stonemason in London, and there he got together with other ex-patriot Welshmen who were concerned that the language and cultural identity of Wales be maintained. Williams became a Bard and assumed the Bardic name 'Iolo Morgannwg' (Iolo of Glamorgan). But Iolo was not content simply to foster modern Welsh culture; he had to invent a pedigree for the Bardic tradition, in which Glamorganshire Bards belonged to an unbroken line stretching back to the ancient Celtic Druids. Iolo's zeal was, of course, fired by the current Druid mania

Notation from Edward Jones' song set for the harp, entitled 'Y Derwydd – The Druid', published in 1802.

infecting English antiquaries. Iolo forged documents (an easy thing to do in the context of the unrigorous scholarship of the time) to prove his case, and he was wholly responsible for the elaborate myth and ritual which has become part of the modern National Eisteddfod.

Welsh Bards and the Eisteddfod

Iolo Morgannwg, in creating this particular pedigree for the Welsh Bards, was tampering

A past Gorsedd ceremony in which the Archdruid stands on the central Logan Stone and performs a ritual in which a sword is withdrawn from its sheath three times. Although the Eisteddfod had existed in some form as early as the twelfth century, the Gorsedd and the trappings and rituals associated with today's Eisteddfod were entirely the invention of Iolo's fertile imagination.

A Gorsedd held in 1903 by the Collège des Bardes de la Bretagne-Armorique, at Brignogan, northern Brittany, France.

with a genuine Welsh tradition which had its genesis in the twelfth century. In medieval times, the Bards enjoyed a rank within a hierarchical society; their poetry was distinctive in its complexity of form, with its rigid metrical structures. The Eisteddfod (literally meaning an Assembly) was set up at least as early as the twelfth century (the Cardigan Eisteddfod took place in 1176) as a court to regulate and validate the musical and poetical work of the Bards, by means of competitions and awards. In the later Middle Ages, Eisteddfodau were held in various Welsh towns, where they performed the additional role of controlling itinerant (and potentially vagrant) Bards, and thus won the favour of the English government.

The Primrose Hill ceremony in 1792, referred to in an extract from the *Gentleman's Magazine* (opening quotation, p. 152), was Iolo's creation but may have been inspired by John Toland's ceremony at Primrose Hill in 1717 (p. 147). The Glamorgan Bard decided to reconstruct a Druidical court of the 'Bards of the Isle of Britain', which involved the 'Gorsedd y Beirdd' (Gorsedd of Bards), a group of people arranged inside a circle of standing stones. The chairing and crowning of poets, with accompanying proclamations, were orchestrated by Iolo.

The ancient medieval Eisteddfod had been languishing for a considerable time. But in 1819, having persuaded Dr Burgess, the Lord Bishop of St Davids (and an Englishman of learning), to lend his support to the revival of regular Eisteddfodau, Iolo organized a three-day

GORSEDD 1933
ROCHE

Eisteddfod held in the grounds of the Ivy Bush Hotel in Carmarthen, and breathed new life into the event by introducing a series of complicated (and invented) ceremonial activities. He brought with him a collection of stones with which he set up a Gorsedd circle and organized a Bardic performance.

Iolo was responsible for the introduction of all the main rituals now associated with the modern Eisteddfod. The Invocation to Peace, the

Gorsedd, the Druids, the Sceptre, Sword, Crown and 'Hirlas Horn' (the Horn of Plenty) all owe their presence to Iolo. He even managed to persuade his somewhat gullible peers that he was the sole survivor of the ancient Order of Glamorgan Druids.

Iolo's forged manuscripts were designed to prove the link between ancient Druids and eighteenth-century Wales, which in its turn endorsed the 'authenticity' of the 'Gorsedd Beirdd Ynys Prydain' (the 'Bardic Circle of the Island of Britain') as a genuine Druidic institution. In his publication, *Poems Lyric and Pastoral* (1794), Iolo proclaimed that the work of the sixth-century Welsh poet Taliesin exhibited a 'complete system of Druidism', despite the fact that the poems (falsely) attributed to Taliesin are not Druidic in content and, moreover, belong to a period no earlier than the thirteenth century.

'Cornish Gorsedd at Roche Rock' near Bodmin, Cornwall, by Herbert Truman, 1933. The central figure on the platform with a white beard is Henry Jenner (1848–1934); the lean figure to the right is thought to be Robert Morton Nance (1873–1959). Both men were leading lights in the Gorsedd.

THE GORSEDD Y BEIRDD

*T*he Gorsedd y Beirdd is an association of poets, writers, musicians and artists who have made a significant and distinguished contribution to Welsh language, literature and culture. Its members are known as Druids, and the colour of their costumes – white, blue or green – is indicative of their various ranks.

The ceremonies of the Gorsedd y Beirdd are held 'under the sun, the eye of light'. The 'Corn Gwlad' (a trumpet) calls the people together from the four corners of the land before chanting the Gorsedd Prayer. The Archdruid performs a ritual in which a sword is withdrawn from its sheath three times. He cries 'Is there peace?', to which the

assembly reply 'Peace'. The ritual is repeated at the competition award ceremonies.

The 'Hirlas Horn' (the Horn of Plenty) is presented to the Archdruid at the Logan Stone (the central stone on which the Gorsedd circle is aligned), by a young local married woman, who urges him to 'drink the wine of our welcome'. A young girl presents him with a basket of 'flowers from the land and soil of Wales' and a group of other girls performs a floral dance, based on a pattern of flower-gathering from the fields.

A local married woman presents the 'Hirlas Horn' to the Archdruid at the Logan Stone, during a ceremony of the Gorsedd y Beirdd.

So I too chose a Welsh name for mine [my house] and it was Taliesin. Taliesin, a Druid, was a member of King Arthur's Round Table.'
From a filmed interview with Frank Lloyd Wright, 1953

THE FAMOUS ARCHITECT Frank Lloyd Wright was the grandson of Richard Lloyd-Jones, a monoglot Welsh-speaking Unitarian preacher, who emigrated with his family to America in 1841. In his grandson's autobiography, published in 1940, Richard Lloyd-Jones is described as a Druidic Patriarch, one of a long line of Welsh Druid ancestors. So Frank, in keeping with his forebears, gave his house in Chicago a 'Druidic' name. For him, not only was Taliesin a Druid, but an Arthurian Druid.

The National Eisteddfod
'Picture the scene. The dimly lit Pavilion is swathed in shadows as the Gorsedd of the Bards march in dignified procession to the stage, their white robes and golden regalia glistening. An air of expectancy prevails as the Druids mount the steps to the stage to join their fellow members already seated in order of rank, a sea of blue and green robes. As the Gorsedd officials take their place on the stage, their

elected leader, the Archdruid, steps forward to address the audience.'
From a leaflet issued by the National Eisteddfod Office

The organizers of the modern Royal National Eisteddfod make it clear in all their literature that there is no connection whatsoever between the Druids who form the present Gorsedd y Beirdd and the ancient Druids of the pre-Roman Celts. It is fully acknowledged that Iolo Morgannwg was the founding father of the modern Eisteddfod.

We have seen that the first regional Welsh Eisteddfod to incorporate Iolo's elaborate rituals was held in Carmarthen in 1819. In 1860, a decision was taken to hold a National Eisteddfod for the whole of Wales, and the first of these took place in Aberdare in 1861.

A cultural Welsh feast
The National Eisteddfod is a cultural fair which takes place at the beginning of August every year and lasts for eight days. It is held at a venue in north and south Wales in alternate years. The Eisteddfod can only take place if it is proclaimed by the Gorsedd y Beirdd at least a year and a day in advance of the proposed event.

Three main ceremonies take place at the National Eisteddfod:

1. The Crowning of the Bard: the crown is awarded to the poet judged to have produced the best volume of poetry in free metre.

2. The award of the Prose medal: for the winner of the Prose Competition.

3. The Chairing of the Bard: the seat of honour is awarded for the best long poem in strict metres.

Competitors submit their work under pseudonyms, and their true identity is revealed to the audience by the Archdruid only after the winner is brought to the stage and dressed in ceremonial robes.

The National Eisteddfod and its Druids are a source of great pride to Wales, and rightly so. Literature and music are still accorded immense value here, and their providers enjoy high status. In this sense (and in this sense only) there is a link between the Druids of the present and the remote past.

PORTRAIT OF A WELSH DRUID

In 1815, Samuel Meyrick and Charles Smith published a book entitled Costume of the Original Inhabitants of the British Isles. *It contains an aquatint of 'An Archdruid in his Judicial Habit': he has the obligatory white beard and long white robe. His head is decorated with an oak wreath and an early Bronze Age gold lunula (a crescent-shaped necklet) worn upside down as a diadem, while a late Bronze Age gold gorget (a collar) encircles his upper chest.*

The Welsh Bards were given a new costume in 1897. It was designed by a Professor Herkomer and was given to them for their use in perpetuity. But the Archdruid, presiding over the Gorsedd y Beirdd in today's National Eisteddfod is clad very similarly to the Druid of Meyrick and Smith's book. The present 'Archdderwydd', John Gwilym, can be seen in his voluminous white robe, a diadem on his head and a massive golden crescent below his throat.

'An Archdruid in his Judicial Habit'; from Meyrick and Smith's Costume of the Original Inhabitants of the British Isles, *1815, based on an engraving by Montfaucon. He holds inscribed wooden rods (an invention of Iolo Morgannwg). The stone altar bears a prehistoric Irish gold ornament and a medieval flagon. The presence of the snake is due to a mistranslated Taliesin poem.*

X
DRUIDS
TODAY

'O, the life of the Druid is the life of the land.
We are one with the dark earth on which we proudly stand
One with the Mother who has suckled us from birth,
Her streams and her rivers, we are one with the earth;
One with the Father, whose oak supports the sky,
Who gazes on us daily with his great, immortal Eye....'
From the poem by Philip Shallcrass (Chief Druid of the British Druid Order),
The Druid and the Land, 1994

MODERN DRUIDRY is part of the Neo-Pagan – or New Pagan – Movement, along with other contemporary religions such as Wicca, Shamanism and Odinism. Shallcrass' poem clearly illustrates several present-day pagan tenets: the sanctity of the landscape; the worship of the Earth as Mother-Goddess and the Sun as Father-God; the sense of being at one with Nature and all living things. Other verses speak of the need to protect the earth from the destruction caused by over-development; and the importance of ancient sites, such as stone circles.

Modern Druids have a firm belief in there being genuine links between past and present. Many see themselves as successors to the original Druids of Caesar's time, and they are drawn to archaeological monuments because they were sacred to their ancestors and are still regarded as holy places.

This final chapter attempts to 'close the circle' (to use a modern Druid phrase): the book began with a discussion of the origins of ancient Druidism; it finishes with an examination of Druidism in the modern world, the perceived links between past and present, and the relationship between modern Druids and other Neo-Pagan groups.

Modern Druids during a dawn ceremony at Stonehenge on the summer solstice.

'Most pagans worship the Triple Goddess of the waxing, full and waning moon and the Horned God of the forests and animal powers. For many, the Goddess is seen as the fertile Earth Mother and the God as the life-giving Sun Father; but whatever forms the Gods and Goddesses are seen to take, they are revered as aspects of the one Divine power.'

From the Pagan Federation Information Pack

The front cover of a modern Druid magazine, The Druids' Voice: Magazine of Contemporary Druidry, the journal of the British Druid Order. This is a quarterly publication and includes poems, articles, advertisements and notice of events and festivals.

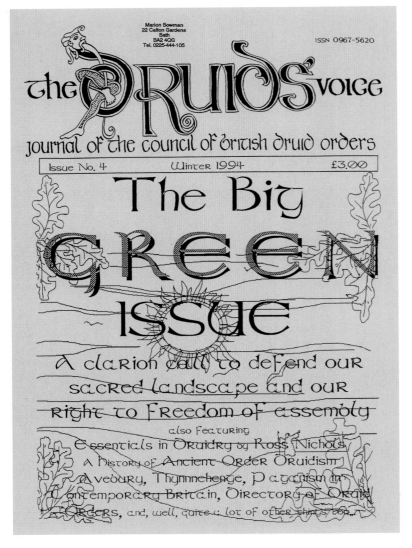

MODERN PAGANISM HAS three central principles:

1. Love for and kinship with Nature
2. The Pagan ethic: 'Do what thou wilt but harm none'
3. Acceptance of the polarity of deity (that is, the equality and balance between male and female divinity

Neo-Paganism has a strong presence in the USA. One of the great American forefathers of the pagan revival there was Gerald Gardner, who was born in 1884. His book *Witchcraft Today* is one of the foundation stones of modern witchcraft (or Wicca). Gardner constructed a Neo-Pagan religion which drew upon such authors as Margaret Murray (*Witchcraft in Western Europe*, 1921) and Robert Graves (*The White Goddess*, 1948). Thus, for Gardner, the Horned God (Cernunnos) and, especially, the Great Goddess of fertility, were paramount.

The British Pagan Federation has its counterpart organizations in America: the Midwest Pagan Council and the Pagan Front are just two of many such co-ordinating groups.

Shamanism

'Shamans are healers, seers, and visionaries … they are in communication with the world of gods and spirits. Their bodies can be left behind while they fly to unearthly realms … shamans are … masters of ecstasy.'

Joan Halifax, *Shamanic Voices*, 1968

The term 'shaman' is Siberian, and Siberia is one of the most important regions in which it is possible to study present-day shamans. But shamanism is central to many other traditional peoples, notably indigenous American cultures. Shamanism is less a cult than a sacred state of being. To a greater or lesser extent, shamanic ritual pervades most modern Pagan movements. The principal goal of the shaman is to achieve an ecstatic state of mind to achieve a direct link with the spirit world. The shaman induces a trance-state, by means of chanting, music or dance, thereby making him/herself receptive to spiritual contact. The shaman may dress up in animal guise to contact the spirits of Nature. The sacred energy thus released gives the shaman power which he or she directs towards healing, divination and other magic. The power endowed by these spirits expresses itself through shamanic visions, dreams, poetry or art.

Odinism

One of the most significant contemporary Pagan traditions in Europe (particularly in Germany, Scandinavia and Britain) is based upon the revival of pre-Christian Norse religion. Central to Odinism are the two divine systems of Norse myth: the sky-gods – known as the Aesir – and the Vanir, the earth-gods, who are concerned with agriculture and fertility.

Odinists make contact with the gods in order to gain power for healing and for spiritual development. Like Druids and Wiccans, they are concerned with environmental issues, and celebrate the seasonal festivals. There is a strict ethical code which emphasizes such values as loyalty, honour, courage and friendship. Although traditionally male-oriented, Odinism is increasingly becoming open to both men and women.

THE PAGAN FEDERATION

The Pagan Federation was founded in 1971 'to provide information on Paganism and to counter misconceptions about the religion'. The Federation's Information Pack defines modern Paganism as:

'... a religion of joy and celebration, a dance with the mysteries of Nature and a journey of self-realization.... Pagans follow a Nature-based spirituality and worship the Old Gods – the deities of pre-Christian times.'

The Pagan Federation is a coordinating body based in London, and its principal role is to provide a network of Pagans and to facilitate communication between the various Pagan groups currently operating within Britain. It organizes conferences and day meetings, and it publishes a quarterly magazine, Pagan Dawn, *which deals not only with Wicca (modern Witchcraft) but also with other Neo-Pagan movements such as Druidry, Odinism and Shamanism. The magazine, like its sister publication* The Druids' Voice, *contains articles by academics and believers (sometimes – but not invariably – one and the same), book reviews, poems, personal advertisements and notices of forthcoming events.*

A modern Native American shaman. Shamanic ritual pervades most Neo-Pagan movements, including Druidry.

'Druidry and Wicca are distinct and separate and the best way to consider them is as brothers and sisters.... Druidry is biased towards a reverence for the Sun, whereas Wicca is biased towards Lunar reverence.... Both, however, work in a circle, with the four quarters and four elements, and celebrate the seasonal festivals.'

Philip Carr-Gomm, *Voices from the Circle*, 1996

'An it harm none, do what you will.'
Wiccan tenet

WICCA IS A MODERN mystery religion which involves an initiatory period of study and reflection. Members of Wicca run introductory courses on the tradition in order to inform interested outsiders and dispel misconceptions about the cult. There is a strong emphasis on the divine element in the female principle. Aspiring Wiccans must be over eighteen years old and must ask for initiation: Wicca does not seek out converts. Novices follow a path of

(Left) White witches at Avebury, in front of one of the defaced stones (p. 178). The witches have just performed a ritual to produce a psychic photofit of the person guilty of the graffiti. The drawing of the man, bottom left, was the result of the ritual.

(Opposite) A Druidess from the cover of the Christmas edition of Le Monde Illustré in 1899, by Leftwich-Dodge. Many Neo-Pagan movements (particularly Wicca) have a strong female component. Some Druidic Orders, such as the Order of Bards, Ovates and Druids (OBOD), promote equality between the sexes, while others are still very male-orientated, not unlike all-male Masonic lodges.

NOËL

The Wheel of the Year

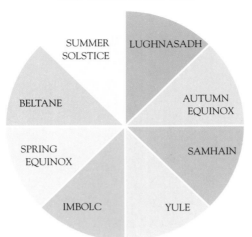

- SUMMER SOLSTICE
- LUGHNASADH
- BELTANE
- AUTUMN EQUINOX
- SPRING EQUINOX
- SAMHAIN
- IMBOLC
- YULE

The modern witch Sybil Leek performing magic at a crossroads (a significant spot at the centre of four cardinal points) near her Hampshire home.

study and ritual, including that associated with divination, incantation, dedication and purification, leading both to a profound communion and harmony with Nature and to spiritual transformation and self-knowledge. Wiccans believe in an all-powerful Earth Goddess and in other Nature deities, including the Horned God. Wicca is open to women (priestesses) and men (priests). A Coven consists of an established group of Wiccans, the members of which teach new initiates. The traditional interval between seeking and being granted initiation is a year and a day.

Wiccan ritual focuses particularly on eight seasonal festivals, known as Sabbats. In this respect, they have much in common with modern Druids (see below). Seasonal celebrations and other ceremonies often take place outside in the open air, so that Nature can more readily be venerated. The purpose of Wiccan ritual is to 'contact the Divine – within and without'.

The British magazine *Pagan Dawn* (formerly called *The Wiccan*) is published quarterly at the four Celtic festivals, which are named after the ancient seasonal ceremonies: Samhain, Imbolc, Beltane and Lughnasadh.

In the United States of America witchcraft is strongly linked to the Feminist Movement. Feminist witches are known as 'Dianic' (from Diana, the Roman goddess of the moon and wild nature), and most of them acknowledge only the Goddess.

The Wheel of the Year

Despite their very separate identities, there are several links between Wiccans and Druids. Both traditions emphasize the centrality of Nature and the Seasons. Members of both see themselves as the earth's guardians and worshippers. Both believe in the sanctity of earth and all living things.

The shared perceptions of Druidry and Wicca are illustrated by the celebration of the eight-fold year, seen as an endlessly rotating wheel – or Wheel of the Year (see above). The eight points in the year's cycle, which are the focus of special rituals, are the summer and winter solstices (midsummer and midwinter), the autumn and spring equinoxes (when day and night are of equal length), and the mid-points between them. These mid-points are called by the old Celtic seasonal names (p. 35) and the cycle is based on the old pagan seasonal celebrations which marked these critical points in the year.

Samhain – Celtic New Year: 31 October to 2 November; equivalent to Hallowe'en; the time for culling of livestock.

Yule – Winter Solstice: 21 to 22 December; equivalent to Christmas.

Imbolc – 1 to 2 February; lambing time.

Spring Equinox – 20/21 March.

Beltane – 1 May; equivalent to our May Day; livestock driven out to hill pasture.

Midsummer – Summer Solstice: 21 to 22 June.

Lughnasadh – 1 August; harvest-time.

Autumn Equinox – 22/23 September.

In this eight-fold festival cycle, Druids have found a 'structure for worship and celebration which has a profound psychological value and elegance' (Philip Carr-Gomm).

THE WICCAN

Journal of The Pagan Federation, Europe's foremost Pagan body

Number 111   **Beltane 1994**   £2

The front cover of the quarterly magazine of Neo-Paganism, The Wiccan, published by the Pagan Federation. The journal has now changed its name to Pagan Dawn, and deals with issues relating to Wicca, Druidry, Odinism and Shamanism.

THE CEREMONIES CONDUCTED by modern Druids generally take place in the open, close to Nature, and, where possible, at ancient cult sites, especially stone circles. Annual celebrations include the seasonal festivals, and central to Druid worship is the ceremony of the marriage between the Sun God and the Earth Mother.

THE GORSEDD BARDS OF CAER ABIRI

The Druid group known as the Gorsedd Bards of Caer Abiri was founded at Avebury (Caer Abiri) on 23 September 1993. The rituals carried out at Avebury (below) are associated with the solar cycle, the annual death and rebirth of the Sun God and his ever-changing relationship with the Earth Goddess. Handfastings and child-blessings take place in the ancient stone circle, as does the admittance of new members.

New initiates gather at the centre of a circle formed by the assembled Druids, who direct the spirit of Bardism (the Awen) towards the newcomers. Once they are perceived to have received this spiritual energy, the new members are blessed by the assembly.

The sixty-strong Gorsedd includes singers, writers and poets, along with members of recognized Druid Orders, Wiccans, Shamans and Christians. The Gorsedd Bards of Caer Abiri welcome 'everyone of good heart'.

PERSONAL CELEBRATION
AT AVEBURY
**'To thee the Creator, to thee,
the Powerful, I offer this fresh
bud, new fruit of the ancient
tree....'**
Extract from the blessing ceremony
of a child at the Avebury Druidic
assembly on the Autumn Equinox,
1993

*The presentation of children is the
equivalent of a Christian baptism,
and serves to acknowledge and
introduce the infant to the Druid
fellowship. 'Handfasting', a
Druidic form of marriage, also
takes place at public gatherings.*

*The 180-ft (55-m) high Cerne
Abbas Giant in Dorset, carved
into the chalk hillside probably in
the Romano-British period. About
70 ft (20 m) above him is a double
enclosure where, it is recorded in
the early 1900s, local villagers
enacted fertility rituals around a
maypole at Beltane (p. 35) on
1 May; the custom was no doubt
inspired by the all-too-evident
virility of the image. The giant's
club has caused him to be linked
with the Irish god, the Daghda, but
he may be a native British
equivalent of the Graeco-Roman
demi-god Hercules.*

A main tenet of Druidry is the promotion of peace. Each ceremony begins with a salutation of 'Peace to the Quarters', a display of the perception that peace radiates out to all parts of the earth from the centre of ritual.

Chief, Pendragon and Scribe

In many Druid Orders, members have 'Order' names, given to them at their initiation. The Chief Druid Ross Nichols was given the name Nuinn (the Irish word for Ash Tree); the Druid names generally reflect some aspect of the natural world, very often trees or plants.

In order to enter some of the stricter orders, an aspiring initiate has to have his/her horoscope cast and studied by the three highest officers: the Triad, known as the Chief, the Pendragon and the Scribe. Initiation rites often take place at a significant date in the Druids' calendar: a popular occasion for this is the May Day Feast of Beltane. The location of the ceremony is also carefully chosen: Glastonbury Tor, Primrose Hill, Parliament Hill and Tower Hill are all favoured locations for initiation and other Druid ceremonies, together with Stonehenge, Avebury and other ancient monuments.

Glastonbury Tor, Somerset, a site where Neo-Pagan rituals and celebrations take place at midsummer and other seasonal festivals. There is no evidence for prehistoric settlement on the Tor, although excavations have revealed material dating to the sixth century AD. *There was an early Iron Age lake settlement on the low-lying land in the vicinity of the Tor.*

'Chief Druid of the British Druid Order, Bard of the Gorsedd of Caer Abiri, Noble Grand Wizard of the Ancient Brother- and Sisterhood of Pre-Cambrian Dormice.'
The affiliations of Philip Shallcrass, Editor of the quarterly magazine *The Druids' Voice*

THE BRITISH DRUID ORDER is just one of the many modern Druid Orders that have grown up in Europe, America and Australia in recent years. Despite their varied rules and customs, the Orders have much in common and are united by the Council of British Druids, a debating forum at which issues concerning the different Orders are discussed. Each Order enjoys full autonomy but the avowed aim shared by all is to spread 'Justice, Philanthropy, Brotherly Love, Unity, Peace and Concord throughout the World'.

Some Druid Orders are small and localized, others have thousands of members. The Ancient Order of Druids (AOD) is one of the oldest and largest of the extant groups, tracing its foundation back to Henry Hurle's Order, established in 1781 (p. 147). The AOD has Lodges all over the world and more than 3,000 members. Most Lodges are for men only, but some female ones now exist. The Order has strong links with Freemasonry and Rotary Clubs, and is actively involved with charitable activities, including Children in Need. It was the Albion Lodge of the AOD that admitted the young Winston Churchill at a ceremony in Blenheim Park in August 1908 (p. 170).

In America, A Druid Fellowship (ADF) (see below) and Keltria are among the most prominent Druid organizations.

A 'WORLD WIDE WEB' OF DRUIDRY

*T*here are Druid Orders all over the world. The raison d'être of the Irish Pagan movement, set up at Samhain in 1993, is the 'Sacred Isle Healing Project' which is dedicated to peace in Ireland and the healing and protection of the land. The École Druidique des Gaulois was created in France in 1988; it believes in the rebuilding of Europe on a common Druidic foundation. Druid Lodges have existed in Germany since 1872; unfortunately some members there are associated with right-wing nationalism and neo-Nazi activities. From Germany, the movement spread to Switzerland, Sweden and Denmark. Neo-Druidism was established in Australia in 1851; there are now Lodges in four of the six states. There is even a group of Hassidic Druids, consisting of former Jews who retain some aspects of their Hebrew tradition while adopting Druidic spiritual doctrine.

In the USA, Druidry has many followers, with the ADF and Keltria being among the most prominent Orders. Other groups include the Schismatic Druids of North America, and the Golden Gate Group in San Francisco, which is an organization for gay and lesbian Druids. This group performs Druidic rituals in a stone circle they have built in the Golden Gate Park, dedicated to Druid members who have died from AIDS.

There are even Druid web-sites on the Internet, connecting the disparate Druidic groups.

The Auberge des Druide (the Druid's Inn), in a village between Perros Guirec and Roscoff in Brittany, France; just one of the many 'Druid' names used today in western Europe.

THE INSULAR ORDER OF DRUIDS (IOD)

'Life is an Art and Science of self-becoming.'

The Insular Order of Druids is a relatively new Order, founded at Stonehenge at the 1993 Summer Solstice. Its 'Mother Grove' (Council) is in Portsmouth and the group began with public meetings in The Druids' Arms, in Binstead Road. When permitted, the IOD celebrate the eight-fold year at Stonehenge. The IOD is concerned with the recreation of 'authentic' Celtic ritual (without the bloodshed, they stress), and members venerate the Earth as Mother. Members are concerned with the attainment of spirituality, which the Druids call 'Awen', and through which people become their true 'Oak Wise' selves.

Members of the IOD describe themselves as a shamanic working group of Druids, who promote the spiritual and cultic skills of adherents, and campaign against religious prejudice. Like the AOD, they maintain an active crusade for the freedom to worship at Stonehenge.

Three grades of Druidry are recognized within the Order: Bard/Fili, Ovate/Vate and Druid. The Bardic grade is concerned with storytelling, music and writing; the Ovates are active in divination and philosophy. The Druid grade promotes the attainment of harmony with the natural world.

The induction of Winston Churchill into the Albion Lodge of the Ancient Order of Druids at Blenheim, near Oxford, in August 1908. The initiation ceremony seems to have been a mixture of civic occasion and inauguration ritual: Druids in white robes and long (false) white beards jostle with civic dignitaries and amused onlookers.

The Order of Bards, Ovates and Druids (OBOD)

'The greatest value of the OBOD postal course is this: it exists, it is available. Precious insights are being passed along. The mysteries are being shared ...'
A Vermont student of the OBOD correspondence course

A large Druid Order – with over 4,000 members – which is perhaps the most active in contemporary Druidry, is the Order of Bards, Ovates and Druids, which was constituted in 1964. The OBOD is a teaching Order which, for more than ten years, has run a correspondence course and workshops on Druidry for over 3,000 people. It is also responsible for the Campaign for Individual Ecological Responsibility, and a Sacred Tree Planting Programme. Unlike the Ancient Order of Druids, the OBOD promotes sexual equality. The OBOD traces its origins to Toland's Primrose Hill ceremony of 1717 (p. 147). The Order publishes a monthly journal, *Touchstone*.

The modern Order has two main aims: to help each individual to develop his/her spiritual, intellectual, emotional, physical and artistic potential; and to cherish and protect the natural world. The Gaelic name of the Order, *Cairdeas Mor Shaoghal Nan Druidh* means 'A Worldwide Fellowship of Druids'.

A Druid Fellowship (ADF)

An independent group interested in finding out about ancient Druids formed A Druid Fellowship in 1983. The ADF later became a Neo-Pagan Order, and is now one of the most widespread Druid groups in the English-speaking world, with a strong presence both in Britain and America. Indeed, the ADF is the largest American Druid Order, with a 51 per cent female membership. The Order has strong links with Wicca. It has a Mother Grove and many daughter groves, consisting of three or more voting members, over the age of eighteen, who live in the same region and who meet at least twice a month to study and practise Druidism.

Some other Druid groups

Druid Orders are sometimes based in particular localities: the Glastonbury Order operates mainly in the southwest of Britain, and celebrates festivals on Glastonbury Tor; the Gorsedd Bards of Caer Abiri belong to Avebury; the Grove of the Four Elements is based in London, as is the London Druid Group. The Ancient Druid Order worships at Stonehenge (when allowed to do so) and at Tower Hill and Primrose Hill in London.

Some Orders are concerned as much with Bardic arts as with Druidry *per se*: the principal aim of the Secular Order of Druids is to establish a National Eisteddfod at Stonehenge; the Bardic Order Group is also concerned with performing arts. The British Druid Order, founded in 1979, models its teachings on the Welsh Bardic Tradition. Like many other Orders, it has three grades of membership: Bard (poet/seer); Ofydd (philosopher) and Derwydd (Druid).

A Midsummer poetry gathering of the Northumbrian Grove of the Order of Bards, Ovates and Druids (OBOD), one of the largest modern Druid Orders.

The Neolithic stone circle at Avebury, Wiltshire, which – like Stonehenge – is a focus for Neo-Druid ritual and spirituality, although it has nothing whatever to do with ancient Druidism.

STONEHENGE PROHIBITED

'Power,
Power of the Stones
Rising from the Earth
Cascading down as light
From the myriad stars
That spackle night's cloak.'
Dylan of the Insular Order of Druids,
Song of the Stones, 1994

'Now people try to tell us we're
no longer free to roam
The holy living landscape that
once we called our home.
They waste our time and money trying
to keep us from the bones
That our blessed Mother gave us
to erect as standing stones.'
Philip Shallcrass, *The Druid and the Land*, 1994

'The Grand Conventional Festival of the Britons' at Stonehenge from Samuel Meyrick and Charles Smith's Costume of the Original Inhabitants of the British Isles, 1815. The erroneous link between Stonehenge and the Druids has led to many romantic notions of the activities which occurred within the stones, including this imaginative view of the ancient Britons and their Druids performing sacrifices at Stonehenge. Today, many Druid Orders still believe that it is their right to perform their rituals at the site, a belief which has led to numerous clashes between Druids and the authorities.

ON 14 SEPTEMBER 1995, *The Times* printed an article about a certain Arthur Uther Pendragon, a self-styled Druid who, the previous day, had been acquitted of taking part in a prohibited assembly at Stonehenge. He had appeared before Salisbury magistrates accused of 'trespassory assembly', an offence under the new British Criminal Justice Act. Uther Pendragon was arrested when he visited Stonehenge for the summer solstice, and his prosecution was the first of its kind under the new act. The hearing was attended by fellow Druids in their ceremonial robes.

The Criminal Justice Act limits the size of assemblies on public property. The human rights organization, Liberty, acted on behalf of Pendragon, and the case failed because although

a gathering of twenty people is the maximum permitted and twenty-seven Druids were present, they split into smaller groups when challenged.

Pendragon, who believes himself to be a reincarnation of King Arthur, took his oath on his sword, Excalibur, and gave his title as Honorary Pendragon of the Glastonbury Order of Druids. His intention had been to celebrate Midsummer Day by performing a dawn ceremony as close as possible to Stonehenge. He customarily maintained all-night vigils here four times a year (at the solstices and equinoxes), followed by rituals at dawn.

'Press Passes and Druids only'

By the late nineteenth century, latter-day Druid groups were using Stonehenge on ceremonial occasions, particularly at the summer and winter solstices. These rituals were a hotchpotch of ancient tradition (gleaned from Classical literature) and invention. In 1900, the then owner of Stonehenge, Sir Edward Antrobus, fenced off the monument after the collapse of an upright. At the next midsummer festival, the police ejected the Chief Druid, who then soundly and

Stonehenge has become a focus for many Neo-Pagan groups who wish to have free access to the monument. (Above) Two Druids stand outside the perimeter fence of Stonehenge while numerous security guards look on, and (left) another Neo-Pagan waits patiently in the hope of gaining entry to the sacred site.

A letter from a member of the British Circle of the Church of the Universal Bond to the Office of Works – to which the responsibilities for Stonehenge had been transferred when Cecil Chubb offered it to the nation – protesting at the restrictions put on the Druid Orders wishing to use Stonehenge for their religious ceremonies.

— Cathoir Ghall. — Glastonbury.

An Druidh Uileach Braithreachas.

Church of the Universal Bond

(BRITISH CIRCLE).

Inheriting the Philosophy and Aspiration of The Most Ancient Faith, by Obedience to the Holy Law, and the Preaching of the Word.

Los Hommes de la Religion Blanche. NANTES, FRANCE.
योग विविधः : एतानिर्विरक्षप्रुषुमातृ विभाग्नि Ma' Ling
體道 توحيد
Canton. China. TRIPOLI N.AFRICA.
המות כרמל Mount Carmel, Lebanon Syria
Glasgow. Dublin. & Llandudno.

THOMAS IRELAND (TAMAS EIRIN),

Corresponding Councillor,

57, CAVENDISH ROAD,

LONDON, S.W. 12.

13th. June, '23.

FROM THE OFFICE OF THE CHOSEN CHIEF, AND THE COUNCIL OF ARCH DASTURS, DRUIDS, BARDS AND OVATES.

To The Right Hon. Sir John Baird,
First Commissioner of H.M. Office of Works,
Storey s Gate. S.W.

Sir,

Pardon my addressing you in person instead of officially. I am now gazing across the Plain where once the people of my faith held sway, and I cannot avoid reflecting upon the great cry that has been raised against the present rulers of Russia by reason of their attack upon religion. It is now that I feel the great wrong that has been done to our people, and, because of this, I am writing to you in order that whatever takes place in the near future, you may possess the necessary facts with which your questions in the House of Commons may be answered.

Our Order has never failed in the past to hold its annual meetings within the enclosure of Cathoir Ghall, (Stonehenge) a place raised in the name of All Father by our forbears. Twenty years ago by reason publicly cursed Sir Edward. But fifteen years later, Stonehenge was under new ownership, and Sir Cecil Chubb gave it to the nation at an official Government ceremony attended by Druids.

Stonehenge continues as a focus for Druidic ritual, especially on Midsummer Day. It has been a sacred place favoured by several Orders, including The British Circle of the Church of the Universal Bond (a remnant of the Ancient Order of Druids originally set up by Henry Hurle in 1781, p. 147).

Because of ever increasing numbers of visitors, the preservation of Stonehenge has been a matter of concern since the 1960s. Only then, too, did vandalism become a problem. In 1962, barbed wire fences were erected to protect the monument, though the Druids were still allowed in for special ceremonies. From the early 1970s, at the summer solstice, the Druids have kept a midnight vigil at the disc barrow on Normanton Down, followed by a long pre-dawn ceremony at Stonehenge, culminating in the blowing of bronze horns to greet the dawning of Midsummer Day. Other ritual activities take place throughout the day. In the 1970s and early 1980s the Druids were allowed in by special arrangement, and a sign at the entrance to the monument read 'Press Passes and Druids only permitted'.

Druids, Stonehenge and the 1990s

The Criminal Justice Act, as we have seen, has curtailed the gathering of large Druid groups at Stonehenge. However, on the evening of 24 June 1995, a party of six adult Druids (three men and three women) and two children entered the monument unopposed and proceeded to perform rituals in celebration of Midsummer Day. To the accompaniment of drums, prayers were addressed to the Ancestral Spirits, the Animal Powers and the Four Quarters of the Sacred Circle. Prayers were also said for the freedom of

King Arthur Uther Pendragon leaves the High Court in London after failing to block a court order which will pave the way for the demolition of Camelot. Uther Pendragon has been involved in many attempts to uphold his Druidic beliefs and rights, including a prohibited gathering at Stonehenge at the summer solstice in 1995.

A gathering at dawn on Midsummer Day of the British Circle of the Church of the Universal Bond at Stonehenge in 1956.

access to the ancient stones. After the ninety-minute-long ceremony, the English Heritage Security Guards ushered out the group and ushered in the next.

This small Druidic group was granted access to Stonehenge after obtaining written permission from English Heritage, and on payment of a fee. Druids object to this, their argument being that Christians and followers of other major religions do not have to pay for entry to churches, mosques, synagogues or Sikh temples. However, the genuine Druids are paying the price for the abuse of the stones by heedless, irresponsible hangers-on, who have climbed the fences, trampled on the stones and have even been caught abseiling down the sarsen uprights.

WHAT IS STONEHENGE?

Stonehenge is an ancient monument which is unique in the world. The site, on Salisbury Plain in Wiltshire (southern England), was in active use from about 3000 to 1000 BC. In its first (Neolithic) phase, it consisted of a 'henge', a circular enclosure bounded by a bank and ditch. By c. 2500 BC, in the late Neolithic, a stone monument was erected comprising two concentric circles of bluestones brought from the Preseli Hills of west Wales, about 150 miles (240 km) away. The entrance of the new stone monument was aligned on the midsummer sunrise. About 100 years after the bluestone settings were erected, a new structure was built, using local stones (known as sarsens), replacing the old bluestone circles. In its final form, c. 1600 BC, it consisted of stone circles and inner horseshoes of sarsens and bluestones, with uprights capped by horizontal lintels, once again oriented towards the midsummer sunrise.

There can be no doubt that Stonehenge was erected so that the midsummer sunrise could be observed by people standing in the centre of the monument. Such observers would also have been able to mark the limits of the rising and setting sun at the summer and winter solstices, and would therefore have been able to calculate the correct times both for religious festivals and for seasonal farming activities. For its original builders, Stonehenge may thus have been both an observatory and a solar temple.

*'Grant, O God/dess/Spirit, thy protection
and in protection, strength
and in strength, humility
and in humility, understanding
and in understanding, knowledge
and in knowledge, the knowledge of justice
and in the knowledge of it, the love of it
and in the love of it, the love of all existences
and in the love of all existences, the love of
God/dess/Spirit and all goodness'*

The prayer which is said to unite all Druids everywhere,
Mathew McCabe (OBOD)

MODERN DRUIDRY ESPOUSES a strong belief in a link between the present and the remote past, hence the focus on megalithic stone circles. Modern Druids venerate the earth, and to them all life is sacred and worthy of protection. For them there is no Heaven as such: they are completely tied to earthly existence. Druidry is a natural rather than a revealed religion and, in fact, it can be both a religion and a philosophy. Many Druids are Pagans but some are Christians: whilst some believe in the old gods of Sun and Earth, others simply perceive spirituality in all living things, and therefore see no conflict between Druidry and Christianity. Druidry prides itself in its ability to build bridges between faiths. The purpose of following the Druidic path is to seek a deeper understanding of Nature, the Planet and oneself. All Druids are deeply committed to the conservationist cause. Some adherents to the cult have a strong belief that Nature is finite and that the world will, sooner or later, come to a sudden end.

The Circle

The concept of cyclicity or circularity is central to Druid belief and practice. Life is perceived as a circle, endlessly turning in a cycle of life, death, regeneration and rebirth. The earth, the year and even the day are seen as cyclical. The pivot of all this is the Sun, which is venerated as a life-force. The human and earthly cycle are seen as closely intertwined.

The symbolism of the circle – representative of wholeness and eternity – pervades all Druid thinking; whenever possible, Druid ceremonies take place at ancient stone circles, although the sacred circle can be made of stones, trees or people. Worshippers stand in a circle for meditation and ritual. The circumference of the circle represents the cycle of life and death; the eight seasonal ceremonies are situated at the eight compass points. At the centre of the circle is the 'still point of Being and No-Being' or 'Place of Integration'. The space inside the circle is the sacred area, in which human beings can reach the spiritual plane.

The Druid Circle of the Year

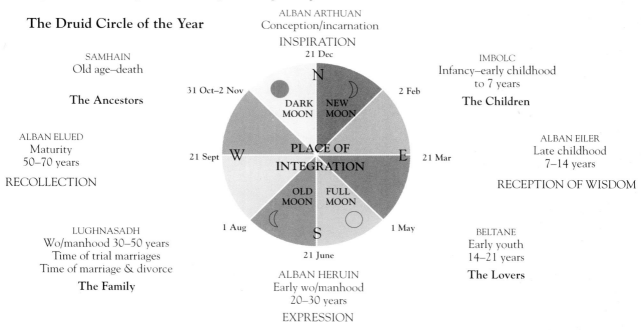

ALBAN ARTHUAN
Conception/incarnation
INSPIRATION
21 Dec

SAMHAIN
Old age–death

The Ancestors

IMBOLC
Infancy–early childhood
to 7 years

The Children

ALBAN ELUED
Maturity
50–70 years

RECOLLECTION

ALBAN EILER
Late childhood
7–14 years

RECEPTION OF WISDOM

31 Oct–2 Nov

DARK MOON NEW MOON

2 Feb

21 Sept W PLACE OF INTEGRATION E 21 Mar

OLD MOON FULL MOON

1 Aug 1 May

LUGHNASADH
Wo/manhood 30–50 years
Time of trial marriages
Time of marriage & divorce

The Family

BELTANE
Early youth
14–21 years

The Lovers

21 June

ALBAN HERUIN
Early wo/manhood
20–30 years

EXPRESSION

Spiritual energy

'The Richness of Place
The Richness of Time
The Treasures of the Tribe
The Treasures of the Ancestors
The Joy of the Journey.'
Philip Carr-Gomm, *The Druid Tradition*, 1991

These are all spiritual forces which Druids believe endow them with energy. Reincarnation is an important Neo-Druid tenet, and the idea of continual rebirth is linked to the recognition of the Spirit of the Journey, which accompanies the transmigrating soul.

A second source of energy is the Spirit of Place, which dwells in the sacred landscape and in all localities within it. Druids believe that all the land possesses sanctity but that particular features are nodal points: wells and stone circles, for instance. Ley lines convey the earth's energy between these centres or 'pulse-points'. Druids practise geomancy, the study of the way ancient sites are placed in relation to the earth's force.

Modern Druids believe that a further energy-source emanates from the Ancestors. Caesar refers to the ancient Gauls' belief in a common ancestor, the god Dis Pater, and, for today's Druids, ancestors provide an important connection between the past and present. There is a belief that ancient holy sites, like Stonehenge and Avebury, are still inhabited by ancestral spirits, and are thus equally sacred to modern Pagan worshippers.

The joy of Druidry

'Summer solstice
day of pleasure
joy to be there
Singing praises
as the year begins to wane.'
Dylan of the IOD, *Song of the Stones*, 1994

Modern Druids (and Wiccans) emphasize the 'fun' element in their religion, as well as its serious messages of peace and conservation. Nature is something to celebrate, to praise and in which to rejoice. The various ceremonies and festivals are not grim, penitential affairs but occasions for gatherings, merry-making and thanksgiving for the glory of Nature and for fellowship.

One of the Avebury stones, defaced in 1996 allegedly by Neo-Pagans.

THE SACRED TREE

Trees are revered as providers of food, air and wood. Present-day Druids have adopted the oak as their tree, seeing it as symbolic of tradition, wisdom and longevity. In this they follow the comments of Classical authors like Pliny and Lucan, who spoke of the close link between Druids and oak trees. Pliny's reference to the association between mistletoe and fertility has also been woven into modern Druid lore: mistletoe-berry juice is symbolic of male sperm.

Some Graeco-Roman writers alluded to other groups, namely the Ovates and the Bards. These also exist within the modern Druid tradition, the word of the Bardic poets being sacred. The Bardic tree is the birch, symbolic of pioneering and new beginnings. Neo-Druid Ovates are particularly responsible for telling the future, and are able to understand 'the hidden dynamics of time'. Ovates use hazel for water-divining, but their sacred tree is the yew, which stands for death, rebirth and eternity.

(Right) The 'Major Oak' in Sherwood Forest, mentioned in the legend of Robin Hood, is an extremely old oak tree which has become a popular shrine visited by many each year.

*'Authorities who govern us have issued fine decrees
To build motorways through wildwoods,
and root up all the trees,
While licences for factories are
granted without heed,
To poison air and water in the holy name of greed.'*
Philip Shallcrass, *The Druid and the Land*, 1994

AT A RECENT British conference on contemporary Paganism, a spokesperson from the Dragon Environmental Project argued that western societies had divorced themselves from the Earth by adopting the philosophy that spiritual and material worlds are completely separate. The Dragon Project representative stated that this schism lies behind the ecological destruction currently taking place. His advice to 'Green' Pagans was to confront the bulldozers and to perform Pagan rituals on threatened land.

The perception of many present-day Druids and other Neo-Pagans is that the sacred landscape is being violated by uncontrolled modern development. As they see it, the problem arises from an imbalance of the relationship between materialism and spirituality. Human beings should be – but are not – in harmony with Nature, thus causing a dysfunction in the well-being of the Planet which will, if not halted, lead to its demise.

A 'Green' religion

We have seen that a central tenet of modern Druidism is the search for an ever-developing personal relationship between themselves and the numinous land. Natural features – such as trees and water – are foci of spirituality and veneration as are ancient monuments, which belong to the ancestors and are perceived as an integral element within the living landscape.

Like the formal conservationist organizations, such as Greenpeace and Friends of the Earth, Druids challenge major new road schemes and other ecological threats to the earth, both because undeveloped land is so scarce (particularly in overpopulated Britain) and because of pollution. Druids also take issue with governments over such matters as the limitation of opportunity for archaeologists to carry out rescue excavations on sites threatened by construction. At the time of writing, the clash between Neo-Pagan conservationists and the Establishment is a topical issue. The proliferation of new road schemes and new building programmes

remains a cause of grave concern to a movement which promotes the preservation of Nature as its fundamental tenet.

This book began with ancient Druids and has ended with modern ones. It is fitting to conclude with a comment by a contemporary Druid:

'… our task is not to try to recreate a Druidry that existed thousands of years ago, but instead to respond to the source and interpret it for today. If we can do this, the gap between ancient Druids and modern ones disappears …'
Philip Carr-Gomm, *Touchstone*, June 1996

Neo-Pagans joined protesters against the building of a new road bypassing Newbury town centre, in southern England. The destruction of ancient woodland by the road has caused anger among ecologically concerned groups.

Directory of Modern Druid Organizations

There are far too many groups devoted to Druidry, Neo-Paganism or the revival of ancient Celtic beliefs throughout the world to provide a complete list here. However, the list that follows is indicative of the widespread nature of the modern Druidic doctrine and the different interpretations given to it and the ancient Druidic past.

Groups in the United Kingdom

Aes Dana
c/o Fiona Davidson
Dun Cauld Cottage
Cauldhame, Kippen,
Scotland FK8 3HL
This group teaches and practises the traditional Bardic arts of music, poetry, song and storytelling, finding in the spirit that inspires these arts a source of spiritual empowerment.

Ancient and Modern Druid Order
Hengist McStone
c/o 1 Crown Walk
Uxbridge, England UB8 1SW

Ancient Order of Druids
c/o Mr R. Hudson
174 Tompkinson Road,
Nuneaton, Warwickshire,
England CV10 8BW
Founded in London in 1781 by Henry Hurle. Although the AOD is on the whole a gentleman's charitable and mutual aid society, it has performed Druid ceremonies at Stonehenge and elsewhere. Winston Churchill was inaugurated into this Order in 1908. The order has had several offshoots during its existence, including the United Ancient Order of Druids, which, along with AOD groups, founded the International Grand Lodge of Druidism in 1913. The AOD has lodges worldwide, including groups in the West Indies and South America. Publications include, *The Druid: The Newsletter of the*

Ancient Order of Druids which is circulated worldwide.

British Druid Order
c/o Philip Shallcrass
and Emma Restall Orr
PO Box 29, St Leonards-on-Sea
East Sussex, England TN37 7YP
Founded in 1979 to teach and practise Druidry as native spirituality, as a shamanic path and as a means to the healing of the self, society and ecosphere. The BDO offers workshops, seminars, courses, open rituals and other gatherings. Publications, including the newsletter *Tooth and Claw* and *The Druids' Voice: Magazine of Contemporary Druidry.*

Charnwood Grove of Druids
c/o Heather and Mark Graham
74 Cobden Street
Loughborough, Leicestershire,
England LE11 1AQ
Locally based grove teaching and practising Druidry as a spiritual path rooted in Celtic tradition and the Earth, open to followers of all religions or none.

Clan Dalriada
Dun na Beatha
2 Brathwic Place
Brodick, Isle of Arran,
Scotland KA27 8BN
This non-Neo-Pagan group focuses on a revival of ancient Celtic religious beliefs, with an emphasis on the lifestyle and daily customs of the ancient Celts, rather than the ritualistic elements common in other Celtic religious groups.

College of Druidism
4a Minto Street
Edinburgh, Scotland EH7 4AN
Founded by Kaledon Naddair a Pictish shaman. Publishes a correspondence course and other literature.

Cotswold Order of Druids
c/o 12 Sochi Court
Edinburgh Place

Cheltenham, Gloucestershire,
England GL51 7RR

Council of British Druid Orders
c/o Liaison Officer
BM Oakgrove
London, England WC1 3XX
Founded in 1989 to promote dialogue between British Druids. Currently has about a dozen member orders. Holds an annual open summer solstice ceremony.

Druid Clan of Dana
c/o Caroline Wise
and Steve Wilson
BM Grasshopper
London, England WC1N 3XX
Founded by Lawrence Durdin-Robertson and Olivia Robertson under the aegis of the Fellowship of Isis to teach and practise Druidry based mainly on Irish tradition. Postal course and other publications, including occasional journal, *Aisling.*

The Druid Order – An Druidh Uileach Braithrearchas, The British Circle of the Universal Bond
23 Thornsett Road
London, England SE20 7XB
This group is traditionally believed to be the product of John Tolland's meeting with British, Irish and French Druids in 1717 in the Apple Tree Tavern in Covent Garden, London. The group 'endeavours to present universal wisdom in a practical form. It is not a cult or a creed, but a system of training in the principles of philosophy, science and religion for those seeking definite instruction. The object is not so much to know as to become.'

Glastonbury Order of Druids
c/o Rollo Maughfling
Dove House, Barton St David
Somerset, England TA11 6DF

Gorsedd Bards of Caer Abiri
c/o BDO, PO Box 29
St Leonards-on-Sea

East Sussex,
England TN37 7YP
Open multi-faith group meeting to celebrate the eight festivals modern Paganism among the stone circles of Avebury, Wilts to promote understanding and kinship between faiths and to encourage reverence and creativity. Irregular newsletter funded by voluntary donation.

Insular Order of Druids
c/o Membership Secretary
Labyrinth, 2 Victoria Road So
Southsea, Portsmouth,
Hampshire, England
PO5 2DF
Founded at the summer solstic 1993, this group teaches and practises Druidry as 'an Art an Science of Self-becoming'. It concerned with the recreation authentic Celtic ritual.

International Grand Lodge of Druidism
c/o A.J. Smith
36 Queens Road
Great Yarmouth,
England NR30 3JR
British lodge of the IGLD whi was founded by representative the UAOD and the AOD fro various countries worldwide; s Germany, Switzerland and Australia for addresses of IGL lodges in those countries.

Iolo Morgannwg Fellowship
c/o Thomas Daffern
Kingsley Hall, Grace Road,
London, England E3 3HJ
Founded to promote research understanding of the life and works of the seminal eighteen century Druid revivalist, Iolo Morgannwg. Membership free open to all.

Irish Wicca
c/o Janet and Stewart Farrar
Herne's Cottage
Ethelstown, Kells,
County Meath, Ireland

Founded in 1970, this Wicca group celebrates the gods and goddesses of the ancient Celts.

London Druid Group
c/o The Secretary
74 Riversmeet, Hertford,
England SG14 1LE
Founded prior to 1939 to research, teach and practise Druidism. Regular open meetings held in London.

Loyal Arthurian Warband
c/o King Arthur Pendragon
10 Sine Close
Farnborough, Hampshire,
England GU14 8HG
Members swear by Excalibur to uphold the principles of Truth, Honour and Justice. LAW campaigns for free access to sacred sites and against environmental damage by road schemes etc. Quarterly newsletter, *Awen*.

Order of Bards, Ovates and Druids
PO Box 1333, Lewes
East Sussex, England BN7 3ZG
Founded in 1964, this is the largest modern Druid Order with members worldwide. OBOD publish a postal course in 36 monthly packages with full tutorial support and a regular newsletter, *Touchstone*. The Order also runs retreats, camps and workshops.

Pagan Federation
BM Box 7097, London,
England WC1N 3XX
Founded in 1971, this Pagan network sponsors events, contacts, conferences etc., to increase the understanding of Paganism, including Druidry, Wicca, Goddess Spirituality and Heathenism. It publishes educational material and a quarterly magazine, *Pagan Dawn*.

Stargrove
BM Stargrove
London, England WC1N 3XX
This group runs an original course on Druidry, under the name of the Druidic College of Albion, with an emphasis on the study of the *Mabinogion* and Bardic star myths. Affiliated to the Druid Clan of Dana within the Fellowship of Isis, Stargrove offers 'a structured approach to a living tradition without dogma'.

United Ancient Order of Druids
c/o Mr P.G. Lester, Druids Hall
8 Perry Road
Bristol, BS1 5QB
This group, an offshoot of Henry Hurle's Ancient Order of Druids, was founded in 1833 as a benefit society. There is an international network of UAOD lodges; however, each lodge is autonomous.

Whitestone
PO Box 118, Horley,
Surrey, England RH6 9FL
This group belongs to the British Council of Druid Orders.

Groups in the United States of America

A Druid Fellowship:
Ar nDraiocht Fein
Office of the Registrar
PO Box 516, East Syracuse,
New York 13057-0516
The largest Neo-Pagan group in America, which offers a wide range of teaching materials and publications.

Carleton College Archives:
International Druid Archives
300 North College Street,
Northfield,
Minnesota 55057
Not actually a Druid Order, but a useful resource for people studying and researching Druidry. Established under the aegis of the Reformed Druids of North America.

Henge of Keltria
PO Box 48369, Minneapolis
Minnesota 55448
Neo-Pagan group dedicated to protecting and preserving Mother Earth, honouring the ancestors, revering the spirits of nature and worshipping the ancient Celtic gods and goddesses. The group provides information and training in Druidism, with a correspondence course and other publications including the quarterly journal, *Keltria: Journal of Druidism and Celtic Magick*.

Reformed Druids of North America
c/o Michael Scharding
Carleton College, Northfield,
Minnesota 55057
Founded in 1963 on the campus at Carleton College, the RDNA have a network of groves throughout America.

Groups in Europe

Assemblées Armorique Atlantique de la Tradition des Druides
c/o Michel Raoult
La Pommeraie-Avalon
29252 Plouezoc'h,
Brittany, France
This group is affiliated with the Council of the British Druid Orders, and has links with numerous other Druid groups in Europe.

Collège des Druides, Bardes et Ovates des Gaules
c/o André Logeat
14 Route de Préval
Perdreauville, 78200 Mantes-la-Jolie, France

Forenede Gamle Druid Orden
c/o Knut Sjövorr
The Old Bakery, Church Road,
Orpington, Kent BR6 7RE
The FGDO is the Norwegian branch of the UAOD.

International Grand Lodge of Druidism
Bro Jurgen W. Rösler
Masurenweg 16
61118 Bad Vilbel, Germany

International Grand Lodge of Druidism
c/o Heinz Hartmann,
Kesslernmatt Strasse 79, 8965
Berikon, Switzerland

Oaled Drouized Kornog
c/o Alain Rouquette
40 Rue de l'Abbesse
Le Diban, 29630 Plougasnou,
Brittany, France
This group focuses on knowledge rather than beliefs. It has many fields of interest: astrology, ecology, history, symbolism, philosophy. The group's ideology is based on ancient pagan celtic tradition; and fights against racism, fascism, xenophobia and sectarianism.

Vereinigter Alter Orden Der Druiden
c/o OSekr. Herr Henning Keßler, Tirolerring 411 24147
Kiel, Germany
The VAOD is the German branch of the UAOD.

Groups in Australia and New Zealand

International Grand Lodge of Druidism
c/o Mr John C. Butler
15 Ash Avenue,
Bellair, South Australia 5052
This group should also be contacted for information on affiliated groups in New Zealand.

Pan-Pacific Pagan Alliance
c/o Kiri White
PO Box 47, Carnegie,
Victoria 3163
Australia

Pan-Pacific Pagan Alliance
c/o Anna Harrop
21 Nelson Street, Helensville
Auckland, New Zealand

Gorsedds

Breudeureizh Drouized (Breton Gorsedd)
c/o M. Bertrand Borne
'An Neizh' Ker Herri,
29380 St Turian, Brittany

Gorseth Kernow (Cornish Gorsedd)
c/o The Institute of Cornish Studies, Trevenson, Pool,
Redruth, Cornwall

GAZETTEER

The list which follows highlights some important sites, monuments and collections that readers of this book will find useful when following up their interest in the Druids and Celtic religion. Readers should note that current exhibitions and museum displays may be temporary, and that some relevant material is held in reserve collections. Serious students should always contact institutions in advance of their intended visits, so that they can receive expert help from museum and exhibition staff.

AUSTRIA The Strettweg cult-wagon can be seen in the Steiermärkisches Landesmuseum Joanneum, **Graz**. The material from Hallstatt is housed in the Naturhistorisches Museum, **Vienna**; the site of **Hallstatt** itself can be visited and includes some reconstructed tombs, and a number of accessible salt-workings. The Keltenmuseum in **Hallein** has some interesting interpretative displays.

BELGIUM The museums at **Liège** and **Tongeren** (Tongres) contain bronzes and monuments pertaining to religion in Belgic Gaul.

CZECH REPUBLIC The Národní Múzeum, **Prague**, houses the stone cult head from Mšecké Žehrovice and the material from the holy spring at Duchcov, in addition to fine collections of Iron Age art. The *oppidum* at **Závist** is worth a visit.

DENMARK The Nationalmuseet, **Copenhagen**, contains the Gundestrup cauldron, Danish bog bodies – Tollund Man and Juthe Fen Woman – and other material associated with Scandinavian Iron Age ritual practice, particularly that connected to solar cults, such as the Trundholm chariot and the sun drum from Balkåkra. The Brå cauldron is in the **Moesgaard** Forhistorisk Museum.

FRANCE The Musée des Antiquités Nationales, Saint Germain-en-Laye, near **Paris**, possesses an outstanding collection of religious sculpture and bronzes from Iron Age and Romano-Celtic Gaul, including the Euffigneix boar-god and the bronze statuette of Arduinna. The monument of the *Nautes Parisiacae*, which depicts the Gaulish gods Esus and Cernunnos, is on display at the Musée du Moyen Age – Thermes de Cluny in Paris. The Coligny calendar is in the Musée de la Civilisation Gallo-Romaine at Lyon. The hoard from Neuvy-en-Sullias, which includes an image of a possible Druid holding a 'Druid's Egg', is at the Musée Historique et Archéologique de l'Orléanais, **Orléans**. A unique group of triple-faced images of gods and a fine carving of Cernunnos, from the Remic tribal capital, are housed at the Musée Saint-Rémi at **Rheims**. The Musée Granet at **Aix-en-Provence** and the Musée d'Archéologie Méditerranéenne (Centre de la Vieille Charité) at **Marseille** house important sculptured monuments from Entremont and Roquepertuse respectively. Both of these sites can also be visited. The Musée Vivenel at **Compiègne** contains material from the sanctuary at Gournay-sur-Aronde. Finds from Alesia, including a stone image of Epona and the votive offerings from the healing sanctuary of Apollo Moritasgus are on view at the Musée Archéologique at **Alise-Sainte-Reine**. The Musée Bargoin at **Clermont-Ferrand** contains the wooden assemblage from the healing spring-shrine of Sources des Roches de Chamalières, and the votive offerings from Sequana's shrine at *Fontes Sequanae* are in the Musée Archéologique at **Dijon**. The Musée Archéologique at **Metz** contains important material from the Gallo-Roman town, including finds from temples and from a large town cemetery at La Horgne-au-Sablon. The material from the Vix burial and sculpted images of the three Mother-Goddesses from Vertault are at the

Musée Archéologique in **Châtillon-sur-Seine**. The Musée Saint-Raymond at **Toulouse** contains an important series of small stone altars from Pyrenean sanctuaries. The Larzac inscription is in the Musée de **Millau**, and the Greek dedication to Taranis from Orgon is in the Musée Calvet at **Avignon**. The Musée des Alpilles, **Saint-Rémy-de-Provence**, houses the religious material from Glanum, including a triple-horned bull and a figurine of the Gaulish hammer-god, as well as numerous altars to local gods. The site of **Glanum** itself is worth visiting to see the spring-sanctuary to Glanis and the Glanicae – the eponymous spirits of the town. The Musée Archéologique at **Beaune** contains a fine collection of iconography, and the Archéodrome nearby displays reconstructions of Caesar's defences at Alesia. The Musée Rolin at **Autun** also houses an important group of Gaulish religious imagery; nearby is the Temple of Janus, the massive remains of a Romano-Celtic temple. **Nîmes** has a significant collection of carved and inscribed altars in its Musée Lapidaire; the natural spring, which was once the focus of the shrine to the spirits called the Nemausicae, can also be seen in the town. The Musée Archéologique at **Saintes**, capital of the Santones, has some interesting images, including a unique set of double Mother-Goddesses and an equally unique wooden statuette of Epona. **Périgueux** in the Dordogne has a small regional museum with one significant object – a priest's headdress. Nearby is the Tour de Vésone, a great round tower that was once the *cella* (the central chamber where an image of a deity was placed) of a large shrine. Important Breton material may be studied at the Musée de Bretagne at **Rennes**. A well-executed, modern and full-size Romano-Celtic temple reconstruction has been erected on the site of a shrine excavated at **Oisseau-le-Petit**, near Poitiers.

GERMANY The Römisches-Germanisches Museum at **Cologne** contains one of the most important German collections of Romano-Celtic religious material from the Rhineland, including several superbly carved monuments to the Rhenish Mother-Goddesses. The Rheinisches Landesmuseum at **Bonn** contains similar material and, in addition, displays the Pfalzfeld pillar, with its mistletoe-leaf crowned heads and objects from Býčiskála cave. The Württembergisches Landesmuseum at **Stuttgart** contains the grave-finds from the Hochdorf Hallstatt chieftain's grave, the altar to Taranucnus from Böckingen, the Jupiter-Giant column from Hausen-an-der-Zaber and wooden figures from the *Viereckschanze* at Fellbach Schmiden. The material from the Reinheim grave can be seen at the Landesmuseum für Vor- und Frühgeschichte at **Saarbrücken**. The Rheinisches Landesmuseum at **Trier** contains finds from major temples to native deities in the territory of the Treveri, including those from the curative shrine of Apollo and Sirona at Hochscheid and the great healing sanctuary of Lenus Mars at Trier itself. The Schleswig-Holsteinisches Landesmuseum in **Schleswig** contains the Windeby Girl bog body.

GREAT BRITAIN
England The British Museum in **London** contains important collections pertaining to priests and ritual in late Iron Age and Roman Britain, including the regalia from the Hockwold temple, the hoards of headdresses from Barkway and Stony Stratford, the deposits at Felmingham Hall, Deal, and Hounslow, the Waterloo helmet, the Aylesford bucket and some of the Snettisham treasure. It is also the permanent home of Lindow Man. The Ashmolean Museum in **Oxford** contains the votive objects from the Woodeaton Romano-Celtic temple. The Cavenham crowns are in **Ipswich** Museum. **Flag Fen** in Cambridgeshire is the site of a

Bronze Age lake village where numerous votive deposits have been recovered from the water. The site has examples of reconstructed Bronze Age houses on an artificial island.The **Norwich** Castle Museum houses some of the Snettisham jewellery and other local cult material. The Roman Baths Museum at **Bath** offers a superlative display of the hot springs, the excavations, plan, reconstructions, monumental sculpture and small finds (including the curse-tablets) from the great temple to Sulis Minerva; remains of regalia and some inscriptions attest directly to the presence of priests at the sanctuary. **Lydney** is the site of an Iron Age hillfort, Roman iron mines and a late Roman pagan temple – an important cult centre with a large temple, a guest house and a bath suite. Finds from the site are housed in a private museum in Lydney Park, and permission is required to visit. In Cornwall, the well-preserved remains of **Chysauster** Iron Age village are worth visiting.

The Corinium Museum in **Cirencester** and **Gloucester** City Museum house important collections of local religious sculpture. The Willingham Fen sceptre is in the University Museum of Archaeology and Anthropology at **Cambridge**. The regalia from the Farley Heath and Wanborough shrines can be seen at **Guildford** Museum. In the Hadrian's Wall area, there are significant collections of native religious material at the University Museum of Antiquities at **Newcastle-upon-Tyne**, the Corstopitum Museum at **Corbridge** and the site museums at **Housesteads**, **Chesters** and Vindolanda (**Chesterholm**). In Cumbria, the City Museum at **Carlisle** and the Senhouse Museum at **Maryport** house good collections of Romano-Celtic religious imagery and epigraphy.

For those interested in the Druid renaissance of the seventeenth and eighteenth centuries, William Danby's 'Druid Temple' folly can be visited in the grounds of Swinton Hall at **Ilton**, Yorkshire. **Stonehenge** and **Avebury** are also sites associated with the revival of interest in the Druids, in addition to being major foci for modern Druid worship. The author wishes to stress, however, that there is no connection between these megalithic monuments and the ancient Druids.

Scotland The National Museums of Scotland in **Edinburgh**, especially the Museum of Antiquities, contain Iron Age and Romano-British religious material, including the wooden figurine from Ballachulish, the Bu sands egg amulet and the cauldrons from Carlingwark and Blackburn Mill. Also in Edinburgh, the Scottish National Gallery of Modern Art has on display the painting by Noel Halle, 'The Druids' Ceremony'. **Glasgow** Museums: Art Gallery and Museum, Kelvingrove displays the painting by Henry and Hornel, 'The Druids: Bringing in the Mistletoe'.

Wales The National Museums and Galleries of Wales in **Cardiff** contain major finds, including the contents of the votive hoards from Llyn Fawr and Llyn Cerrig Bach. Thomas Jones' painting 'The Bard' can be seen in the Art Gallery here. The Museum of Welsh Life at St Ffagans, Cardiff, has a full-size reconstruction of an Iron Age village, and, at the time of writing, a replica of the Sarn-y-Bryn-Caled timber circle is being erected here. St Ffagans also houses archives pertaining to Iolo Morgannwg, William Price and the Gorsedd y Beirdd. A modern Gorsedd circle can be seen outside the National Museums and Galleries of Wales in Cathays Park, Cardiff. The Royal National Eisteddfod office at Llanishen, also in Cardiff, provides information on the timing and location of the annual National Eisteddfod (which alternates between north and south Wales) and can also provide details of the International Eisteddfod held annually at **Llangollen.**

In north Wales, the Oriel Ynys Mon at **Llangefni**, Anglesey, houses some of the Llyn Cerrig finds. **Machynlleth** in mid Wales is the home of Celtica, a walk-through audio-visual exhibition designed both to educate and entertain. The exhibition presents the history, culture and beliefs of the ancient Celts, and includes a section on the Celtic Otherworld showing the mythical and magical aspects of Celtic religion in which the Druids participated. The **Pontypridd** Historical and Cultural Centre provides information on local history and culture, including latter-day Welsh Druidism. The excavated foundations of a Romano-Celtic temple are on view in **Caerwent** and in the church is an altar to the local god Ocelus. **Newport** Museum and Art Gallery houses more religious material from the Roman town. An extensive reconstructed Iron Age settlement can be visited at **Castell Henllys** in west Wales.

IRELAND The main collections of Iron Age religious antiquities are in the National Museum of Ireland in **Dublin**, which houses the Loughnashade trumpets, the Broighter hoard, the Petrie Crown and many other important finds. At Trinity College Library, Dublin, manuscripts containing versions of some Irish myths can be viewed. The **Cork** Public Museum contains one of the late Iron Age horned headdresses. It is possible to visit the royal sites of Emhain Macha (**Navan** Fort) near Armagh and **Tara** in County Meath. The Cathedral Church of Saint Patrick is in the town of **Armagh**. **Dun Aengus** on Inishmore, one of the Aran Islands, is a spectacular site which may have combined secular and religious functions. Some of the holy wells associated with Saint Brigit are worth visiting (for example the one at **Kilaire**, County Westmeath). The church at **Ballylynan**, County Laois has stained glass windows depicting Saint Brigit and Saint Patrick.

ITALY The museums at **Brescia**, **Bologna** and **Milan** all house important collections of Iron Age Celtic art. Do not miss the **Val Camonica** rock art, the most accessible of which can be seen in the Parco Nazionale delle incisioni rupestri di Capodiponte near Brescia. Here you can also visit the Museo Didattico d'Arte Preistorica and the Archeodromo Centro di Archaeologia Sperimentale, which displays a reconstructed prehistoric settlement.

LUXEMBOURG The Musée National d'Histoire et d'Art in the town of **Luxembourg** contains the finds from the Treveran *oppidum* at **Titelberg** (which is also worth visiting) and, in particular, the rich grave furnishings and equipment from the late Iron Age cemetery between Goeblingen and Nospelt. Relevant material of Roman date includes the many images of Epona from Dalheim.

NETHERLANDS The Rijksmuseum van Oudheden at **Leiden** houses the numerous stone monuments set up to the local North Sea goddess Nehalennia from the temples at Domburg and Colijnsplaat. The Simpelveld sarcophagus is also on display here.

SPAIN While there are many museums which contain Iron Age and Roman-Celtic religious material, of particular note are the Museo Arqueológico Nacional in **Madrid** and the archaeological museum in **Cordoba**, which contains finds from local shrines, together with examples of *verracos* (large stone images of animals) from Celtiberian hillforts. The Iron Age town at **Numantia** is well worth a visit: finds from the site include some very rare painted pottery depicting Celtic divinities.

SWEDEN Visitors should make a point of visiting the rock-art centre and museum at **Tanum** near Oslo Fjord.

SWITZERLAND Material from the great Iron Age religious hoard from La Tène may be seen at the Musée Schwab at **Biel** and at the Musée Cantonal d'Archéologie at **Neuchâtel**. An important collection of Romano-Celtic cult material is contained in collections at the Bernisches Historisches Museum, **Bern**, including the inscribed bronze statuette of the bear-goddess Artio and the finds from the shrine at Thun-Allmendingen on Lake Thunersee.

FURTHER READING

Chapter 1: Finding the Druids
Arnold, B. and Blair Gibson, D., (eds.) *Celtic Chiefdom Celtic State*, Cambridge University Press, New Directions in Archaeology, Cambridge 1995.

Brown, P. Graves, Jones, S., and Gamble, C., S. (eds.), *Cultural Identity and Archaeology: the Construction of European Communities*, Routledge, London and New York 1995.

Chapman, M., *The Celts. The Construction of a Myth*, St Martin's Press, London 1992.

Cunliffe, B., *The Celtic World*, Constable, London 1992; reissue of 1979 Bodley Head edition.

Evans, D. Ellis, 'The Early Celts: the Evidence of Language', in Green, M.J. (ed.), *The Celtic World*, pp. 8–20, Routledge, London 1995.

Green, M.J. (ed.), *The Celtic World*, Routledge, London 1995.

James, S., *Exploring the World of the Celts*, Thames and Hudson, London and New York 1993.

Chapter 2: The Celts and the Supernatural
Chadwick, N., *The Druids*, University of Wales Press, Cardiff 1966.

Green, M.J., *The Gods of the Celts*, Alan Sutton, Gloucester 1993 (2nd edn).

Green, M.J., *Symbol and Image in Celtic Religious Art*, Routledge, London 1992 (2nd edn).

Green, M.J., *Dictionary of Celtic Myth and Legend*, Thames and Hudson, London and New York 1992.

Hatt, J-J., *Mythes et Dieux de la Gaule I*, Picard, Paris 1989.

Henig, M., *Religion in Roman Britain*, Batsford, London 1984.

Ross, A., *The Pagan Celts*, Batsford, London 1986.

Wait, G., *Religion and Ritual in Iron Age Britain*, British Archaeological Reports, Oxford, British Series, No. 149, 1985.

Webster, J., '*Interpretatio*: Roman word power and the Celtic Gods', *Britannia* vol. 26, pp. 153–161, 1995.

Chapter 3: The Druids in Classical Literature
Chadwick, N., *The Druids*, University of Wales Press, Cardiff 1966.

Dunham, S.B., 'Caesar's perception of Gallic social structures', in Arnold, B. and Blair Gibson, D. (eds.), *Celtic Chiefdom Celtic State*, pp. 110–115, Cambridge University Press, Cambridge 1995.

Piggott, S., *The Druids*, Thames and Hudson, London and New York 1975 (new edn).

Rankin, H.D., *The Celts and the Classical World*, Croom Helm, London 1987.

Rankin, H.D., 'The Celts through Classical Eyes', in Green, M.J. (ed.), *The Celtic World*, pp. 21–33, Routledge, London 1995.

Tierney, J.J., 'The Celtic Ethnography of Poseidonius', *Proceedings of the Royal Irish Academy*, vol. 60, pp. 189–246, 1960.

Wiseman, A. and Wiseman, P. (trans.), *Julius Caesar: the Battle for Gaul*, Chatto and Windus, London 1980.

Chapter 4: Digging up Druids
Bradley, R., *The Passage of Arms*, Cambridge University Press, Cambridge and New York 1990.

Creighton, J., 'Visions of power: imagery and symbols in late Iron Age Britain', *Britannia*, vol. 26, pp. 285–301, 1995.

Cunliffe, B., *Iron Age Communities in Britain*, Routledge, London and New York 1991 (3rd edn).

Fox, C., *A Find of the Early Iron Age from Llyn Cerrig Bach, Anglesey*, National Museum of Wales, Cardiff 1946.

Green, M.J., *The Sun Gods of Ancient Europe*, Batsford, London 1991.

Green, M.J., *Celtic Art: Reading the Messages*, Weidenfeld and Nicolson, London 1996.

Kaul, F., *Thracian Tales on the Gundestrup Cauldron*, Najade Press, Amsterdam 1991.

Megaw, R. and Megaw, V., *Celtic Art from its Beginnings to the Book of Kells*, Thames and Hudson, London and New York 1989.

Meid, W., *Gaulish Inscriptions*, Archaeolingua, Budapest 1992.

Nyberg, H., 'Celtic ideas of plants', in Huttunen, H-P. and Latvio, R. (eds.), *Entering the Arena: presenting Celtic Studies in Finland, Etäi 2*, pp. 85–114, 1993.

Olmsted, G.S., *The Gundestrup Cauldron*, Latomus, Brussels 1979.

Olmsted, G.S., *Gods of the Celts and the Indo-Europeans*, Archaeolingua, Innsbruck 1994.

Piggott, S., *The Druids*, Thames and Hudson, London and New York 1975 (new edn).

Raftery, B., (ed.), *Celtic Art*, UNESCO/Flammarion, Paris 1990.

Raftery, B., *Pagan Celtic Ireland*, Thames and Hudson, London and New York 1994.

Ross, A., 'Ritual and the Druids', in Green, M.J. (ed.), *The Celtic World*, pp. 423–444, Routledge, London 1995.

Stead, I.M., Bourke, J.B. and Brothwell, D., *Lindow Man: the Body in the Bog*, British Museum Publications, London 1986.

Stead, I.M., 'The Snettisham Treasure: Excavations in 1990', *Antiquity* vol. 65, no. 248, pp. 447–464, 1991.

Stead, I.M., 'The Metalwork', in Parfitt, K., *Iron Age Burials from Mill Hill, Deal*, pp. 58–111, British Museum Press, London 1995.

Taylor, T., 'The Eastern Origins of the Gundestrup Cauldron', *Scientific American no. 266 (3)*, pp. 66–71, March 1992.

Wait, G., 'Burial and the Otherworld', in Green, M.J. (ed.), *The Celtic World*, pp. 465–488, Routledge, London 1995.

Chapter 5: Sacrifice and Prophecy
Brunaux, J-L., *The Celtic Gauls: Gods, Rites and Sanctuaries*, Seaby, London 1988.

Cunliffe, B., *Danebury: Anatomy of an Iron Age Hillfort*, Batsford, London 1983.

Cunliffe, B., *Danebury*, Batsford/English Heritage, London 1993.

Glob, P.V., *The Bog People*, Faber and Faber, London 1969.

Grant, A., 'Economic or symbolic? Animals and Ritual Behaviour', Garwood, P., Jennings, D., Skeates, R. and Toms, J. (eds.), *Sacred Profane*, pp. 109–114, Oxford University Committee for Archaeology, monograph no. 32, 1991.

Green, M.J., *Animals in Celtic Life and Myth*, Routledge, London and New York 1992.

Meniel, P., *Chasse et élèvage chez les Gaulois (450–2 av. JC)*, Errance, Paris 1987.

Stead, I.M., Bourke, J.B. and Brothwell, D., *Lindow Man: the Body in the Bog*, British Museum Publications, London 1986.

Turner, R.C. and Scaife, R.G. (eds.), *Bog Bodies: New Discoveries and New Perspectives*, British Museum Press, London 1995.

Chapter 6: The Female Druids
Allason-Jones, L., *Women in Roman Britain*, British Museum Press, London 1989.

Davidson, H.E., *The Lost Beliefs of Northern Europe*, Routledge, London 1993.

Davies, S., *The Four Branches of the Mabinogion*, Gomer Press, Llandysul 1993.

Ehrenberg, M., *Women in Prehistory*, British Museum Press, London 1989.

Fradenburg, L.O. (ed.), *Women and Sovereignty*, Edinburgh University Press, Edinburgh 1992.

Green, M.J., *Celtic Goddesses: Warriors, Virgins and Mothers*, British Museum Press, London 1995.

Jones, G. and Jones, T. (trans.), *The Mabinogion*, Dent, London 1976.

Kelly, P., 'The *Táin* as Literature', in Mallory, J.P. (ed.), *Aspects of the Táin*, pp. 69–102, Universities Press, Belfast 1992.

Kraemer, R.S., *Her Share of the Blessings*, Oxford University Press, Oxford and New York 1992.

Markale, J., *Women of the Celts*, Cremonesi, London 1975.

Meid, W., *Gaulish Inscriptions*, Archaeolingua, Budapest, 1992.

Pelletier, A., *La Femme dans la société gallo-romaine*, Picard, Paris.

Philpott, R., *Burial Practices in Roman Britain: a survey of grave treatment and furnishing AD 43–410*, British Archaeological Reports, British Series, Oxford, no. 219, 1991.

Wood, J., 'Celtic Goddesses: Myth and Mythology', in Larrington, C. (ed.), *The Feminist Companion to Mythology*, pp. 118–136, Pandora Press/HarperCollins, London 1992.

Chapter 7: Sacred Places and Their Priests

Brunaux, J-L. (ed.), *Les Sanctuaires Celtiques et le Monde Méditerranéen*, Archéologie Aujourd'hui, Protohistoire-Editions Errance, Paris 1991.

Cunliffe, B. (ed.), *The Temple of Sulis Minerva at Bath. Vol. 2. The Finds from the Sacred Spring*, Oxford University Committee for Archaeology, monograph no. 16, 1988.

Cunliffe, B. and Davenport, P., *The Temple of Sulis Minerva at Bath. Vol. 1: The Site*, Oxford University Committee for Archaeology, monograph no. 7, 1985.

Cunliffe, B., *Roman Bath*, Batsford/English Heritage, London 1996.

Deyts, S., *Les Bois Sculptés des Sources de la Seine*, XLII supplément à *Gallia*, 1983.

Deyts, S., *Le sanctuaires des Sources de la Seine*, Musée Archéologique, Dijon 1985.

Downey, R., King, A. and Soffe, G., 'The Hayling Island Temple and religious connections across the Channel', in Rodwell, W. (ed.), *Temples, Churches and Religion in Roman Britain*, pp. 289–304, British Archaeological Reports, British Series, Oxford, no. 77, 1980.

Fitzpatrick, P., 'The deposition of La Tène Iron Age metalwork in watery contexts in southern England', in Cunliffe, B.W. and Miles, D. (eds.), *Aspects of the Iron Age in Central Southern England*, pp. 178–190, Oxford University Committee for Archaeology, monograph no. 2, 1984.

France, N.E. and Gobel, B.M., *The Romano-British Temple at Harlow, Essex: a record of the excavations carried out by members of the West Essex Archaeological Group and the Harlow Antiquarian Society between 1962 and 1971*, West Essex Archaeological Group, Harlow 1985.

Thevenot, E., *Divinités et sanctuaires de la Gaule*, Fayard, Paris 1968.

Venclovà, N., 'Celtic Shrines in Central Europe: a sceptical approach', *Oxford Journal of Archaeology*, pp. 55–66, vol. 12, no. 1, March 1993.

Webster, J., 'Sanctuaries and Sacred Places', in Green, M.J. (ed.), *The Celtic World*, pp. 445–464, Routledge, London 1995.

Wheeler, R.E.M. and Wheeler, T.V., *Report on the Excavations … in Lydney park, Gloucestershire*, Society of Antiquaries of London, London 1932.

Woodward, A., *Shrines and Sacrifice*, Batsford/English Heritage, London 1992.

Woodward, A. and Leach, P., *The Uley Shrines. Excavation of a Ritual Complex on West Hill, Uley, Glos, 1977–9*, English Heritage, London 1993.

Chapter 8: Druids in Irish Myth

Edel, D. (ed.), *Cultural Identity and Cultural Integration: Ireland and Europe in the Early Middle Ages*, Four Courts Press, Dublin 1995.

Green, M.J., *Celtic Myths*, British Museum Press, London; University of Texas Press, Austin 1993.

Kinsella, T., *The Táin*, Dolmen, Dublin 1969.

Mac Cana, P., *Celtic Mythology*, Newnes, London 1983.

McCone, K., *Pagan Past and Christian Present*, An Sagart, Maynooth 1990.

Minahane, J., *The Christian Druids. On the Filid or Philosopher-poets of Ireland*, Sanas Press, Dublin 1993.

O'Rahilly, T.F., *Early Irish History and Mythology*, Centre for Advanced Studies, Dublin 1946.

Raftery, B., *Pagan Celtic Ireland*, Thames and Hudson, London and New York 1994.

Chapter 9: Druids Resurrected

Carr-Gomm, P., *The Druid Tradition*, Element Books, Shaftsbury 1991.

Daniel, G.E., *The Origins and Growth of Archaeology*, Penguin, Harmondsworth and Baltimore 1967.

Humphreys, E., *The Taliesin Tradition*, Black Raven Press, London 1983.

Hunter, M., *John Aubrey and the Realm of Learning*, Duckworth, London 1975.

Jones, M., *Eisteddfod – A Welsh Phenomenon*, private publication, Aberaeron 1986.

Owen, A.L., *The Famous Druids*, Oxford University Press, London 1962.

Piggott, S., *Celts, Saxons and the Early Antiquarians*, the O'Donnell Lecture 1966, Edinburgh University Press, Edinburgh 1967.

Piggott, S., *Ruins in a Landscape: Essays in Antiquarianism*, Edinburgh University Press, Edinburgh 1976.

Piggott, S., *William Stukeley: An Eighteenth-Century Antiquary*, Thames and Hudson, London and New York 1985.

Piggott, S., *Ancient Britons and the Antiquarian Imagination*, Thames and Hudson, London and New York 1989.

Royal National Eisteddfod of Wales, *Eisteddfod. An Introduction and Guide to non-Welsh Speakers*, Royal National Eisteddfod of Wales, Cardiff undated.

Smiles, S. *The Image of Antiquity: Ancient Britain and the Romantic Imagination*, Yale University Press, 1994.

Chapter 10: Druids Today

Carr-Gomm, P., *The Druid Tradition*, Element Books, Shaftsbury 1991.

Carr-Gomm, P., *The Druid Renaissance*, Thorsons, London 1996.

Chippindale, C., *Stonehenge Complete*, Thames and Hudson, London and New York 1994 (rev. edn).

Matthews, J. (ed.), *The Druid Source Book*, Blandford Press, London 1996.

Nicholls, R., 'Essentials in Druidry', *The Druids' Voice*, issue no. 4, pp. 10–11, Winter 1994.

Pagan Federation, *The Pagan Federation Information Pack*, Pagan Federation, London 1993 (2nd edn).

Russell, J.B., *A History of Witchcraft: Sorcerers, Heretics and Pagans*, Thames and Hudson, London and New York 1981.

Shallcrass, P., 'Druids, Dongas and Diggers, Vates, Bards and Bulldozers', in *The Druids' Voice*, issue no. 4, pp. 20–21, Winter, 1994.

Talking Stick, *Magical Directory*, Talking Stick, London 1993.

Williams, T., 'A Brief Treatise on the History of International Ancient Order Druidism', *The Druids' Voice*, issue no. 4, pp. 6–9, winter 1994.

ACKNOWLEDGMENTS

Sources of texts

Sources of translations for Classical texts:

Aelius Lampridius – *Severus Alexander*; Vopiscus – *Aurelianus*: D. Magie, *The Scriptores Historiae Augustae*, Loeb Classical Library II 1980; III 1932.

Ammianus; Laertius – *Lives of the Philosophers*; Pomponius Mela – *De Chorographia*: N. Chadwick, *The Druids*, University of Wales Press 1966.

Athenaeus – *Deinosphists*; Caesar – *Gallic War*; Diodorus Siculus – *Library of History* (quotations on pp. 76, 85); Strabo – *Geography* (quotations on pp. 105, 109, 124): J.J. Tierney, 'The Celtic Ethnography of Posidonius', *Proceedings of the Royal Irish Academy* 1960.

Cicero – *De Divinatione*: W. Falconer, *Cicero De Divinatione*, Loeb Classical Library 1922.

Dio Cassius – *Roman History*: E. Cary, *Dio's Roman History*, Loeb Classical Library VIII 1926/26.

Diodorus Siculus– *Library of History*: C.H. Oldfather, *Diodorus of Sicily*, Loeb Classical Library 1939.

Lucan – *Pharsalia*: R. Graves, *Lucan Pharsalia*, Penguin 1956.

Pliny – *Natural History*: H. Rackham, *Pliny Natural History*, Loeb Classical Library IV 1945.

Pliny – *Natural History* (quotations on pp. 41, 46): W.H.S. Jones, *Pliny Natural History*, Loeb Classical Library VII 1956; VIII 1963.

Strabo – *Geography*: H.L. Jones, *The Geography of Strabo*, Loeb Classical Library II 1923; III 1924.

Suetonius – *Life of Claudius*: R. Graves, *Suetonius The Twelve Caesars*, Cassell 1957.

Tacitus – *Annals*: M. Grant, *Tacitus The Annals of Imperial Rome*, Penguin 1956.

Tacitus – *Germania* and *Agricola*: H. Mattingly, *Tacitus on Britain and Germany*, Penguin 1948.

Tacitus – *Histories*: K. Wellesley, *Tacitus The Histories*, Penguin 1964.

Later Celtic and medieval texts:

Extracts from *The Táin*, pp. 102, 123, 127, 128, 129: from T. Kinsella, *The Táin*, Dolmen Press, 1969.

Extract from the Second Branch of the *Mabinogion*, p. 66: from Jones, G. and Jones, T., *The Mabinogion*, Dent, 1976.

Extracts from Irish Myths: the *Book of Invasions*, p. 132; and the *Fate of the Children of Tuirenn*, p. 130: from T. F. O'Rahilly, *Early Irish History and Mythology*, Centre for Advanced Studies, Dublin 1946.

Extract from *The Story of Da Derga's Hostel*, p. 125: from T. Sjöblom, 'Advice from a Bird-man: Ritual Injunctions and Royal Instructions in TBDD', in A. Ahlquist *et al.* (eds.), *Celtica Helsingiensia*, pp. 233–251, Societas Scientiarium Fennica 1996.

Miscellaneous extracts: fifteenth-century poem, p. 124; seventh-century Irish Penitential, p. 134; *Life of Saint Berach*, p. 134; *Life of Saint Brigit*, p. 136; *Life of Saint Patrick*, pp. 136, 137: all from Minahane, J., *The Christian Druids. On the Filid or Philosopher-poets of Ireland*, Sanas Press 1993.

Archaeologický Ústav Čsav. 58c Musée Historique et Archéologique de l'Orléanais, Orléans. 58b Photo © Tony Rook. 59tc Národní Muzeum, Prague. 59tr Copyright British Museum. 59br British Museum, London. Photo J.V.S. Megaw, Flinders University of South Australia, Adelaide. 61b National Museum of Ireland, Dublin. 62t © Cambridge University Museum of Archaeology and Anthropology. 64t Fenland Archaeological Trust. 64b Photo Philip Macdonald. 65a The National Museum of Wales, Cardiff. 65b Castle Museum, Norwich. 66 The National Museum of Wales, Cardiff. 67t Nationalmuseet, Copenhagen. 67b © The Trustees of the National Museums of Scotland 1997. 68 Rijksmuseum van Oudheden, Leiden. 69 Historisches Museum der Pfalz, Speyer. 70–71 © U.G.C., U.K. 72a Musei Capitolini, Rome. 72b Römisch-Germanisches Museum, Cologne. Photo Miranda J. Green. 72–73 Private Collection. Photo Jean-Loup Charmet, Paris. 74l Nationalmuseet, Copenhagen. 75 Photo Jean-Loup Charmet, Paris. 76 Copyright Camelot Research Committee. 77tl Centre Camille Jullian, CNRS Photo Chéné. 77b Photo Danebury Trust. 79l Photo Miranda J. Green. 80 Copyright British Museum. 81 Gardner Films. 82 Nationalmuseet, Copenhagen. 83a Schleswig-Holsteinisches Landesmuseum, Schleswig. 83b Nationalmuseet, Copenhagen. 85a Bibliothèque des Arts Décoratifs, Paris. Photo Jean-Loup Charmet, Paris. 85br Worthing Museum and Art Gallery. 86bc Musée Historique et Archéologique de l'Orléanais, Orléans. 87tl Photo London Underground Ltd. 87bc Photo Danebury Trust. 88 The National Museum of Wales, Cardiff. 89a Bodleian Library, Oxford. 89b (see 37). 90 Musée Archéologique, Dijon. Photo Miranda J. Green. 91 The Pierpont Morgan Library, New York. 92–93 Steiermärkisches Landesmuseum Joanneum, Graz. Photo AKG London/Erich Lessing. 94 Reconstruction by Gaynor Chapman. 95b Musée Archéologique, Châtillon-sur-Seine. 96l Musée Archéologique, Dijon. Photo Miranda J. Green. 96c Landesmuseum für Vorgeschichte und Frühgeschichte, Saarbrücken. 96r Musée de Bretagne, Rennes. Photo Jean Claude Housbin. 97br Newport Museum and Art Gallery (County Borough of Newport). 98 Copyright British Museum. 99 Facsimile by A. Vernhet from W. Meid, Gaulish Inscriptions, Archaeolingua 1992. 103b Photo Frank Gibson. 104l Musée Archéologique, Clermont-Ferrand. Photo Bayle, Chamalières, from Miranda Aldhouse Green, Celtic Art: Reading the Messages, The Everyman Art Library (Weidenfeld and Nicolson Ltd), 1996, courtesy Calmann and King Ltd, London. 104r Rheinisches Landesmuseum, Bonn. Photo Miranda J. Green. 106–107, 108tl Photos Miranda J. Green. 108bl Copyright British Museum. 108br Michael Fulford, Reading University. 109a Photo Miranda J. Green. 109b Prähistorische Staatssammlung, Munich. 111a Harlow Museum. 111b Musée d'Archéologie Méditerranéenne (Centre de la Vieille Charité), Marseille. Photo Miranda J. Green. 112tl, bc, br Roman Baths Museum, Bath. 113 John Ronayne. Bath Archaeological Trust. 114a Bath Archaeological Trust. 114bl Roman Baths Museum, Bath. 115t From W. Meid, Gaulish Inscriptions, Archaeolingua 1992. 115b Photo John Morgan, University of Wales, Cardiff. 116c Ipswich Borough Council Museums and Galleries. 116b Roman Baths Museum, Bath. 117ar Photo Miranda J. Green. 118bl, 119l © Department of Archaeology, City of Bristol Museum and Art Gallery. 119r Musée Archéologique, Dijon. 120 Photo Michael Herity. 122–123 Photo Aerofilms. 124l National Museum of Ireland, Dublin. 126b National Museum of Ireland, Dublin. 127 Images Colour Library, London. 128 Photo Irish Tourist Board. 129b National Gallery of Scotland, Edinburgh. 130l National Museum of Ireland, Dublin. 131t Viewfinder Colour Photo Library, Simant Bostock. 131ar Rowley's House Museum, Shrewsbury. Photo Miranda J. Green. 132a © National Trust. 132–133 Commissioners for Public Works in Ireland, Dublin. 134 Dudley Wright, Druidism, The Ancient Faith of Britain, London 1924. 135 Ashmolean Museum, Oxford. 136r, 137 Photos Irish Tourist Board. 138–139 Bibliothèque des Arts Décoratifs, Paris. Photo Jean-Loup Charmet, Paris. 140 J. Britton, Memoir of John Aubrey, 1845. 141 John Aubrey, Monumenta Britannica (c. 1675), Bodleian Library, Oxford. 142a, 142b Bodleian Library, Oxford. 143 William Stukeley, Stonehenge, 1740. 144al John Wood, Essay Towards a Description of Bath, 1749. 144br William Stukeley, The History of the Religion and Temples of the Druids, Bodleian Library, Oxford. 145 © Mick Sharp. 146a The Laing Art Gallery, Newcastle-upon-Tyne. 146b Bodleian Library, Oxford. 147 Salisbury and South Wiltshire Museum. 148a Private Collection. Photo Jean-Loup Charmet, Paris. 148b University of Pennsylvania, Philadelphia. 149 Fitzwilliam Museum, Cambridge. 150l Aylett Sammes, Britannia Antiqua Illustrata, 1676. 150r Henry Rowlands, Mona Antiqua Restaurata, 1723. 151 Elias Schedius, De Dis Germanis, Amsterdam 1648. 152 Henry Inman. 153a Notation from Edward Jones, The Bardic Museum of Primitive British Literature, 1802. 153b, 154l Museum of Welsh Life, Cardiff. 154–155 The Royal Institution of Cornwall, Truro. 156 Museum of Welsh Life, Cardiff. 157 S.R. Meyrick and C.H. Smith, Costume of the Original Inhabitants of the British Isles, 1815. 158–159 Viewfinder Colour Photo Library, Paul Walters. 160 The Druids' Voice, Winter 1994. (Courtesy Marian Bowman, Bath). 161 Haddon Library Collection, Cambridge University Museum of Archaeology and Anthropology. 162 Calyx Photo Services, Swindon. 163 Bibliothèque des Arts Décoratifs, Paris. Photo Jean-Loup Charmet, Paris. 164b Associated Press, London. 165 The Wiccan, Beltane 1994. 166 Viewfinder Colour Photo Library, Stuart Baynes. 166–167 Department of the Environment (Crown Copyright reserved). 168 Janet and Colin Bord/Fortean Picture Library. 169 Photo Miranda J. Green. 170 The Oxford Times. 171a Courtesy Mathew McCabe, OBOD. 171b Photo © British Tourist Authority. 172–73 S.R. Meyrick and C.H. Smith, Costume of the Original Inhabitants of the British Isles, 1815. 173a, 173b Calyx Photo Services, Swindon. 174 Public Record Office, London. 175a PA News London. Fiona Hanson. 175b Photo J.V.S. Megaw, Flinders University of South Australia, Adelaide. 176 © English Heritage/Skyscan. 177 After Philip Carr-Gomm, The Druid Tradition, Element Books, Shaftsbury 1991. 178a Calyx Photo Services, Swindon. 178b J. Allan Cash Ltd. 179 © Peter Bloodworth.

INDEX

Page numbers in *italic* refer to illustrations and captions. There may also be textual references on these pages.

A Druid Fellowship (ADF) 169, 170
Aberdare Eisteddfod 156
Aedui, tribe of 10, 31, 44, 60, 90, 115
Aelius Lampridius 97
Aesir (sky-gods) 161
afterlife 51, 68–9, *see also* immortality; rebirth; reincarnation
Albion Lodge of AOD 17, 169, 170
Alesia, Burgundy 14, 28, 29
Alexander Severus *see* Severus Alexander
Alexandria 41
altars 32
Altartate Glebe, Monaghan 66
Ambiani 65, 121
Ambigatus, King 31
Ammianus Marcellinus 41, 48, 50, 51
amphitheatre (legionary fortress): Caerleon 46
amphorae 68
amulets 46, 58
ancestor-worship 30, 49, 178
Ancient Order of Druids (AOD) 17, 147, 169, 175
Andraste 29, 78–9, *79*
Anglesey (Mona) 40, 41, 108, 147, *150*; Llyn Cerrig Bach *13*, 53, 64, 65; Roman attack on 15, 52, 53, 64, 73, 93
anguinum 46
animal sacrifices 7, 25, 32, 65, *71*, 84, 85–7, 89, 109; bulls 18, *19*, *72*, 74, 85, *130*
animals: in farming 34–5, 36, 37, 85; hunting of 101; images of 9, 25, 29, 34, *121*; and shamans 33; spirits of 24, 29, *see also* dogs; horses
Annwn (Otherworld) 103
antiquarians 139, 140, 141, 146
Antiquaries, Society of 144
Antium calendar 37
antlered god *see* Cernunnos
antlered headdresses 33, 59
Antrobus, Sir Edward 172–5
Anvallus 115
Apollo 23, 26, 90, *91*, 144
Apollo Belenus 15, 26, 90
Apollo Cunomaglus 29, *118*
Apollo Vindonnus 90

Aquae Arnemetiae (Buxton, Derbyshire) 25
Aquae Sulis see Bath
Aquitaine 15
arbitrators: Druids as 10, 44–5, 65, *see also* mediators
archaeology 8, 53, 55–69
Ardbrinn, County Down 63
Ardennes 29
Arduinna (boar-goddess) 29
Ares 45
Argentomagus, France *115*
Ariovistus, King 44
Arnemetia 107
Arrian 30
art: afterlife 69; Celtic 19, *33*; La Tène *12–13*, 63; Minerva 23; Swedish rock 63
Arthur, King *43*
Artio (bear-goddess) 24, 29
Arverni 34
ash tree 109
Ashill, Norfolk 109
Asklepios (healer-god) 119
astrology 50
astronomy 10, 50, 89, 148
Athenaeus: *Deinosphists* 34
Aubrey, John 17, *142*, 146; *Monumenta Britannica* 140, *141*, 144
augury 88, 90
Augusta, Princess Dowager 142-3
Augustan Histories (*Scriptores Historiae Augustae*) 15, 97
Augustus, emperor 14, 31, 48
Ausonius (poet) 15, 32, 90
Autumn Equinox 164, 165
Autun, France 37, 48, 115
Avebury, Wiltshire 141, *142*, 144, *146*, 148, *162*, 168, *171*, *178*; Gorsedd Bards of Caer Abiri 166, 167, 170
Aylesford, Kent *33*, 59

Badbh (warrior-goddess) 98, *100*, 102, *128*
badges of office 8, 60–3
Balkåkra 'sun drum', Sweden 57
Ballachulish, Argyll, Scotland: female wooden figure *24*
Ballyedmond, Galway 66
Ballylynan, County Laois *137*
banquets 19, 34, 68, 69
Bardic Order Group 171
Bards 15, 49, 88, *124*, 125, *126*, 132, 140, *146*, 147, 152, 157, 166, 170, 178; and Eisteddfod 153–4, 155, *see also* Order of Bards, Ovates and Druids
Bath: *Aquae Sulis* 19, 24, 25, 28,

32, *42*, 112–14, 115, *116*; Circus of 144
Bayeux, Druid stock of 15
bear-goddess (Artio) 24, 29
Beire-le-Châtel, France 90
Belatucadrus 28
Belenus (Apollo Belenus) 15, 26, 90
Bellovaci 44, 65, 121
Beltane 35, 37, 164, 165, *167*, 168
Berecynthia 37
Bible: Old Testament 41, 121, 125, 137, 140, 142, 143
Bibracte, Burgundy 48
birch 83, 178
birth 30
Bituriges 31, 115
Black Magic 46, 83, 98
Blackburn Mill, Berwickshire 67
Blake, William *51*, 147, 148; *Prophetic Books* 148, *149*; *Songs of Innocence and Experience* 149
Blenheim 169, *170*
Bliesbrück, Germany 121
boar-god (Euffigneix) 29, *30*
boar-goddess (Arduinna) 29
boars: figurine *31*; sacrifice of 85
Böckingen, Germany 25
Bodmin, Cornwall 155
bog burials 53, 73, 80–4
Bohuslän, Sweden 63
Boii 76
Bolards, Burgundy 90, 118
bone, animal 19, 57, 86, 120, *121*
bone, human 19, 30, 52, 57, 76, 77, 86, 98–9, 111
Bonn, Germany 104
Book of Invasions 35, 126, 132
Bordeaux 15, 90
Borlase, William: *Antiquities of Cornwall* 144
Borre Fen 82
Boudica 15, 29, 53, 58, 78–9, *79*, 95–6, 140
Bourg-en-Bresse, France 37
Brå cauldron 66
Brandon, Suffolk 73, *81*, 109
Brigantes 96
Brignogan, Brittany 154
Brigstock, Northamptonshire 63, 116
Britain 10, 13, 31, 39, 40, 41, 44; Druid revival 17; uprisings against Rome 52, 53, *see also* Boudica *and* individual locations
British Druid Order 159, *160*, 171
Britons 11, 23
Brittany 13, 15, *44*, 96, 148, *154*, 169

Broighter, County Derry 126, *130*
bronze: cauldrons 66, 68; figurines 9, *19*, *25*, *31*, 49, 62, *63*, *125*; grave goods *51*, 60–1, 95; head: bull-horned god 34; helmets *108*; hoards *31*, 58; musical instruments 63; objects 8, *13*, *37*; shield-boss 53; sickle 46; stag *25*; statue *14*; statuette: St Maur *26*
Bronze Age 55, 56, 57, 64, 110
brooch (*fibula*) 60
Brough, Yorkshire 62
Brunaux, Jean-Louis 30, 64
Bryher, Isles of Scilly 103
Bu Sands, Orkney 46, 58
bulls: sacrifice of 18, *19*, *72*, 74, 85; *Tarbhfhess* ('bull sleep') *19*, *130*
Burgess, Dr (Bishop of St Davids) 154
Burgundy 10, *14*, 27, 28, 29, 48, 90, 94, 95, 115, *118*
burials *51*, 79, 98, 99, 110, 142; alive 82–4; funerary rituals 30; Hochdorf, Germany: chieftain's tomb 19, *33*, 69; King's Barrow chariot burial, Yorkshire 86; megalithic passage grave *132*; noble ladies 94, 95, 96; old women 98–9; tombs: banquets represented in 19; Trundholm 'sun chariot' 55, *57*; warriors/noblemen 60, 68–9, 69, 86, 93, 104, *see also* bog burials; cremation burials
Butser Iron Age Farm Project, Hampshire 37
Buxton, Derbyshire: Aquae Arnemetiae 25
Býčiskála, Bohemia *19*, 76, 84, 86

Caesar, Julius 10, 11, 14, 20, 40–1, 44, 45, 50–2, 60, 65, *71*, 72, 78, 97, 101, 107, 124, 140, 178; *Gallic War* 8, 10, 23, 26, 31, 32, 37, 41–2, 48–50, 68, 72, 75, 79, 85, 89, 108, 115
Caerleon, south Wales 46
Caerwent, south Wales 24, 28, 86, 97
Cairnhill, Aberdeenshire 58
Calan Mai (Beltane) 35
calendars 37, 50; Circle of the Year *177*; Wheel of the Year 164–5, *see also* Coligny calendar; farming (calendar)
Calpurnius Receptus (priest) *114*
Cambry, Jacques 148
Camonica Valley, Italy 77

Camulodunum (Colchester) 53, 96
cannabis 33
cannibalism 52, 73
Caratacus 96
Cardiff, Wales 79, 152
Cardigan Eisteddfod 154
Carlingwark, Kirkudbright 67
Carman, Leinster 36
Carmarthen Eisteddfod 154, 156
Carnac, France 73, 148
Carnutes 32, 108, 115; assembly 34, 45, 65
Carr-Gomm, Philip 162, 165, 179
Cartimandua 95, 96
Cassiterides islands 103
Cathbadh of Ulster 8, 90, 102, 125, 128, 129, 132, 133, 134
cats 89
cattle 19, 35, 87, 121, 130
cauldrons 66–7, 68, 69, 93, 97, 103, 104, 131, see also Gundestrup cauldron
Cavenham, Suffolk 60–1, 60, 116
caves 14, 48, 84, 86
Celtic: art 19, 33; Iron Age 19, 107; language/culture 13; myths 121; nationalism 15; religion 18, 19, 23–37; sanctuaries 115–16
Celtic society: decline of 14; Druids in 8, 10, 10; women in 94–6
Celtic world, geography of 11–13
Celts 11, 124, 126; Graeco-Roman literature 12, 13, see also Romano-Celtic
Cenabum 115
cereals: in bog bodies 81, 82
ceremonial regalia 8, 60–3, 116
ceremonies 34–6
ceremony and celebration 166–8
Cerne Abbas Giant, Dorset 167
Cernunnos (Horned God) 23, 58, 59, 160
Chadwick, Nora: The Druids 31
chalk figurine 60, 61
Chamalières, France 104, 118–19
Charon (infernal ferryman) 69
Chartist movement 152
Chartres, France 32
Chedworth, Gloucestershire 28
Christianity 24, 31, 41, 89, 109, 123, 124, 143, 147, 166, 167, 176, 177; Celtic 13; in Ireland 15, 17, 50, 134–7
Chubb, Sir Cecil 174, 175
Church of the Universal Bond 147, 174, 175
Churchill, Winston 17, 169, 170
Chyndonax see Stukeley, William
Cicero 50, 88, 90; De Divinatione 44
Cimbri 66, 67, 97

Circle of the Year 177
Claudius, emperor 15, 97
Clement of Alexandria 40, 41, 50
Cocidius 28
Cockersand Moss, Cumbria 28
Cogitosus: Vita Brigitae 135
coins 28, 65, 67, 69, 96, 97, 111, 112, 118
Coligny calendar 8, 37, 89
College of Pontiffs 37
Cologne, Germany 28, 72
Conaire, King 125, 133
Conall Cernach (warrior) 129
Conchobar of Ulster, King 8, 89, 90, 102, 128, 129, 132, 134–5
Connacht 8, 100, 127, 128, 130, 133
Conwy, River 146, 148
Cooke, William 148
Corinth 95
Corleck, County Cavan 28
Cormac of Ulster 129, 133
Cormac (writer) 35, 89
Cornwall 13, 133, 144
Council of British Druids 169
Covent Garden, London 147
craftsmanship, god of 36
cremation burials 56, 59, 68, 111
Cricklade 49
crime: punishment for 72, 73, 81, 82, 83
Criminal Justice Act 172, 175
crops 34, 37; fertility of 24; harvest 30, 36, 37
crosses, stone carved 13, 32
crows 121
Cú Chulainn 36, 100, 101, 102, 128–9, 128
curses: lead 32, 46, 73, 81, 99, 109, 114
Cyril of Alexandria 41

Da Derga's Hostel, Story of 125, 130
Daghda (god) 36, 167
Dáire, King 133
Danby, William 144, 144
dancing 9, 55, 63
Danebury, Hampshire: Iron Age hillfort 30, 76, 77, 86, 87
Dante: Divine Comedy 51
Danube, River 11
dark places underground, divine power of 29
Deal, England 60
decapitation 98–9
deer 29
defixiones see lead curses
Deiotarus, King 31
'Deirdre of the Sorrows', tale of 129
Delphidius 15
dendrochronology 56, 121
Denmark: bog burials 82-4, see also Gundestrup cauldron

Devon 133
Diana (goddess of the moon) 164
Dijon 142; Fontes Sequana 28, 55, 115, 116, 117, 118, 119
Dinéault, Brittany 96
Dinnschenchas ('History of Places') 35, 36, 109, 123
Dio Cassius 31, 58, 78-9, 95
Dio Chrysostom 44, 50; Oratio 88
Diocletian, emperor 15, 88, 97
Diodorus Siculus 14, 31, 40, 41, 49, 51, 52, 68, 115; Library of History 7, 39, 45, 50, 72–3, 76, 85, 88
Diogenes Laertius 39, 46; Lives of the Philosophers 48
Dionysiac Maenads 105
Dis Pater 49, 89, 178
disease: Apollo 23; protection against 35, see also healer gods/goddesses; healing
Divitiacus 10, 31, 44, 50, 60, 88, 90
Dobunni 65
Dogra, chief Druid 133
dogs 89, 121; burials 64; healing symbols 119; sacrifice of 85, 86, 87
Doonwell, Ireland 107
Dorset 99
Dragon Environmental Project 179
Drayton, Michael: Polyolbion 140
Druids: in Celtic society 8, 10; Council of British 17; history 14–21; meaning of 9; organization 32; reborn 17; and Romans 52–3; and social order 44–5; timeline 20–1, see also archaeology; female Druids; myths; prophecy; sacrifices
Drunemeton ('Oak Sanctuary') 32, 108
Duchcov, Bohemia 66–7
Dumnorix 10, 44
Dun Aengus, Galway: Iron Age fort 120

earth: worship of 159, 177
Earth Mother 166
earth-goddess 37, 164, 170
earth-gods 161, 177
Eburones 108
Edward I, King 88, 146, 148
Eggs, Druid's 46, 58
Eisteddfod 7, 17, 152, 153–5, 153, 156–7, 171
Emhain Macha 128, 129, see also Navan Fort
English Heritage 176
engravings 9, 10, 17
Entremont, Lower Rhône Valley 26, 76–7, 77
environmental issues 161, 179
Epidaurus, Peloponnese 119

Epona (horse-goddess) 24, 27, 29, 58, 131
equites (knights) 10, 44, 68
Erik Bloodaxe, King 83
Erne, Loch 102
Essarois 90
Esus ('Lord') 27, 75, 78
Etruria 95
Etzelsdorf, Bavaria 56–7, 57
euhages (seers) 50
Euripides: The Bacchae 105
Exmoor 144
eyes: healing of 46, 90, 115, 116, 118, 119

Fagus ('Beech Tree') 108
Farley Heath, Surrey 62
farming: animals 34–5, 36, 37, 85; calendar 34–7; harvest 30, 36, 37, see also crops
feasts see banquets
Fedelma (prophetess) 101, 102
Fellbach Schmiden, Stuttgart 121
Felmingham Hall, Norfolk 31, 63
female bog burials 82–4, 83
female Druids 93–105
Fenian Cycle 8, 36, 101, 109, 125
Ferghus (warrior) 129
fertility 19, 24, 35, 160, 161
festivals 34–6, 37
Fianna 101, 134, see also Finn
figurines 58, 60, 61, 104, 121, see also bronze (figurines)
Filidh (seers) 15, 89, 124
Finn (leader of Fianna) 8, 36, 101–2, 109, 125–6, 126, 127
Finnegas the Bard 125, 126
fire 50; Beltane 35; Hill of Slane 137; human sacrifice 78; of Mide (Ireland) 126; sacrifices 56; Wicker Man ceremony 75
Flag Fen, Cambridgeshire 64
Flamen Dialis 32
Flavian dynasty, Roman empire 111
Fletcher, Jon: Bonduca 140
Floriacum (Fleury) 58
Fontes Sequana, Dijon 28, 55, 115, 116, 117, 118, 119
food/drink 30, 55
forests 14, 24
France 9, 12, 19, 25–7, 29, 30, 36–7, 55, 58, 64–5, 73, 76–7, 78, 86, 90, 94–6, 99, 105, 108–11, 115, 118, 140, 142, 148, 154, 169
freemasonry 169
funerary rituals 30

Gaels (Celts) 124, 126
Galatae 11
Galatia 31, 39
Galatians 32, 45, 108
Gallagh, Galway 80

Gallic (Gaulish) language 8, *12*, *37*, 97, 99, 107, 115
Gardner, Gerald: *Witchcraft Today* 160
Gaul 14, 15, 18, 23, 31, 32, 34, 39, 40, 41, 42, 44, 45, 58, 67, 89; Caesar's campaigns *10*; religion 28; and Rome 52
Gaulish culture 10
Gaulish language (Gallic) 8, *12*, *37*, 97, 99, 107, 115
Gaulish society 10
Gauls 11, 39, 48; religion 23, 24, 25, 27; and sacrifices *71*
Gerald of Wales (Giraldus Cambriensis) 131
Germany 19, 25, 28, 29, 30, 32, 33, 48, 56–7, 59, 69, *72*, 78, 79, 90, 95, 96, *104*, 109, 115, *121*, 140
gessa (divine injunctions) 124, 125, 133
Glamorgan: Order of Glamorgan Druids 155
Glamorganshire 153
Glanis 29
Glanum 29, 49
Glastonbury Order of Druids 172
Glastonbury Tor, Somerset *168*, 170
Gloucester, Nine Witches of 99, 100
gods/goddesses 29–30; and farming 37; identifying 26–8, *see also* religion; sacrifices; votive offerings *and* individual deities
Golden Gate Group (San Francisco) 169
Gorsedd ceremonies 17, *18*, *153*, *154*, 155, 156, 157, 166, 170
Gournay-sur-Aronde, Picardy: shrine 19, 30, 64–5, 76, 86, 87, 110, *111*, 116, 120–1, *121*, 130
Graeco-Roman literature 11, 12, 13, 14–15, 20–1, 31, 39–53, 46, 94, 107, *see also* individual writers
Graeco-Roman religion 26
Grannus (Apollo) 26
Grauballe Man 82
grave goods 60; bronze *51*, 60–1, 95; meaning of 68–9; of noble ladies *94*, *95*, 96
Graves, Robert: *The White Goddess* 160
Gregory of Tours 37, 109
Grey, Thomas: *The Bard* *146*, 148
groves, sacred 7, 14, *41*, 48, 55, 73, 107, 108–9, 147
Gundestrup cauldron 19, *33*, 59, *67*, *74*, 78
gutuatri (Celtic religious officials) 32, 115
Gwilym, John 157

Hades 51, 108
Hadrian, emperor 115
Hadrian's Wall 28
Halifax, Joan 160
Hallein 12
Hallowe'en 36
Hallstatt: chieftain's tomb: Hochdorf 19, *33*, 69; objects 109
Hallstatt cemetery (Austria) 12
Harald, King (Danish) 83
Harlow, Essex: shrine 110–11, *111*, 116, 121
Hassidic Druids 169
Hayling Island, Hampshire 87, 108
hazel 73, 80–1, *81*, 109, 178
head hunting 24, 76, *77*, 97
headdresses 8, 55, 56, 60–2, *60*, *116*; antlered *33*, 59
heads: bronze: bull-horned god *34*; decapitation 98–9; human: decorative *19*
healer-goddesses *see Fontes Sequana*
healer-gods *118*, 119
healing 18–19, 23, 46, 90, 115, 116–19; eye disease 46, 90, 115, 116, *118*, 119
hearth and home, spirit guardians of 30
Hecataeus of Miletus 14
Heidelberg, Germany 59
helmets, bronze *108*
Herbert, Rev Algernon 148
Hercules *167*
Herkomer, Professor 157
Herodotus 11, 14
Hertfordshire *33*, 59; Mars Toutatis 27, *see also* St Albans
Hill of Slane: fire 137
'Himbas Forosnai' (prophecy) 89, 102
Hippolytus 40, 41, 46, 50, 51, 88
'Hirlas Horn' (Horn of Plenty) 7, 155, 156
historians: Druids as 48
Hochdorf, Germany: Hallstatt chieftain's tomb 19, *33*, 69
Hochscheid, Germany 90
Hockwold-cum-Wilton, Norfolk 60, 73, *116*
Hohmichele, Germany 79
Holzerlingen, Germany 30
Holzhausen, Bavaria 121
Hook's Cross, Hertfordshire *33*, 59
Hoppstädten, Germany 79
Horn of Plenty ('Hirlas Horn') 7, 155, *156*
Horned God 23, *34*, 58, 59, 160, 164
horse-goddess (Epona) 24, 27, 29, 58, *131*
Horsens, eastern Jutland 66
horses *121*; legend of the white mare *131*; sacrifice of 84, 85, 86, 87
hound-lord (Apollo Cunomaglus) 29
human bodies, ritual dismembering 30
human sacrifices 7, *10*, 14, *19*, 25, 32, 39, 40–1, 52, 55, 71–4, 76, 78–9, 84, 87–8, 97, 105, 140, *see also* bog burials
hunter-gods 29–30, *29*
hunting 101
Hurle, Henry 147, 169, 175

Iceni 53, 58, 78, 79, 95–6
Imbolc 35, 37, 164
immortality 51
Insular Order of Druids 170, 172
Internet 169
Inverness: 'Druid Temple' 144
Ireland 13, *28*, 32, 49, 50, 55, 56, 63, 90, *107*, 108, *120*, 121; bog body 80; Druidic survival 15–17; festivals 34–6; Petrie Crown 61; sacred vessels 66; witchcraft 100, *see also* myths; Ulster
Irish Pagan movement 169
Iron Age 21, 23, 24, 25, 26, 28, *33*, 37, 64–5, *124*; bog burials 80, 82–3; burial 51; Celtic 19, 107; female burials 95; 'Hallstatt' *12*; headdresses 60; jewellery 58; La Tène 12–13, 67, 79; metalwork 12, *13*, 63; sanctuaries/shrines 110, *111*; structures 56; votive objects 53; wooden figures *24*
Italy *12*, 37

jewellery 58–9, 60, *94*, 95, 110, 114; in cauldron 66–7; grave goods 69, 96; human heads on 19, *see also* amulets; pendants; torcs
Johnson, Dr Samuel 144
Jones, Edward (harper) 152, *153*
Jordan Hill, Weymouth 121
Judas Men 75
judges: Druids as 10, 14, 32, 44–5
Jupiter 23, 25, 26, 28, 32, 78
Juthe Fen Woman, Jutland 83, 84
Jutland 67

Keltoi 11
Keltria 169
Keshcarrigan, Ireland *124*
Kew Gardens, Kew 142, *143*
Kildare: St Brigit's monastery 102, *137*
Kimmeridge, Dorset 98–9
Kings Arms, Poland Street, London 147
King's Barrow chariot burial, Yorkshire 86

La Tène: art 12–13, 63; Bliesbrück, Germany *121*; Iron Age 12–13, 67, 79; Lake Neuchâtel, Switzerland 12, *13*, 109
landscape, divine power of 24, 29, 107, 178
Lankhills, Winchester: cemetery 98
Larzac, France 99
Latin 8, *12*, 89, 99, 133
Le Châtelet, Haute-Marne, France 25, 62
Le Donon, temple of (Vosges) 29
le Fèvre, Jean 140
Le Touget, Gers, France 29
Leabhar na h-Uidhre (*Book of the Dun Cow*) 8
lead curses 32, 46, 73, 81, 99, 109, *114*
Leckhampton, England 60
Leinster 135
Lemington, England *132*
Lemovices 108
Lenus Mars (Trier) 115
ley lines 178
Libenice, Bohemia 57, 109
light, god of 36
Lindow Man 53, 80, *81*, 82
Lingones 90
Liptovska Mara 110
Liscus of the Aedui 115
Livy 76
Llangollen Eisteddfod 152
Lloyd-Jones, Richard 156
Llyn Cerrig Bach, Anglesey *13*, 53, 64, 65
Llyn Fawr, south Wales 66, 109
Loegaire, King 136–7
Logan Stone *153*, 156
Loire, Maenads of *105*
London: Druid Group 170; Roman town (Londinium) 53, 96, *see also* Primrose Hill
lotus motif 59
Louernius 34
Loughnashade, Armagh, Ireland *61*, 63
Lourdes 118
Lowbury Hill, Oxfordshire *108*, 121
Lucan 14, *24*, 25, 31, 40, *41*, *43*, 49, 50, 51, 52, 68, 178; *Pharsalia* 27, 40, 51, 55, 73, 75, 78, 107, 108
Lucas, Vrain 148
Lucretius 41
Lugh 36, 130, 132
Lughnasadh 35, 36, 37, 164, *165*
Luna (moon-goddess) 19, 114
lunar amulets 19
Luxembourg: burial 68
Luxeuil 29
Lydney, Gloucestershire 28, 115, 118, *119*

Mabinogion 24, 66, 100
McCabe, Mathew 177
Macha (warrior-goddess) 102, 131
Maenads of the Loire *105*
magic 7, 46; Black Magic 46, 83, 98
magicians 14, 31, 46
Mailly-le-Camp, Champagne 58, 65
Manching, Bavaria *109*
Marne, River 25
marriage 30
Mars 23, 26
Mars Mullo (Romano-Celtic god) 115
Mars Toutatis *27*
Marseille *43*, 55, 76–7, 107
Martin, Jean 148
Marvell, Andrew 140, 148
mathematics 50
Matrona (Mother): River Marne 25
Matronae Aufaniae 29
Mavilly, France 90, *118*
Meath 35
Medb, Queen of Connacht 89, 94, 95, 97, *100, 101*, 102, 123, 128
mediators 32, 36, 121, 124, 125, 130, *see also* arbitrators
medicine: and plants 18–19, 46, *see also* healing
megalithic monuments 139, *142*, 144, 147, *148*
megalithic stone circles 17, *141*, 144
Mela, Pomponius 14, 39, 49, 50, 103–4, *103*, 105; *De Chorographia* 48, 51
Mercury 23, 26
Merlin *43*
metalwork: grave goods 68, 69; hoard: Anglesey 53; Iron Age 12, *13*, 63; jewellery 58–9; solar ritual 55, 56–7; votive offerings 25, 64, 65, 66, *109*, 114, *see also* bronze; cauldrons
Meyrick, Samuel 157, *172*
Mide (Druid) 35, 126
Midwest Pagan Council (USA) 160
Minerva 23, 26
Mirebeau, northern France: sanctuary 19
mistletoe 7, 18–19, 46, 47, 59, *148*, 178; in bog burials 80, 81
Mithras 74
Moldau Valley 110
Mona *see* Anglesey
Mont Lassois 95
moon-worship 18, 19
Morgan, Owen 152
Morgannwg, Iolo (Bard) 17, 152–5, 156, *157*
Morgannwg, Myfyr 152
Moritasgus (Apollo) 26

Morrigán (warrior-goddess) 36, 98, 100, 102, *128*
Mother-Goddesses 27–8, *27*, 99, *104*, 159
mountains, divine power of 24, 29
Moux, Burgundy 90
Msecke Zehrovice, Bohemia 59
Muirchú: *Life of Saint Patrick* 136, 137
Muntham Court, Sussex 62, 85, 86, 116, 121
Murray, Margaret: *Witchcraft in Western Europe* 160
musical instruments 55, *61*, 63
Mythological Cycle 8, 15, 123, 124, 133
myths 49; Celtic 121; Irish 8, 15, 19, 24, 34, 35, 51, 63, 66, 68, 73, 81, 89, 93, 94, 98, 101–2, 103, 109, 123–37; Norse 161; Welsh 8, 24, 51, 66, 68, 93, 102, 103, 152–5

Navan Fort (Emhain Macha), Armagh, Ireland 36, 56, 63, 108
Nemausus 29
Nemesis (god of justice and vengeance) 46
Nemetona 107
Neo-Paganism 159, 160–1, *162*, 170, *173*, *179*
Neptune (water-god) 73
Nero, emperor 15, 95
Nerthus (earth-goddess) 37
Nettleton Shrub, Wiltshire *118*
Neuchâtel, Lake (Switzerland): La Tène 12, *13*, 109
Neumagen, Germany 48
Neuvy-en-Sullias, France 9, *25*, 55, 58, 86
Newgrange, Ireland *132*
Niall, King 133
Nicander of Colophon 30
Nîmes 28, 29
Nitrobriges 58
'Noble Savages', Druids as 14, *40*, 41, 50, 139, 143, 146
Nodens (god) 28, *119*
Normanton Down: disc barrow 175
Nôtre Dame, Paris 78

oak: Drunemeton ('Oak Sanctuary') 32, 108; in structures 56; trees 9, *18*, 108, 109, 121, *144*, *178*
Odinism 159, 161
Oenghus (god of love) *127*
ogam (writing) 133
Ogilvie, Rev Dr John 139
oracles 88, 90, 91, 97
oral traditions 7, 14, 15, 24, 32, 48–9, *48*, *see also* Ulster Cycle
Order of Bards, Ovates and Druids (OBOD) 17, 143, 147, *162*,

170, *171*, 177
Orgon, southern France 78
Otherworld 103, 105
Ovates 170, 178
oxen: sacrifice of 19, 86, 87

Pagan Federation, British 160, 161
Pagan Front (USA) 160
Partholón 126
Patmos, island of *115*
Paulinus, Gaius Suetonius (Roman governor) 15, *52*, 53, 64, 73, 93
Pendragon, Arthur Uther 172, *175*
Peredur 99, 100
Petrie Crown 61
Pfalzfeld St Goar, Germany *19*, 59
philosophers 14, 39, 40, 50
philosophy 10
Phoebicius (priest) 15, 90
Piggott, Stuart 46, 146, 148
pigs 29, 87, 89
Pliny 14–15, 18–19, *19*, 40, *41*, 50, 52, 59, 73, 81, 108, *148*, 178; *Natural History* 8, 9, 18, 40, 41, 46, 50, 58
politics: and religion 31, 44
Polybius 11, 58
Polyhistor 41
polytheism 24
Posidonius 14, 20, 34, 40, 41, 50, 75, 105
Postumus (Roman general) 76
Prasutagus, King 53, 78, 95, 96
prayer 32, 55
Preiddu Annwfn (Welsh mythic poem) 103
priest-physicians 116
priestesses 102, 164; virgin 103–4
priests 8, 31, 32, *33*, 42, 49, 56–7, *56*, 62; and sacred places 107–21
Primrose Hill, London 7, 147, 152, 154, 168, 170, 171
prophecy/prophets 7, 15, 31, 35, 71, 88–91, 124, 125, 130
prophetesses 15, 97, *101, 102*, 143
Pufendorf, Esaias 140
purification ritual 35
Pythagoras 41, 50, 51, 88

rag trees *107*, 108
Rákos Csongrád, Hungary *125*
raven war-goddess *see* Morrigán
ravens 90; figurine *31*
rebirth 51, 69, 178
reincarnation 51, 178
Reinheim, Germany 95, 96
religion: Celtic 18, 19, 23–37; doctrine 49; Graeco-Roman *26*; and politics 31, 44, *see also* gods/goddesses
Remi (Gaul) 28
Renaissance 140–1
Ribemont-sur-Ancre 76, 86, 111,

116
ritual: cannibalism 52; funerary 30; head hunting *24*; murder 71, 72, 73, 76–7, 83; and the priesthood 56–7; shafts 109, 121
rivers, divine power of 29
rocky ourcrops, divine power of 29
Rodenbach, Germany: chieftain's burial 69
Rollright Stones, Chipping Norton 144
Roman: religion 23, 32
Roman literature: on Celts 24, *see also* Graeco-Roman literature
Roman period 118; army 53; calendar 37; emperors, persecution of Druids by 14–15; empire, collapse 15
Romano-British period 86, 98, *111*
Romano-Celtic period 26, 60–1, *60*, *62*, 118; culture 13; gods 115
Romans: and Druids 52–3
romanticism 148
Roquepertuse, France 26, 36, *52*, 76–7, 110, *111*
Rotary Clubs 169
Rowlands, Rev Henry 146, 147, *150*
Rudiobus 58, 86

Sabrina (River Severn) 25
sacerdotes 32, 42
sacred places, and priests 107–21
sacrifices 8, 10, 32, 57, 71–88, 111, 120, *see also* animal sacrifices; human sacrifices
St Albans (Verulamium) 53, 76, 96
St Berach 134
St Beuno 8
St Brigit 8, 15, 35, 50, 102, 123, 135–6, *136*, *137*
St Maur, Oise, France 26, 109
St Patrick 8, 15, *17*, 123, 134, 135, 136–7, *137*
Salisbury magistrates 172
'salt-route' (*Salzkammergut*) 12
Saluvii *52*, 77
Samhain 35, 36, 37, 164, 169
Sammes, Aylett: *Britannia Antiqua Illustrata* 140, *150*
Samnitae 105
Sarn-y-Bryn-Caled, Welshpool, Wales 56
satire 35, 49, *124*
Sava (wife of Finn) 125–6, *125*
Scáthach of Ulster 102
sceptres 8, 19, 55, *62*, 116, 155
Schedius, Elias: *De Dis Germanis* 150, *151*
Schifferstadt 57
Schismatic Druids of North

America 169
Scotland 13, 35, 46, 58, 66, 133, 144; cauldrons 66, 67
seer-poets (Filidh) 15, 89, *124*
seers 7, 15, 32, 49, 50, 93, 109, 124, 171; female 101
selago plant 46
Sena, island of 103
Senilis, Titus Flavius *119*
Sequana: Burgundian healing-goddess 27; *Fontes Sequana*, Dijon 28, 55, *115*, 116, *117*, *119*; River Seine 24, 25
Severus Alexander, emperor 15, 88, 97
Shallcrass, Philip 159, 169, 172, 179
Shamanism 33, 159, 160, *161*, 166
shape-shifters, Druid *127*
sheep 35, 37, 87, *121*
Sherwood Forest *178*
shield-boss: bronze *53*
shrines/temples 107–21; ceremonial banquets 19, *see also* individual sites
Siberia 160
sickle, golden/bronze *47*
Silbury Hill *146*
Silchester, Hampshire *63*
Sirona (goddess) 90, 115
sky-gods 27, 28, 161
Smith, Charles 157, *172*
Snettisham, Norfolk *59*, 65
Soissons: noble burial 86
Souconna (River Saône) 25
South Cadbury, Somerset: Iron Age hillfort 76
Sovereignty, Goddess of 131–2, *132*
speech, power of 35, *124*
spring-god (Nemausus) 29
stags, images of 25, *121*
Stanton Drew: Druidic University 144
Star Carr, Yorkshire 59
Stoic philosophy 41, 50
Stone of Fál *131*
Stonehenge 7, 17, *18*, 56, 139, *140*, 141, *142*, 144, 147, 148, 159, 168, 170, *171*, *172–6*, 178
Strabo 14, 15, 20, 31, 32, 49, 50, 52, 68, 72, 74, 78, 108, 115; *Geography* 8, 40, 41, 45, 66, 71, 75, 76, 97, 105, 109, 124
Stratford, east London 86
Strettweg, Austria 93, 104

Stukeley, William 17, *18*, 89, 141, *142–3*, 144, *146*, 147, 148, 150, 152; *Itinerarium Curiosum* 142
Sucellus (Celtic hammer-god) 49
Suebi 58
Suetonius (historian) 14, *15*; *Life of Claudius* 52
Sulis Minerva: shrine at Bath 19, 24, 25, 28, 32, *42*, 112–14
summer solstice 170
sun: divine power of 24, *25*, 29; gods 26, 61, 166, 177; solar ritual 55, 56–7, *57*; worship of 159, 162, *see also* wheel

Tacitus 14, 15, 23, 40, *41*, 48, 52, 95, 96, 97, 108, 143, 147; *Agricola* 94; *Annals* 40, 53, 64, 73, 93, 94; *Germania* 37, 58–9, 82, 83; *Histories* 88, 97
Táin Bó Cuailnge (Cattle Raid of Cooley) 8, 24, 95, 100, 102, 123, 127, 128, 129, 130
Taliesin (poet) 152, 155
Tara, Ireland: assembly of 34, 35, 36; pagan feast at 137; royal site 123, 132; Stone of Fál 131
Taranis (Taranucnus): thunder-god 24, *25*, 27, 75, 78
Tarbhfhess ('bull sleep') 19, 130
Tartigny, France 86
Tayac, western Gaul 65
teachers, Druids as 7, 14, 15, 48–9, 124
Teigngrace, Devon: male wooden figure 24
Teutates 27, 75, 78
thunder-gods 24, 25, 26, *27*, *see also* Taranis
Tiberius, emperor 14–15, 40, 115
Timaeus 14, 41
Timagenes 41, 50
Titelberg, Gaul 67, 68
Titus Flavius Senilis *119*
Toland, John 141, 146–7, 154, 170
Tollund Man, Denmark 82
torcs (neckrings) 57, 58–9, *59*, 65, 67, 95, 104, *130*
'totem': Wavendon 62
Touchstone 170, 179
Toulouse 101
Tours, France 109
Tower Hill, London 168, 171
Transmigration of Souls 51
trees 29, 37, *108–9*, 168, *178*; dendrochronology 56, 121;

mistletoe 46, *47*; rag *107*, *108*; sacred *178*; willow 27, 78, *see also* oak
Tresco, Isles of Scilly 103
Treveri (tribe) 28, 79
tribal history/identity 24, 28, 32
Trier, Germany *27*, 28, 78, 115
Trinovantes 53, 78, 96, 121
trumpets 55, *61*, 63
Trundholm 'sun chariot' burial 55, 57
Tuatha Dé Danann 8, 124, 126, 130, 131, 132, 133

Ucuetis 28
Uisneach, Meath 126
Ulster 8, 36, 56, 63, 90, 100, *102*, 125, 127, 128–9, *133*, *see also* Cathbadh of Ulster
Ulster Cycle 8, 15, 24, 89, 90, 94, 95, 100, 123, 128, 129
United Ancient Order of Druids 147
United States 160, *161*, 164, 169, 170

Vacallinehae 29
Vaison, Lower Rhône Valley 29
Valerius Flaccus 51
Vanir (earth gods) 161
Vates (seers) 32, 49, 124
Veleda (prophetess) 97, 143
Venutius 96
Vercingetorix 14
vernacular: myths 24, 94; traditions: Irish 13, 34; traditions: Welsh 13, *see also* Irish language; Welsh language
Vertault, Burgundy, France 27
Verulamium (St Albans) 53, 76, 96
Vespasian, emperor 88
Vestal Virgins 103
victory gods 52
Viereckschanzen 121
virgin priestesses 103–4
Viromandui 65, 121
Vix, Burgundy 94, 95
Vopiscus of Syracuse 97
votive offerings 25, 46, *53*, 55, 57, 63, 64–5, 66, 76, 77, 104, 108, 109, 111, *112*

Wales 7, 13, *24*, 28, 35, 46, 86, 99, 109, 133, *146*, 148, 156–7;

sacred vessels 66; witchcraft 100, *see also* myths
Wanborough, Surrey 61, 116
wands: ceremonial 62–3
war 30, 45; craft 101, 125; exemption from 32; prisoners of 73, 76, 97; trumpets 63
war-goddess 36
war-gods 23, 26, *26*, 36, 77
warrior aristocracy, Gaul *10*
warrior-goddesses 36, 96, 98, *100*, 102, *128*, 131
warrior-gods 77
water: divine power of 25, 50, *see also* cauldrons
water-god (Neptune) 73
Waterloo Bridge, London *108*
watery places 108–9, 121; divine power of 29; spirits of 24; votive offerings 64, *see also* Bath; bog burials; cauldrons; *Fontes Sequana*; wells
Wavendon Gate, Buckinghamshire: totem 62
weapons 71, 76, 86, 102, 111; grave goods 60; as votive wells 109, 121, 178
Wetwang, Yorkshire *51*, 79
wheel: depiction of *31*; solar symbol 25, 28, 62; symbols 60, 61
Wheel of the Year 164–5
wheel-god, solar 67
Wicca 159, 161, 162–5, *162*, 166, 170, 178, *see also* witchcraft
Wicker Man, the 71, 75, 78
Wiesbaden, Germany 115
Williams, Edward *see* Morgannwg, Iolo
Willingham Fen, Cambridgeshire 62
willow tree 27, 78
Windeby Girl, Schleswig-Holstein 83, 84
witchcraft 93, 98–100, 129, 160; Nine Witches of Gloucester 99, 100, *see also* Wicca
Wood, John *144*
Woodeaton, Oxfordshire 63, 65
Wordsworth, William: *The Prelude* 148

yew 69, 108, 109, 178

Závist, Bohemia: Iron Age hillfort *110*